EXPANDING YOUR HORIZONS

A CAREER GUIDE

■ ■ ■ ■ ■ ■ ■ ■

JUDI MISENER

Head of Program, Co-operative Education
Scarborough Centre for Alternative Studies
Scarborough, Ontario

SUSAN KEARNS

Head of Student Retention
Scarborough Centre for Alternative Studies
Scarborough, Ontario

McGraw-Hill Ryerson Limited

Toronto   Montreal   New York   Auckland   Bogotá   Caracas
Lisbon   London   Madrid   Mexico   Milan   New Delhi
Paris   San Juan   Singapore   Sydney   Tokyo

Expanding Your Horizons
A Career Guide

ISBN 0-07-551392-7

3 4 5 6 7 8 9 10   2 1 0 9 8 7 6 5

Printed and bound in Canada

Canadian Cataloguing in Publication Data
Misener, Judi, (date)
     Expanding your horizons : a career guide

Includes bibliographical references and index.
ISBN 0-07-551392-7

1. Vocational guidance – Canada. 2. Occupations –
Canada. 3. Youth – Counseling of – Canada.
I. Kearns, Susan. II. Title.

HF5382.5.C2M58 1993   371.4′25′0971   C92-095756-0

Publisher: Andrea Crozier
Associate Editor: Karen Ross
Senior Supervising Editor: Marilyn Nice
Production Editor: Claudia Kutchukian
Permissions Editor: Jacqueline Russell
Cover and Interior Designer: Avril Orloff
Part Illustrator: Nicholas Vitacco
Text Illustrator: Stephen MacEachern
Typesetter: Pages Design Ltd.

Cover photograph of climbers in the Bugaboos, British Columbia, by Wilhelm Schmidt/Masterfile

This book was manufactured in Canada using acid-free and recycled paper.

▼ ▼ ▼
Contents

Preface

*I*nstitutions around the world are undergoing major restructuring. Educators are critically examining not just what they do but why they do it. Are you, as a student, gaining the knowledge, skills, and attitudes necessary for your future? What is the best way to teach for learning? How do you learn best?

Community-based co-operative education, or work experience, programs are still relatively new in Canadian education. Our experience has taught us that these programs provide many answers to the critical questions above. As a result, this mode of learning will continue to grow in importance.

Expanding Your Horizons: A Career Guide enables you to develop the knowledge, skills, and attitudes needed for your future. The text guides you through your experiences, enables you to critically examine yourself and your environment, and helps you to make decisions about what is best for your future, particularly for your future careers. The text provides suggested journal entries, case studies, and integrated activities that challenge you to question current practices in the workplace. Your experiences in the workplace form the foundation while the text provides the framework for your learning.

In **Part 1, Planning Your Career**, you will examine how to approach and interpret information and experiences, and you will complete a detailed process of self-assessment. Trends are then studied to assist you in predicting your future work environment. Understanding yourself as an individual and the possibilities the future workplace holds for you enables you to begin the process of career planning. You will begin to research career options and make informed career goals and plans.

Part 2, Developing Your Career Skills, will help you to learn the practical skills needed to have a successful career. These skills include communicating clearly and accurately; finding employment; producing effective résumés, covering letters, and application forms; and developing successful interviewing techniques.

Part 3, Quality of Work Life, explores in detail issues that affect the workplace and addresses the question of responsibility in terms of labour relations, human rights, health, and safety.

Part 4, Exploring the Workplace, critically examines the knowledge, skills, and attitudes needed to succeed in the workplace. Individual, company, and societal ethics, as well as interpersonal relations, are explored. This part concludes with reflection on the workplace experiences and how your experiences affect your evolving career plan.

Upon completion of this text, you should be able to understand, through close analysis of personal and work experiences, how you can shape your future.

▼ ▼ ▼
Acknowledgements

I would like to thank my family, Bill, Erin, and Meaghan, for understanding why the creation of this book was so important to me.

Judi Misener

I would like to thank Lindsay, Ashley, and Peter, whose support helped me to turn a wish into reality.

Susan Kearns

We would like to thank our colleagues who believe in co-operative education and who, over a relatively short period of time, have created excellent opportunities for students.

We would also like to express appreciation to Andrea Crozier and Karen Ross of McGraw-Hill Ryerson for their continued support, enthusiasm, and commitment in developing a textbook that fully explores co-operative education, or work experience.

Finally, we would like to thank the following people for reviewing the manuscript and providing worthwhile suggestions:

Sue Cooper-Twiss
Chinguacousy Secondary School
Brampton, Ontario

Sharon Crabb
Fredericton High School
Fredericton, New Brunswick

Dale Gullekson
Bev Facey Composite High School
Sherwood Park, Alberta

Janet Lucier
Catholic Central High School
London, Ontario

Frank J. Matys
St. Joseph's High School
Barrie, Ontario

Peter Phelan
Simcoe County Roman Catholic
Separate School Board
Barrie, Ontario

Jim Turk
Director of Education
Ontario Federation of Labour
Toronto, Ontario

▼ ▼ ▼
Using the Text

Students and teachers who are involved in co-operative education, or work experience, share a unique mode of learning. The activity-based text of *Expanding Your Horizons: A Career Guide* explores and expands this experience through a variety of features, which are outlined below.

JOURNAL ENTRIES

The ideas and information in each chapter are personalized for you through the journal entries. These opportunities for reflection further your understanding of the value of the workplace in lifelong learning and the integration of classroom theory and workplace experiences.

ACTIVITIES

A number of activities, such as surveying, interviewing, debating, and role-playing, provide opportunities for reflection, discussion, writing, interaction, and inquiry in each chapter.

MAKE THE CONNECTION

The Make the Connection activities are designed to integrate school and workplace experiences. They provide opportunities for you to interact with your classmates, observe the dynamics of the workplace, and think critically about the impact of present actions on your future goals.

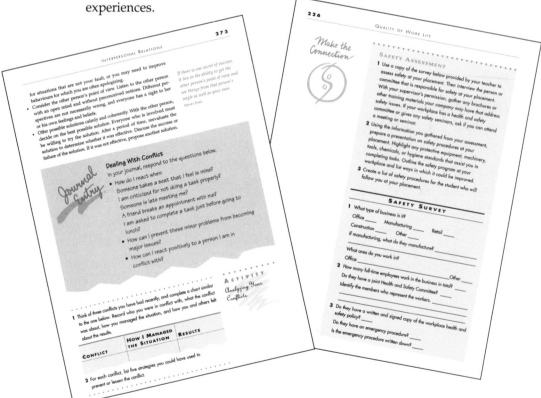

CASE STUDIES

Realistic and practical case studies offer insight into situations related to the workplace. They include hypothetical incidents and real-life articles, which are reinforced by the questions and activities that follow each case study.

WHAT HAVE YOU LEARNED?

The questions in the What Have You Learned? sections, which appear at the end of each chapter, reinforce and review key concepts. Group discussion of individual responses will help to extend your knowledge.

MARGINAL QUOTES

The marginal quotes are designed to provoke thought. They include literary quotes, statistics, opinions, and student, teacher, and supervisor reflections.

GLOSSARY

The glossary, which follows the final chapter, provides a quick reference for key terms used in the text.

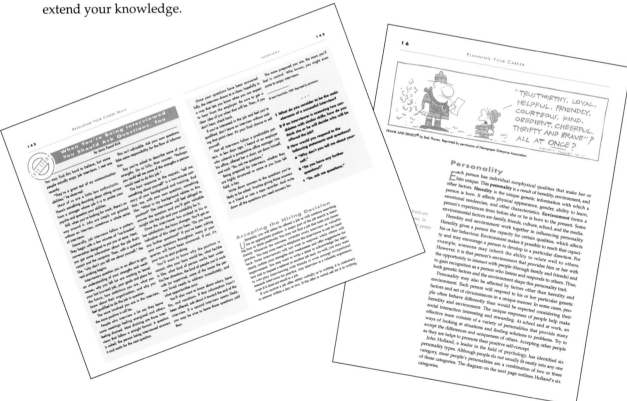

PART 1

PLANNING YOUR CAREER

Destiny is not a matter of chance,
it is a matter of choice.

ANONYMOUS

LEARNING THROUGH WORK EXPERIENCE

After completing this chapter, you should be able to:

▼ ▼ ▼

- Appreciate the relationship between learning in school and learning in a workplace.
- Understand the five components of a co-operative education, or work experience, program.
- Identify the outcomes of work experience.
- Recognize your responsibilities as well as those of your teacher and your supervisor.

▼ ▼ ▼

placement	monitoring	employee
journal	log sheet	employer
training plan		

Why Experience Work?

Experience is the process that links education, work, and personal development.
John Dewey

Every experience relies on that which has gone before and modifies in some way the quality of that which follows.
John Dewey

Immediate, concrete experiences serve to arouse observation, prompt reflection, and spur action.
D.A. Kolb and L.H. Lewis

Work experience provides opportunities to critically analyze the workplace and the role of work in our society. Co-operative education, or work experience, programs involve a method of learning that links schools and workplaces through an active relationship among students, teachers, and members of the community. These programs enrich, enhance, and reinforce knowledge as they integrate school subjects with workplace learning.

There are many benefits to being a student in a work experience program. Not only do you develop useful and marketable skills to help you proceed into a career, but you are also exposed to up-to-date, relevant information and technology in an area that interests you. The practical experience also provides a unique setting in which to learn more about yourself and to help you plan for your future. With workplace experience, you will be able to develop a career plan based on realistic, practical information, and you will be better equipped to make a smooth transition from school to work. You will also be able to answer questions such as: What types of occupations interest me? What strengths and skills do I have that need to be improved? What knowledge, skills, and attitudes will I need in the future?

At your assigned workplace, or **placement,** you will put into practice what you learn in school and, through journal writing and classroom activities, you will reflect upon and critically analyze work-related issues and your personal goals. Working with your classmates will provide opportunities to share experiences and reflect on the role of work in your life.

A C T I V I T Y
Getting to Know One Another

1 In order to get to know your classmates, divide a sheet of paper into as many squares as there are people in your class. In the upper left-hand square, write your name, your favourite leisure activity, and an occupation (or area of work) that appeals to you.

2 Move around the classroom and fill in the remaining squares with information on the same topics from your classmates. Share your information with them. Try to remember each person's name and, if possible, one piece of information each person shared.

Erin Bettens	Alka Singh	Meaghan Rutherford
Jazz dancing	Volleyball	Playing the piano
Journalism	Coaching	Owning her own business

3 As a class, form a circle. One person begins by introducing himself or herself. The next person introduces the first person again, then introduces himself or herself. Continue around the circle, prompting one another if necessary.

. . . .

The Learning Cycle of Work Experience

A co-operative education, or work experience, program typically involves five components (see the diagram of the learning cycle on the next page):

1 *School subjects taken prior to or at the same time as work experience.*
These subjects, such as science or English, provide the knowledge and skills that you will put into practice at your placement.

2 *The placement, which is chosen with your needs, career plans, and school subjects in mind.*
An ideal match between you and your placement will provide you with appropriate challenges and training. Ideally, you will function in certain roles and perform certain tasks; be exposed to new people, situations, and ideas; and enjoy the process of learning about work and acquiring new knowledge.

3 *Structured personal reflection and classroom integration sessions, which provide opportunities to consider work experiences in relation to school subjects.*
It is important that you process what is happening, draw conclusions, and develop new behaviours or change old ones. As you strive to understand new experiences, these sessions can transform your experiences into learning.

Your classroom sessions will combine individual and group activities, case studies, and journals. Activities such as presentations, essay writing, role-plays, and discussions provide you with opportunities to synthesize your knowledge and share others' experiences. Case studies help you to understand and analyze workplace experiences by presenting realistic situations. A **journal** is a collection of your writings that reflects your feelings and attitudes. In a journal, you challenge your experiences in a private document. Include your observations, reactions, feelings, questions, and judgements about the workplace and about yourself. You may wish to express yourself not only in words but also through pictures and cartoons.

4 *Evaluation and monitoring.*
Your progress at the placement will be evaluated by your teacher based on your training plan, using a variety of evaluation techniques. This individualized **training plan** will be developed by you, your teacher, and your supervisor before you begin your placement, and it will outline your tasks and learning objectives. Once you are at the placement, your teacher will meet with you and your supervisor during

Reflection is the critical examination of experience.
L. JOPLIN

The Learning Cycle

What You Bring to Your Work Experience

- School subjects
- Past experiences
- Self-concept and personality
- Needs, values, and interests
- Knowledge, skills, and attitudes
- Career goals and plan

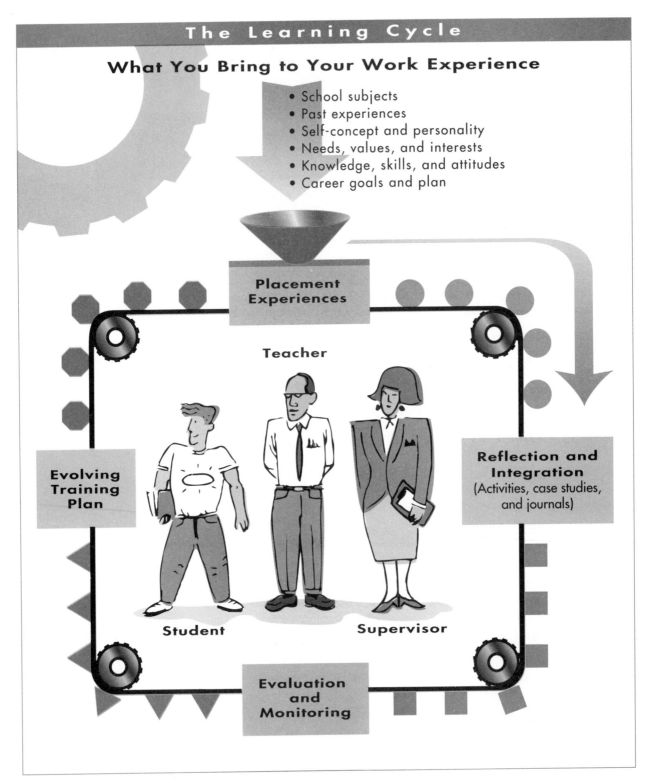

Placement Experiences

Teacher

Evolving Training Plan

Reflection and Integration
(Activities, case studies, and journals)

Student   Supervisor

Evaluation and Monitoring

Adapted from *Alternate Strategies for Providing Work Experience*, James R. Stone III and Renee L. Wonser, Minnesota University, Minnesota, 1990.

monitoring sessions. Your teacher's observations when visiting the placement will be part of your evaluation. Your placement supervisor will assess your progress using a form that closely resembles the performance review used by many companies and organizations. You will also be involved in self-assessment, particularly when you analyze the feedback you receive. You may be required to complete daily or weekly **log sheets** to record the tasks you do and the hours you spend at your placement.

5 *Evolving training plan.*

Your training plan will be continually assessed and revised as needed throughout your placement. For example, you may be given additional responsibilities or further training.

A C T I V I T Y
Analyzing Your Past Experiences

1 With a partner, discuss how your past experiences will be valuable to you at your placement. Consider experiences such as courses completed at school, part-time jobs, family responsibilities, and personal relationships.

2 Complete a chart like the one below in your notebook. Outline your past experiences and how each experience could benefit you at your placement.

PAST EXPERIENCE	BENEFIT FOR WORK EXPERIENCE

Outcomes of Work Experience

Through experiences at your placement, you will develop many new skills, such as listening effectively, thinking creatively, acting independently, and motivating yourself. These skills will help you in your future career. As you progress through your career, you will need to constantly strive to acquire the necessary skills that will help to maintain and advance your career.

A survey of Canadian companies conducted by The Conference Board of Canada resulted in a list of skills that are important for Canadian workers (see page 8). These include the necessary academic and personal management skills that are required to get, keep, and progress on a job, as well as the teamwork skills that are needed to work with others on a job. Co-operative education is an excellent way to develop the skills you will need to be successful in the future.

EMPLOYABILITY SKILLS PROFILE

THE CRITICAL SKILLS REQUIRED OF THE CANADIAN WORK FORCE

Academic Skills

Those skills that provide the basic foundation to get, keep, and progress on a job and to achieve the best results

Canadian employers need a person who can:

Communicate

- Understand and speak the languages in which business is conducted
- Listen to understand and learn
- Read, comprehend, and use written materials, including graphs, charts, and displays
- Write effectively in the languages in which business is conducted

Think

- Think critically and act logically to evaluate situations, solve problems, and make decisions
- Understand and solve problems involving mathematics and use the results
- Use technology, instruments, tools, and information systems effectively
- Access and apply specialized knowledge from various fields (e.g., skilled trades, technology, physical sciences, arts, and social sciences)

Learn

- Continue to learn for life

Personal Management Skills

The combination of skills, attitudes, and behaviours required to get, keep, and progress on a job and to achieve the best results

Canadian employers need a person who can demonstrate:

Positive Attitudes and Behaviours

- Self-esteem and confidence
- Honesty, integrity, and personal ethics
- A positive attitude toward learning, growth, and personal health
- Initiative, energy, and persistence to get the job done

Responsibility

- The ability to set goals and priorities in work and personal life
- The ability to plan and manage time, money, and other resources to achieve goals
- Accountability for actions taken

Adaptability

- A positive attitude toward change
- Recognition of and respect for people's diversity and individual differences
- The ability to identify and suggest new ideas to get the job done—creativity

Teamwork Skills

Those skills needed to work with others on a job and to achieve the best results

Canadian employers need a person who can:

Work With Others

- Understand and contribute to the organization's goals
- Understand and work within the culture of the group
- Plan and make decisions with others and support the outcomes
- Respect the thoughts and opinions of others in the group
- Exercise "give and take" to achieve group results
- Seek a team approach as appropriate
- Lead when appropriate, mobilizing the group for high performance

Why Do You Want to Experience Work?

Determining reasons why you make decisions is important. In your journal, respond to the questions below to determine your reasons for experiencing work. You can use these reasons to measure your progress and accomplishments during your placement.

- What do I think will be the benefits for me of my work experience?

- What knowledge, skills, and attitudes do I want to demonstrate at the end of my placement? Why?

Working as a Team

Three key people are involved in making your work experience a successful one: you, your teacher, and your placement supervisor. Each person has a certain role and has specific responsibilities. All must work as a team.

Your responsibilities to your supervisor are similar to the responsibilities of an employee to an employer. An **employee** is a person who works for an organization or another person for pay, while an **employer** is an organization or a person that hires one or more employees. Although you will not actually be an employee at your placement, the rules for employees apply to you. Your responsibilities include:

- Communicating well with your teacher and your supervisor.
- Arriving on time and ready to work every scheduled day.
- Identifying and respecting your placement's health and safety regulations.
- Following the dress code at your placement.
- Being willing to learn new skills and apply them.
- Completing assigned work tasks.
- Completing journal entries and other school assignments.
- Actively participating in the classroom sessions by critically analyzing your experiences.
- Analyzing feedback from your teacher and your supervisor.
- Showing your ability to work with others as a team player.
- Showing initiative and resourcefulness.
- Working steadily and showing self-discipline.

Co-operative education has given me hands-on experience and insight into what people are like at work.
STUDENT

This experience is helping me establish career goals by introducing me to parts of the world of work I had not discovered.
STUDENT

- Demonstrating maturity and good judgement.
- Reporting unavoidable absences promptly to your teacher and your supervisor.
- Contacting your school if you have an accident.
- Learning as much as you can every day.

The responsibilities of your teacher include:

- Finding a placement for you and striving for a placement that meets your needs and relates to your school subjects.
- Assisting the placement supervisor in developing a training plan for you.
- Creating an atmosphere of trust and respect.
- Providing feedback to both you and your supervisor.
- Discussing your progress with you and your supervisor.
- Frequently visiting you at your placement.
- Working closely with you and your supervisor.
- Acting as a mediator, if required, should problems occur.
- Collecting and marking your assignments.
- Evaluating your work and assigning your final mark.
- Completing required forms for insurance purposes.
- Evaluating the co-operative education program annually.

The responsibilities of your placement supervisor include:

- Welcoming you to the placement.
- Providing you with a thorough orientation and identifying his or her expectations.
- Informing co-workers about your role at the placement.
- Providing a healthy and safe work environment that is free from discrimination.
- Helping you become an important member of the work team.
- Providing a meaningful learning experience that relates to your school subjects.
- Explaining procedures carefully and thoroughly.
- Outlining rules concerning hours of work, breaks, lunch time, appropriate dress, and other company policies.
- Helping to develop a training plan for you with your teacher.
- Evaluating your progress.
- Signing your insurance forms.
- Meeting frequently with you and your teacher.
- Reporting work accidents to your teacher immediately.

This program is the best way to teach students how to learn.
TEACHER

I value the one-to-one relationships I have with my students when I monitor their progress.
TEACHER

The schools cannot be solely responsible for the education of our youth—it is too important a job.
SUPERVISOR

The students are very welcome here. We depend on them.
SUPERVISOR

1 Divide your class into three groups. One group discusses the student's responsibilities at the placement, another discusses the teacher's responsibilities, and the third discusses the supervisor's responsibilities. Clarify the student's, teacher's, and supervisor's expectations, and discuss your reactions to these expectations. Brainstorm to identify any additional student, teacher, or supervisor responsibilities, and compile a list of concerns and suggestions about them.

2 Present your group's lists of additional responsibilities and concerns/suggestions to the class. Be prepared to answer questions about your lists.

Strategies for Success

In your journal, complete the statements below.

- I am going to have a successful work experience because . . .
- In order to have a successful experience, I will . . .

WHAT HAVE YOU LEARNED?

▼ ▼ ▼

1 Describe the relationship between school and work experiences.

2 Why is reflection an important part of learning through work experiences?

3 What do you think is meant by this formula: past + present = future?

4 How can you get the most out of your placement?

▼ ▼ ▼

CHAPTER 2

PERSONAL DISCOVERY

WHAT YOU WILL LEARN

After completing this chapter, you should be able to:

▼ ▼ ▼

- Understand the process of self-assessment.
- Assess who you are in terms of your self-concept, personality, needs, and values.
- Determine what you are capable of doing by assessing your interests and skills.
- Consider who you want to be and examine the process of change in yourself.

TERMS TO REMEMBER

▼ ▼ ▼

self-assessment	needs	technical skills
self-concept	hierarchy of needs	self-management
personality	values	skills
heredity	interests	transferable
environment	skills	skills

Self-Assessment

Although all humans have the same basic needs, individuals vary tremendously. To fully understand yourself, you need to analyze and reflect upon who you are, what you are capable of doing, and who you want to be. **Self-assessment** is a process of determining who you are and how you change over time. As you progress through your school and work experience, you will continue to develop and to learn new things about yourself. For example, a person who becomes successful in several sports may develop confidence in his or her physical abilities and build a strong competitive nature. A person who is forced into temporary unemployment may better understand the importance of work in his or her life. People's feelings and attitudes are constantly changing. Awareness of who you are physically, mentally, and emotionally and how you are changing will help you to make decisions about your future lifestyle and career.

Awareness of who you are develops by learning about several aspects of yourself. How do you view yourself? How do you think other people view you? The answers to these questions form your self-concept. What qualities or characteristics do you possess? When you examine your characteristics, such as ambition, courtesy, patience, and optimism, you are learning about your personality. What needs motivate your decisions, and what values influence you? By analyzing your skills and interests, you can better form career goals that suit you. This process of self-assessment will help you make choices that are right for you in order for you to achieve personal and job satisfaction.

To see what is in front of one's nose is a constant struggle.
GEORGE ORWELL

Self-Concept

How you feel about yourself, your **self-concept,** is extremely important. A newborn child has no initial self-concept; as the child grows, her or his self-concept develops based on life experiences and social interaction. Awareness of your self-concept will help you to successfully become the person you want to be.

How you believe others feel about you is part of your self-concept as well. A person tends to become the kind of person that others expect. For example, if your placement supervisor states that you have much potential and ability, you may tend to work harder in order to fulfill this expectation. Everyone thinks of you in a slightly different way, however. For example, an employer may see you as responsible and a quick learner but slightly lacking in organizational abilities, whereas a friend may see you as a good listener and a fun person to be with.

People who have a poor self-concept often have lower expectations and unconsciously fulfill these expectations. For example, if something bad happens to them, these people tend to blame themselves even if the situation is not their fault. If something good happens to them, they may assume it was due to chance. People who think that they will not succeed

We should look long and carefully at ourselves before we pass judgement on others.
MOLIÈRE

may influence their success in a negative way. This is called a self-fulfilling prophecy. People may also mask a poor self-concept by constantly criticizing others. They act as though they consider themselves to be better than anyone else.

They can because they think they can.
VIRGIL

People with a positive attitude toward themselves, who tell themselves that they can accomplish their objectives, tend to develop a good self-concept. Ideally, you should see yourself in a realistic and favourable light. If you think well of yourself, you will be better able to fulfill your expectations of success. When relating to others and yourself, remember that everyone is unique and has value as a person in spite of slight imperfections. We all have enormous potential and are capable of accepting others and of being accepted by them.

What Is Your Self-Concept?

In your journal, respond to the questions below.

- What do I like about myself?
- How do I feel about my physical appearance?
- How would I describe my ability to learn?
- How do I feel when someone asks my opinion?
- What is my proudest moment?
- What is my greatest defeat?
- What would I like to improve about myself?

ACTIVITY
How Are You Perceived?

You can compare how you think about yourself and how others think about you by examining your behaviours. Copy the chart below on a sheet of paper and complete it using this five-step process:

1 Under the Self column, rate yourself on each behaviour. The rating codes are: 5—always, 4—usually, 3—sometimes, 2—seldom, and 1—never.

2 Fold back the sheet to hide the Self column.

3 Ask a friend to rate your behaviours under the Friend column.

4 Fold back the sheet to hide the Friend column.

5 Ask a person in authority (such as a teacher, parent, or work supervisor) to rate your behaviours under the Authority column.

After completing the chart, discuss with a partner the behaviours that show a difference of opinion. Why do you think these differences exist? Discuss which behaviours you would like to change and how you can make these changes.

BEHAVIOUR	AUTHORITY	FRIEND	SELF
Ambitious			
Cheerful			
Confident			
Considerate			
Co-operative			
Dependable			
Good leader			
Hard worker			
Helpful			
Neat			
Optimistic			
Outgoing			
Patient			
Respectful			
Self-centred			
Serious			
Shy			

FRANK AND ERNEST® by Bob Thaves. Reprinted by permission of Newspaper Enterprise Association.

Personality

Certain personality traits are important for job success. In general, employers prefer people who are dependable, self-motivated, able to get along with others, flexible, and committed.

Each person has individual nonphysical qualities that make her or him unique. This **personality** is a result of heredity, environment, and other factors. **Heredity** is the unique genetic information with which a person is born. It affects physical appearance, gender, ability to learn, emotional tendencies, and other characteristics. **Environment** forms a person's experiences from before she or he is born to the present. Some environmental factors are family, friends, culture, school, and the media.

Heredity and environment work together in influencing personality. Heredity gives a person the capacity for certain qualities, which affects his or her behaviour. Environment makes it possible to reach that capacity and may encourage a person to develop in a particular direction. For example, someone may inherit the ability to relate well to others. However, it is that person's environment that provides him or her with the opportunity to interact with people (through family and friends) and to gain recognition as a person who listens and responds to others. Thus, both genetic factors and the environment shape this personality trait.

Personality may also be affected by factors other than heredity and environment. Each person will respond to his or her particular genetic factors and set of circumstances in a unique manner. In some cases, people often behave differently than would be expected considering their heredity and environment. The unique responses of people help make social interaction interesting and rewarding. At school and at work, an effective team consists of a variety of personalities that provide many ways of looking at situations and finding solutions to problems. Try to accept the differences and uniqueness of others. Accepting other people as they are helps to promote their positive self-concept.

John Holland, a leader in the field of psychology, has identified six personality types. Although people do not usually fit neatly into any one category, most people's personalities are a combination of two or three of these categories. The diagram on the next page outlines Holland's six categories.

The Six Personality Types

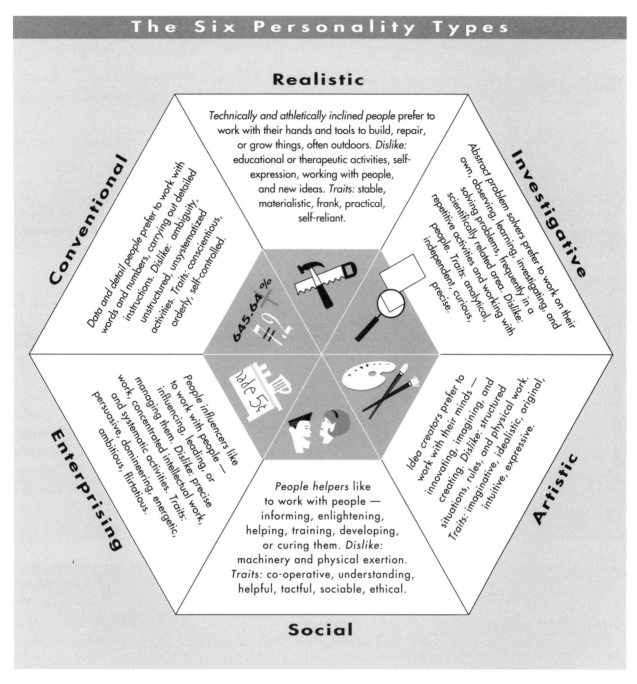

Realistic

Technically and athletically inclined people prefer to work with their hands and tools to build, repair, or grow things, often outdoors. *Dislike:* educational or therapeutic activities, self-expression, working with people, and new ideas. *Traits:* stable, materialistic, frank, practical, self-reliant.

Investigative

Abstract problem solvers prefer to work on their own, observing, learning, investigating, and solving problems, frequently in a scientifically related area. *Dislike:* repetitive activities and working with people. *Traits:* analytical, independent, curious, precise.

Conventional

Data and detail people prefer to work with words and numbers, carrying out detailed instructions. *Dislike:* ambiguity, unstructured, unsystematized activities. *Traits:* conscientious, orderly, self-controlled.

Enterprising

People influencers like to work with people — influencing, leading, or managing them. *Dislike:* precise work, concentrated intellectual work, and systematic activities. *Traits:* persuasive, domineering, energetic, ambitious, flirtatious.

Artistic

Idea creators prefer to work with their minds — innovating, imagining, and creating. *Dislike:* structured situations, rules, and physical work. *Traits:* imaginative, idealistic, original, intuitive, expressive.

Social

People helpers like to work with people — informing, enlightening, helping, training, developing, or curing them. *Dislike:* machinery and physical exertion. *Traits:* co-operative, understanding, helpful, tactful, sociable, ethical.

A C T I V I T Y

Determining Your Personality

1 In your notebook, create a chart like the one that follows. Describe your physical appearance, ability to learn, emotional tendencies, an activity you enjoy, an activity you are good at, a moment you are proud of, and an activity you would like to do in the future. Then determine how heredity and your environment have affected you.

2 Based on the information summarized in your chart and your knowledge of yourself, consider which of Holland's personality types apply to you.

PERSONAL QUALITIES	DESCRIPTION	INFLUENCE OF HEREDITY	INFLUENCE OF ENVIRONMENT
Physical appearance			
Ability to learn			
Emotional tendencies			
Activity you enjoy			
Activity you are good at			
Moment you are proud of			
Activity you would like to do in the future			

Needs

*C*ertain **needs** or necessities motivate everyone. For example, when you feel the need for food, you are motivated to eat. People work to satisfy a number of needs. Many people work for a sense of identity. When you ask people what they do or who they are, they often reply by saying something like: "I am a student" or "I work as a sales representative." Another reason people may work is for dignity and social recognition. People may also work for money to satisfy needs such as food and shelter, or to satisfy wants such as luxury cars and designer clothes.

The needs that motivate our decisions can be very complex. Abraham Maslow, a psychologist, identified a number of psychological and physical needs that motivate human action. He stated that these needs are the true motivators of humans, although the needs can be ignored or suppressed. Maslow created a model called the **hierarchy of needs** that outlines the priority of these needs in pyramid form. According to Maslow, human beings are motivated by a number of basic needs, which are apparently unchanging and instinctive. These basic needs must be met before higher-level needs become major influences on a person. Once a level of needs is satisfied, other, higher needs begin to dominate a person. Once these new needs are met, still higher needs emerge, and so on. Maslow referred to people who have fully achieved their potential and met all their needs as self-actualized people.

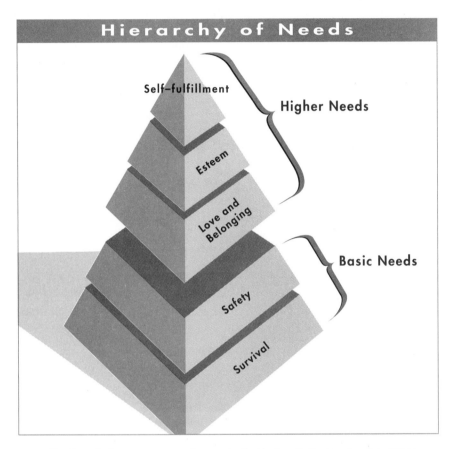

"Hierarchy of Needs" from *Motivation and Personality* by Abraham H. Maslow. Copyright 1954 by Harper & Row, Publishers, Inc. Copyright © 1970 by Abraham H. Maslow. Reprinted and redrawn by permission of HarperCollins Publishers.

SURVIVAL NEEDS

The most basic and powerful needs are for physical survival, such as food, water, sleep, oxygen, and shelter. A person who is lacking food and love will seek food first and ignore all other needs until this need is satisfied.

SAFETY NEEDS

Once survival needs are basically satisfied, safety needs emerge. Protection from harm, injury, and abuse are safety needs. Without safety needs, a person may be anxious and insecure. Such a person seeks order and stability to satisfy safety needs.

LOVE AND BELONGING NEEDS

When the survival and safety needs are met, needs for love, affection, and belonging emerge. A person will forget about the basic needs that have been satisfied and seek a place in his or her group (such as family, friends, or co-workers) and healthy relations with others. A healthy relationship, according to Maslow, involves mutual trust, equality, and lack of fear.

ESTEEM NEEDS

These needs refer to self-esteem and esteem from other people. Self-esteem includes needs such as confidence, competence, achievement, and independence. Esteem from others includes respect, recognition, acceptance, attention, and appreciation.

SELF-FULFILLMENT NEEDS

You must begin to think of yourself as becoming the person you want to be.
D. VISCOTT

Once a reasonable satisfaction of love and esteem needs has been achieved, a person can develop her or his potential through continuing personal growth. Maslow described this need as "the desire to become more and more what one is, to become everything that one is capable of becoming." Seeking new experiences, learning new skills, developing talents, and taking courses all help a person to feel fulfilled. Once all needs have been met, self-actualization is achieved.

A person's needs are generally desired in the order listed in Maslow's hierarchy, from bottom to top. However, there are exceptions. Some people may prefer to seek self-esteem instead of healthy relationships. A person who has been unemployed for a long time may have suppressed higher needs after years of seeking only basic needs. People who have been secure in their basic needs for a long time can withstand the loss of these needs for a length of time. Maslow also stated that the hierarchy of needs does not occur precisely. For example, the need for love may emerge before the need for safety is completely met. Most people only partially satisfy their basic needs. The unsatisfied needs affect behaviour significantly, while satisfied needs have little effect. In other words, a want that is satisfied is no longer a want. Needs affect human behaviour, as do self-concept, personal experiences, heredity, and other factors.

A C T I V I T Y

Identifying Levels of Needs

1 In small groups, identify five examples for each major need (survival, safety, love and belonging, esteem, and self-fulfillment), and rank them in order of importance.

2 In your notebook, indicate where you are in terms of fulfilling each of the needs identified by your group.

3 Write a profile of a self-actualized person.

Values

Values are the moral principles that you use to make decisions. Understanding your values and acting in accordance with them will help to bring you personal satisfaction. A person's values may include showing concern and caring for others, a desire for world peace, working toward a clean and healthy environment, or material success.

Your values are affected by many people and your environment, such as your family, friends, school, religion, culture, society, and the media. For example, your parents may influence your values in terms of education by encouraging you to attend college or university. Every new experience challenges and shapes your values. Although your values are influenced in many ways, you can shape them and the decisions you make in your life.

The greatest thing in the world is to know how to be one's own.
MONTAIGNE

ACTIVITY
What Do You Value?

1 Below is a list of values that might influence your choice of occupation. Read the list carefully and then create a chart like the one that follows in your notebook. Place each value under the appropriate category in the chart.

- Helping others (making a contribution to the betterment of people and society).
- Influencing people (being able to change people's attitudes or opinions).
- Knowledge (being able to learn new things).
- Creativity (being able to contribute original ideas, develop new procedures or programs, or use imagination).
- Variety (having different tasks and responsibilities that make the work different from day to day).
- Stability (having a work routine and job duties that are predictable and not likely to change).
- Security (never having to worry about job loss or loss of income).
- Physical challenge (being physically active all of the time).
- Recognition (being known for the work one does: fame).
- Accomplishment (being able to see the results of one's work and the effect of one's contribution).
- Leisure time (having enough time for one's hobbies and activities).
- Family life (having enough time to spend with one's family).
- Responsibility (being in a leadership position, being able to make decisions).
- Adventure (being able to do exciting and sometimes dangerous things).
- Independence (being able to work on one's own without supervision).
- Needing little schooling (being able to enter an occupation without spending much time in school).
- Working alone (being able to work without much contact with others).
- Working with others (having companionship on the job).

- Travel (being able to travel to different parts of the country/world as part of one's job).
- Income (the amount of money paid or received for the work).
- Religious concerns (having an occupation that is compatible with your religious beliefs).

THINGS I VALUE VERY MUCH	THINGS I VALUE A LITTLE	THINGS I DO NOT VALUE

2 Study the first column of your chart, and list at least five occupations that might be a suitable match for you in terms of your values. Study the third column, and list at least five occupations that are not suitable for you.

Reproduced with kind permission of Guidance Centre, The Ontario Institute for Studies in Education.

• •

Journal Entry

Influences on Your Values

In your journal, respond to the questions below.

- What values do I share with a family member, a friend, and a neighbour or member of the community?
- What values are unique to me?
- Who or what influences my values? How do they influence me?

Interests

Analyzing your **interests**—the activities, pastimes, and subjects you enjoy—can help you to understand who you are and what occupations may be appropriate for you. People whose jobs relate to their interests tend to be happier and more satisfied.

Interests can be categorized in terms of information, people, and things. Interests in information refer to working with facts, data, and numbers; for example, accounting. Interests in people include working with and helping people; for example, counselling or providing a service. Interests in things refer to working with tools, specialized equipment, computers, and building materials, and also include physical activities; for example, construction work or landscaping. Many quizzes are available to help you analyze your interests. They can be a useful way to determine occupations that may suit you.

Our deeds determine us, as much as we determine our deeds.
GEORGE ELIOT

A C T I V I T Y
Analyzing Activities You Enjoy

1 Quickly list 20 activities you enjoy. Once your list is complete, create a chart like the one below. Place a check mark in the appropriate column to classify the activity according to whether it involves information, people, or things and whether it involves being outdoors or indoors. An activity may involve more than one category.

2 Count the check marks in each column and write the totals at the bottom.

3 In small groups, discuss what you have learned about yourself from your totals. What conclusions can you form?

ACTIVITIES I ENJOY	INFORMATION	PEOPLE	THINGS	OUTDOORS	INDOORS
1					
2					
3					
4					
5					
6					
7					
8					
9					
10					
11					
12					
13					
14					
15					
16					
17					
18					
19					
20					
Totals	_____	_____	_____	_____	_____

On a copy of the following quiz provided by your teacher, mark an X in the Yes or the No column for each question. There are no right or wrong answers. Answer each question honestly, and take as much time as you need. If some questions are hard to answer, discuss them with a partner. This quiz will assess your interests at this particular moment in your life. Your interests will continue to change, so you may want to take this quiz again at a later date.

	Yes	**No**
1 Do you like to have a lot of freedom when you do an assignment or a job?	___	___
2 Do you like to be a leader?	___	___
3 Do you like to finish one job before you start the next?	___	___
4 Are you generally co-operative?	___	___
5 Do you like to work on projects by yourself?	___	___
6 Do you keep your things neat and tidy?	___	___
7 Do you enjoy writing poetry or stories?	___	___
8 Would you enjoy selling things, from apartment rentals to newspaper advertisements?	___	___
9 Do you plan carefully before you start to do something?	___	___
10 Are social activities very important to you?	___	___
11 Would you like to work on research projects?	___	___
12 Do you like to follow directions carefully?	___	___
13 Are you sensitive to your own feelings?	___	___
14 Do you usually look on the bright side of things?	___	___
15 Do you like to build things and/or repair them?	___	___
16 Are you able to explain things clearly to other people?	___	___
17 When you learn something new, do you often try to find out more about it?	___	___
18 Do you have clerical ability?	___	___
19 Do you like to create things, for example, inventing gadgets or designing posters?	___	___
20 Would you describe yourself as being ambitious?	___	___
21 Are you uncomfortable when a lot of people pay attention to you?	___	___
22 Can you discuss difficult subjects with people without hurting their feelings?	___	___
23 Would you want to work in a science laboratory?	___	___
24 When you do a project or another job, do you do it carefully, one step at a time?	___	___
25 Do you have musical, artistic, or dramatic ability?	___	___

26 Do you like speaking in front of a group of people?   ____ ____

27 Do you enjoy working with tools and machinery?   ____ ____

28 Are you able to help people who are upset or worried?   ____ ____

29 Do you read scientific books or magazines?   ____ ____

30 Would you like to prepare letters and written reports?   ____ ____

31 When you have been assigned a project or task, do you like to do it differently from most other people?   ____ ____

32 Are you a person who likes to try new things or experiences?   ____ ____

33 Do you see yourself as a practical person?   ____ ____

34 Are you a good listener?   ____ ____

35 Do you like solving mathematical or chess puzzles?   ____ ____

36 Do you arrange your papers, files, or books in an organized way?   ____ ____

37 Do you express your emotions easily?   ____ ____

38 Do you think you can sell an idea or a product?   ____ ____

39 Do you often take part in sports or athletics?   ____ ____

40 Can you meet new people easily?   ____ ____

41 Do you dig deeply into topics to satisfy your curiosity or to solve problems?   ____ ____

42 Do you see yourself as being calm rather than emotional?   ____ ____

43 Are you basically independent?   ____ ____

44 Are you good at arguing your point of view?   ____ ____

45 Do you think you have mechanical ability?   ____ ____

46 Do you enjoy giving information to other people?   ____ ____

47 Would you rather find out something for yourself than take another person's word for it?   ____ ____

48 Would you like to work at a job where you would operate a computer or other machine?   ____ ____

49 Do you have a good imagination?   ____ ____

50 Would you be interested in organizing a club or another group?   ____ ____

51 Would you rather work at a task than socialize with people?   ____ ____

52 Would you describe yourself as generous?   ____ ____

53 Are you more of a thinking than an emotional person?   ____ ____

54 Do you enjoy working with numbers?   ____ ____

55 Are you able to design, invent, or create things?   ____ ____

56 Have you considered starting your own business?   ____ ____

57 Do you like working with your hands, doing things such as plumbing repairs, fixing cars, sewing, or wallpapering?   ____ ____

58 Are you interested in looking after people when they are sick?   ____ ____

59 Do you have mathematical abilities?   ____ ____

60 When you are given an assignment, do you like to show how well you can do it?   ____ ____

How to Score the Quiz

The chart below contains 60 numbers, one for each of the questions you have just answered. For every question you answered Yes, mark an X on the corresponding number on a copy of the chart provided by your teacher. For example, if you answered Yes for question 1, you should put an X on number 1. Then count the number of Xs on each line. Write that number in the space at the right. The lines with the most Xs are your strongest interest areas.

Artistic/ Creative	1	7	13	19	25	31	37	43	49	55	___
Enterprising	2	8	14	20	26	32	38	44	50	56	___
Practical	3	9	15	21	27	33	39	45	51	57	___
Social	4	10	16	22	28	34	40	46	52	58	___
Investigative	5	11	17	23	29	35	41	47	53	59	___
Orderly	6	12	18	24	30	36	42	48	54	60	___

Artistic/Creative

You enjoy music, art, drama, and literary activities. You are creative. You dislike rules and structures and show emotions more openly than most people.

Enterprising

You enjoy sales, leadership, and management. You like power and status and can use your verbal skills to direct and influence others.

Practical

You would rather do things than just socialize. When you run into problems you want concrete solutions; you try them out to see if they work. You may feel uncomfortable working out answers in theory only.

Social

You like being with other people and helping them, or maybe doing work that involves others. You seek close relationships with people and probably have good interpersonal skills. You may feel unhappy when working alone or doing physical jobs.

Investigative

You like working with ideas. You analyze and think things through. You prefer to work independently. You would rather let others do the persuading to have people accept your ideas.

Orderly

You like keeping things tidy, perhaps doing forms and reports in business or economics. You enjoy working with details, you have good self-control, and you identify with power, status, and well-structured programs.

Connect your interests to the possible jobs on the chart on page 28. Select your strongest category across the top of the chart, and then select your second-strongest category along the side of the chart. Find the intersection of these categories—these jobs should relate to your interests.

Scarborough Board of Education

Answer the following questions in your notebook:

1 What are the benefits of this interest quiz for you?

2 How can an interest quiz be misleading? How accurate do you think this interest quiz was for you?

3 Of the jobs within your interest areas, which ones appeal to you? Add at least three more jobs to your interest areas.

. . . .

Skills

A skill is a practised or natural ability to do something well; for example, speaking, organizing, or teaching. Some experts think that each person has up to 700 different skills, although it would be difficult for many people to identify these skills. In today's job market, it is important to be able to identify your skills and know how they apply to a particular job or task. As well, determining your skills can help you to more realistically direct your future career.

Skills can be classified into three main categories: technical skills, self-management skills, and transferable skills. **Technical skills** are the specific areas of technical knowledge and ability that a person needs in order to do a particular job. Many jobs require certain technical skills; for example, a computer programmer knows the technical aspects of computers and a car mechanic knows engines and engine repair. Technical skills are usually learned through some kind of training, either through formal education or on the job. These skills often need to be updated as technology changes over time.

Self-management skills are a part of personality and are continually learned. These skills are also transferable, since they help a person to manage or cope with situations. For example, the ability to work with

We are human becomings rather than human beings.
AARON J. UNGERSMA

CAREER CHART

	ARTISTIC/CREATIVE	ENTERPRISING	PRACTICAL	SOCIAL	INVESTIGATIVE	ORDERLY
ARTISTIC/CREATIVE		Choreographer, Artistic director, Interior decorator, Advertising manager, Film producer/director	Graphics, Photographer, Sculptor, Photographer's helper, Sign writer, TV camera operator, Audio-visual technician, Drafter	Model, Teacher, Economist, Musician, Actor, Production manager (theatre, film radio, TV)	Composer, Architect, Sculptor, Sign writer	Theatre technician, Electronics, Props, Costumes, TV and film technician, Grip, Camera person, Set dresser
ENTERPRISING	Film producer, Disc jockey, Announcer, Baker, Lawyer, Craftsperson (arts and crafts), Working chef, Interior designer		Pharmacist, Pharmacy assistant, Dietary assistant, Salesclerk, Tradesperson, Carpenter/plumber	Museum curator, Systems analyst, Buyer, Auctioneer, Real estate, Sales manager	Market research analyst, Insurance investigator, Private investigator, Security, Quality control	Auctioneer, Buyer, Manager, Market research analyst, Real estate agent, Sales agent, Insurance inspector
PRACTICAL	Furniture refinisher, Cook, Painter, Cabinetmaker, Mould maker, Photo engineer, Printer, Baker	Plumber, Roofer, Small engine mechanic, Animal breeder, Mechanic		Taxi driver, Meat cutter, Kitchen helper, Server, Chef, Baker, Police officer	Welder, Grounds keeper, Iron worker, Small engine mechanic, Jeweller, Appliance service person, Radio and TV technician	Dental hygienist, Driller, Lather, Truck driver, Letter carrier, Maintenance, Motor mechanic, Packager, Assembler, Construction labourer
SOCIAL	Flying instructor, Minister, Priest, Rabbi, Speech therapist, Preschool teacher, Teacher, Childcare worker	Counsellor, Dietitian, Home economist, Host restaurant, Driving instructor, Employment counsellor	Childcare worker, Employment counsellor, Orderly, Nurses' aid, Waiter		Community organization worker, Social worker, Sociologist, Probation officer, Police officer	Orderly, Community organization worker, Cashier, Server, Nurses' aid, Waiter, Host, Probation officer, Police officer
INVESTIGATIVE	Doctor, Chemist, Law clerk, Taxidermist, Mathematician, Scientist, Research	Pharmacist, Optometrist, Electronics technician, Lawyer, Chemical lab technician, Inventor	Electronics technician, Camera repair person, Chemical lab technician, Computer operator, Geological technician	Doctor, Optometrist, Psychologist, Social worker, Librarian, Veterinarian, Order processor/picker		Word processor, Camera repairperson, Lawyer, Law clerk, Librarian, Instrument repairer
ORDERLY	Administrative assistant, Library technician, Drafter, Computer programmer, Designer	Hotel clerk, Stock clerk, Travel agent, Sewing machine operator	Coding clerk, Keypunch operator, Order filler, Bank teller, Sewing machine operator, Business machine operator	Switchboard operator, Travel agent, Receptionist, Library, Credit clerk, Bookkeeper	Clerk typist, Methods analyst, Travel agent, Bookkeeper, Accounting clerk, Stock clerk	

Scarborough Board of Education

others and the ability to adapt to new situations are self-management skills. These skills are rarely part of a company's training program and are usually mastered throughout a person's life. Since these skills are usually not obtained through formal education or training, people often do not recognize them.

Transferable skills are skills developed through everyday experiences such as school, employment, or other activities. These skills are common to many situations and can be easily applied to new jobs or industries. Both technical and self-management skills can be transferable. Examples of transferable skills include word processing, making decisions, and communicating effectively.

A C T I V I T Y
Rating Your Skills

1 Rate yourself in terms of each skill described below on a copy of the list provided by your teacher. Use the following scale: 4—superior, 3—above average, 2—average, and 1—limited.

2 With a partner, compare your results. Discuss the similarities and differences in your skills.

Academic	**Rate**

Reasoning. Thinking logically, solving problems, understanding ideas, putting facts together and drawing conclusions from them, and evaluating or organizing information. Essential for learning and performing complex tasks.   ____

Alertness. Reacting to a situation quickly. Required for troubleshooting, consulting, repairing, and emergency action.   ____

Memory. Recognizing and recalling things. Valuable in occupations that call for recognizing people or recalling details.   ____

Creativity. Thinking of a new idea, product, or way of doing things. Includes designing improved methods, researching, artistic endeavours, writing, and media.   ____

Judgement. Seeing all the essential factors in a situation and their relationships to the desired outcome.   ____

Analysis. Breaking down a complex thing into smaller parts.   ____

Organization. Placing elements in appropriate relationships to one another. The elements may be machinery, people, and facts or ideas.   ____

Communication

Fluency. Ability to speak and write easily, rapidly, and smoothly.   ____

Vocabulary. Understanding word meanings, and choosing the right words to convey meanings. Essential for understanding, communicating, and summarizing.   ____

Listening. Understanding, interpreting, and summarizing what one hears.   ____

Reading. Understanding, interpreting, and summarizing what one reads.   ____

English usage. Knowledge of grammar, spelling, punctuation, and formal rules of writing.   ____

Writing. Organizing and expressing ideas or conveying feelings through the written word.   ____

Languages. Skill in learning and using new languages.   ____

Numerical

Computing. Facility in simple arithmetic operations.   ____

Comprehension. Understanding number relationships.   ____

Mathematics. Handling numbers in the abstract, understanding and resolving formulae, and expressing problems in formulae.   ____

Estimating. Assessing distances, sizes, and costs and predicting outcomes.   ____

Social

Understanding. Being sensitive to what people feel and think, understanding their needs and motives, and appraising complexities of personal relations.   ____

Persuasion. Influencing others to agree with an idea or follow a course of action.   ____

Negotiating. Working with others toward an amicable decision.   ____

Technical

Precision. Speed and accuracy in recording, comparing, remembering details, computing, classifying, and coding.   ____

Observation. Noticing details and small differences; for example, in colour, form, position, size, or touch.   ____

Attention. The ability to concentrate and observe.   ____

Space. Imagining how things will look when fitted together or taken apart, or when an object is viewed from a different angle. ____

Mechanical understanding. Seeing quickly how mechanical devices operate, what to expect of a machine, whether it is operating properly, and how it may be repaired. ____

Mechanical ingenuity. Designing mechanisms that will accomplish specific movements and seeing possible uses for a device. ____

Aesthetic

Art talent. Ability to identify what is pleasing and why, creativity in developing a pleasing arrangement, and memory for visual experience. ____

Musical talent. Sensitivity to fine differences in intensity, pitch, time, and rhythm; strong emotional reaction to music; and ability to play an instrument. ____

Dramatic talent. Ability to perform through words and gestures in a variety of settings. ____

Physical

Strength. Stamina to do the job. ____

Dexterity. Speed and accuracy in moving objects and using tools and machinery. ____

Co-ordination. Skill in using one's hands together (hand-to-eye co-ordination). ____

Precision. Delicate, highly controlled movements. ____

- -

1 Gather the information you have accumulated about yourself throughout this chapter. Then create a copy of the form that follows. Complete the form in order to summarize the aspects that you think are most important for you to consider when you start planning your career.

2 Create a collage that tells people who you are.

A C T I V I T Y
Who Are You?

WHO AM I?

My five strongest personality traits are:

My five strongest needs are:

My five most important values are:

My five main interests are:

My five strongest skills are:

Based on this information, how do I feel about myself?

Directing Change

Your self-concept, personality, needs, values, interests, and skills are continually evolving as you move through life and experience new things. Since who you are and what you are capable of doing are continually changing, you can control and direct these changes. In your journal, complete the statements below.

- The person I wish to become is a person who . . .
- The steps I can take to become that person are . . .

HOW HAVE YOU CHANGED?

Once you have been at your placement for a number of weeks, consider how your work experiences have influenced your self-assessment. Use the Who Am I? form that you completed (page 32) to help you reassess who you are.

1 How have your self-concept, personality, needs, and values changed based on your placement experiences?

2 What new interests and skills do you have?

3 What skills do you want in the future?

Make the Connection

WHAT HAVE YOU LEARNED?

▼ ▼ ▼

1 Describe how a positive and a negative self-concept can affect a person.

2 a What factors affect personality?

b How do these factors affect personality?

3 Describe Maslow's hierarchy of needs.

4 How do people's values influence the decisions they make?

5 How might your interests and skills be enhanced at your placement?

6 a Identify two jobs that may be suitable for you.

b List five technical, self-management, and transferable skills you have that relate to each job.

7 Why is periodic self-assessment important?

CHAPTER 3

FUTURE TRENDS

WHAT YOU WILL LEARN

After completing this chapter, you should be able to:

▼ ▼ ▼

- Analyze futurists' predictions.
- Consider the implications of these possible trends on future careers.
- Consider the implications of the six-wave economy.
- Interpret the effect of changing demographics on the work force.
- Examine paradigm shifts and resistance to shifts.

TERMS TO REMEMBER

▼ ▼ ▼

futurist	demography	paradigm
trend	information age	paradigm shift
prediction		

Predicting Change

*I*n a future full of uncertainty, change is constant. Change in today's world is occurring faster than in any previous generation. How can a person not only cope with change, but also create change if it is necessary? Although there are no guarantees, reading literature written by **futurists** (predictors of the future) and observing current societal **trends**, or general directions in which a society is developing, will help indicate the future for your personal life as well as for your career choices. Futurists examine and make **predictions,** or forecasts, of what will happen in the future in order to make decisions about the present and direct the future. In other words, people may use predictions to either justify current situations or to encourage change. **Demography** is the statistical science dealing with the distribution, density, and vital statistics of human populations. Studying these population characteristics, or demographics, also helps in determining trends. By understanding and assessing predictions or images of the future, a person can learn to cope with and direct change and, thus, work to achieve a desirable future.

In 1982 in his book *Megatrends,* John Naisbitt predicted the following shifts in thinking that have dramatically affected people in industrialized nations.

PAST PRACTICE	1980 DEVELOPMENTS
Industrial Society • Producing goods	*Information Society* • Working with information • Phenomenal growth of technology (satellites, computers, and television)
Forced Technology • Computers were resisted and misunderstood • Unions were concerned that new technology would cost jobs	*High Tech/High Touch* • With the introduction of new technology is a corresponding movement toward the personal; for example, high technology within hospitals has led to more neighbourhood clinics, and airplanes have led to more meetings between people
National Economy • Self-sufficient national economies • A world industrial leader	*World Economy* • An interdependent world economy • Trade among all countries
Short Term • Management makes the current quarter stronger at the expense of the future	*Long Term* • Sacrifice now in order to have a healthy future • A struggle between short-term profits and long-range plans

Centralization
- National governments have power
- Head offices and plants located in major cities
- Population concentration in the cities
- Conformity

Decentralization
- Provincial and local governments have more power
- Independent regional offices and plants in small towns and rural areas
- People live in small towns and commute to work
- Regional diversity

Institutional Help
- Governments, medical establishments, corporations, and schools developed
- Belief that only with the strength of large institutions could we effectively counter life's blows
- Food, jobs, and shelter are supplied by institutions

Self-Help
- Learning to trust and rely on the individual
- Running, jogging, and health food
- Alternative schools and organizations

Representative Democracy
- Politicians are elected to represent the public in government
- Consumers and workers accept what the corporations tell them

Participatory Democracy
- The public must be part of the decision making
- Politicians must be accountable
- Consumers start to complain and form activist groups
- New attention to workers' rights

Hierarchies
- Pyramid structure with one person at the top and power decreasing downward
- Everyone agrees with the "boss"
- Vertical power structure

Networking
- People talking to one another and sharing ideas, information, and resources
- Horizontal power lines
- Strong belief in social equality
- Team approach

Either/Or
- Either married or did not marry
- Either worked 9 to 5 or did not work
- Mass markets and mass-market advertising
- Major television networks
- White Anglo-Saxon dominance

Multiple Options
- Wide diversity in lifestyle, consumer goods, and family structure
- Personal choices
- Cable television
- Ethnic diversity

1 Divide into groups of three or four and discuss the predictions for 1980 from *Megatrends* listed on pages 36–37.

2 Analyze the accuracy of each prediction. List at least two examples to support the prediction or to demonstrate the inaccuracy of the prediction. If your group needs more information before determining accuracy, ask a history or economics teacher or do some library research.

3 If a prediction has proven to be inaccurate, discuss why you think it did not come true.

Journal Entry

Images of the Future

Consider predictions and images of the future to which you have been exposed (for example, from fictional movies and TV shows or from political predictions). In your journal, respond to the questions below.

- How have I been influenced by these images? For example, have they encouraged me to make changes, foster expectations, or justify current situations?

Predictions for the Future

Analyzing futurists' predictions can help a person to make long-term personal and career decisions. *Megatrends 2000* by John Naisbitt and Patricia Aburdene and *The Popcorn Report* by Faith Popcorn are two futurist publications.

MEGATRENDS 2000
John Naisbitt and Patricia Aburdene's book *Megatrends 2000* includes the following predictions.[1]

A Global Economic Boom in the 1990s
The world is moving away from a system of trade among countries to a single world economy. The borders between countries, tariffs, and trade regulations will no longer exist in the marketplace. The North American Free Trade Agreement and the European Common Market are examples of the initial elimination of borders. This global marketplace will be tremendously prosperous.

The greatest thing in this world is not so much where we are, but in what direction we are moving.

O.W. HOLMES

---

[1] Text excerpt as adapted with the authors' approval, from *Megatrends 2000: Ten New Directions for the 1990s,* by John Naisbitt and Patricia Aburdene. Copyright © 1990 by Megatrends Ltd. By permission of William Morrow & Company, Inc.

A Revival of the Arts

There will be a fundamental and revolutionary shift in leisure time and spending priorities. During the 1990s, the arts—drama, dance, music, and visual arts—will gradually displace sports as society's major leisure activity. The arts will have a prominent place on television, and people will attend more live performances.

A Transformation of Communist Socialism

Traditional communism in areas such as the former Soviet Union and Eastern Europe is being modified to adapt to the twenty-first century. In the past, communist governments owned the means of production and controlled the distribution of goods. Most communist countries are letting go of that control. The reasons for this change include the new global economy, the trend to decentralization, the high cost of government social programs, and the new importance of the individual.

Global Lifestyles and Cultural Nationalism

A thriving world economy, global telecommunications, and expanded travel will enable people around the world to enjoy similar lifestyles. But Naisbitt and Aburdene point out that "even as our lifestyles grow more similar, there are unmistakable signs of a powerful countertrend." A strong desire to assert one's culture and language will develop, along with a rejection of foreign influence.

Privatization of the Welfare State

There will be a move away from the government as provider and a move toward individuals taking more control over their own lives. Since World War II, governments have become more involved in social welfare programs, such as welfare payments, housing and food programs, and medical assistance. Governments have taken care of those who are unable to care for themselves. In the future, companies that were once run by the government will be owned by members of the public—in other words, government-run companies will be privatized. Countries will shift away from welfare programs, and individuals will participate in training and work programs in order to receive assistance until they are fully employed. The shift will be to individuals and what individuals can do for themselves, not what can be done for them. All over the world, countries are trying to outline society's responsibilities to citizens.

Rise of Pacific Rim Nations

The Pacific Rim is a vast region that includes all the countries touched by the Pacific Ocean. These countries will grow and become more economically powerful. The major cities of the Pacific Rim, such as Los Angeles, Sydney, Vancouver, and Tokyo, are taking the focus of world trade away from the old, established cities of the Atlantic.

The computer will change the hierarchical, pyramidal, managerial system. We originally needed this system to keep track of people and the tasks people did. The computer can now fulfill this need, and so our institutions will be restructured horizontally.

JOHN NAISBITT

A survey to determine the percentage of office workers using computers at work showed 88 percent of Canadian office workers use computers compared to 85 percent in the United States, 80 percent in the European Community, and 64 percent in Japan.

Decade of Women in Leadership

For the last two decades, women have filled two-thirds of the millions of new jobs created by the **information age** (which refers to the explosion in the past two decades in industries that create, process, and distribute data) and will continue to do so well into the next century. As workers, professionals, and entrepreneurs, women are prevalent in the information age. In the 1990s, conventional thought will concede that women and men function equally well as business leaders, and women will achieve leadership positions denied them in the past.

Age of Biology

We are poised on the threshold of a great era of biotechnology, which is technology that involves biology or the science of life in all its forms. Through biotechnology, species can be altered at a genetic level. For example, fish like the carp have been genetically altered to grow faster, and in the future, insect-resistant crops may be grown. Many people have ethical concerns about this manipulation of nature. Two questions that arise from the developments in this area: Will the intrusion of technology in nature transform people's perception of life itself? Will future generations see life as just another usable computer program? The power to bring about good will also open the door to serious potential problems. Increased biotechnology will lead to increased development, discussion, and debate of ethics.

Triumph of the Individual

The unifying theme of all the trends is the triumph of the individual. It is not an "every person for himself or herself" individualism but an ethical philosophy that elevates the individual to the global level. Each person is responsible for concerns such as preserving the environment, preventing nuclear warfare, and eliminating poverty.

A C T I V I T Y
*Analyzing Predictions
from Megatrends 2000*

1 Divide into nine groups, with each group analyzing one prediction from *Megatrends 2000*. Determine whether you agree or disagree with the prediction.

2 Share your group's analysis in a presentation to the class, including why you agree or disagree with the prediction. If you agree, explain how the prediction might be expanded. If you disagree, provide alternative predictions.

THE POPCORN REPORT

In her book *The Popcorn Report*, futurist Faith Popcorn has theorized about the trends that follow,[2] which she expects to make a great impact on our society.

---

[2] From *The Popcorn Report* by Faith Popcorn. Copyright 1991 by Faith Popcorn. Used by permission of Doubleday, a division of Bantam Doubleday Dell Publishing Group, Inc.

Cocooning

Cocooning is the need to withdraw into a small, familiar space protected from the outside world. In the 1980s, cocooning meant staying home, which resulted in the growth in popularity of takeout food, VCRs, and mail-order services. Today, cocooning is an emotional as well as a physical withdrawal. It is no longer exclusively about a place (the home) but a state of mind (self-preservation). People's "cocoons" are now armoured (for example, security systems are becoming more popular), and safety is a major concern. People's cars are becoming secondary self-contained cocoons.

You have to see the future to deal with the present.
FAITH POPCORN

Fantasy Adventure

There is a desperate need to escape physically into our cocoons for comfort and to escape emotionally into our fantasies for release of stress. People are seeking a risk-free, momentary, wild and crazy retreat from the world. The adventure could be very small, such as eating exotic foods, or it could involve indoor rock climbing and tours of exotic countries.

Small Indulgences

Instead of large, expensive luxury items, consumers will pamper themselves with small, affordable luxuries, such as creams, oils, and fancy pens.

Egonomics

Egonomics refers to personalizing products and services for a consumer; for example, kitchen counters of different heights or customized book publishing. People will want to feel unique, not self-centred as in the 1980s "me generation." Customizing will become more and more popular as people seek ways to express individuality.

Cashing Out

After years of commuting to work and working in a fast-paced environment, the trend is for people to go somewhere else to work at something they want to do and to do things the way they want to do them. More people will work at home, and more city people will move to the country. People will evaluate what is real, what is honest, what is quality, and what they value. They will trade in the rewards of traditional success in favour of a slower pace and quality of life. There will be a tremendous growth in small businesses and a reduction in large corporations.

Trends never end. And the future is never here.
FAITH POPCORN

Down-aging

As a major part of the population ages, the definition of what constitutes "old" will change. For example, today's attitude toward being 40 years old is similar to the past attitude toward being 30 years old. Although plastic surgery, hair colouring, and anti-aging creams will still be in demand, older people will be more inclined to accept their age and ignore it in favour of character. People will have more fun, act more childlike to relieve stress, and develop a good sense of humour.

Staying Alive

There will be a constant search for methods of preventing disease and aging. People will take extremely good care of themselves, including self-health care, proper nutrition, and organic foods. In the future, most food will be grown in laboratories in clinically controlled conditions. Technology will monitor people's vital signs daily and customize people's diets for complete health. By maximizing the performance of their bodies, people will also maximize their quality of thought.

The Vigilante Consumer

Consumers will become angry if products are anything but top quality. Any claims made by a company about a product that prove to be untrue will cause a violent reaction against the company and the product through boycotts, protests, letters, telephone calls, and so on. Companies will have to respond because consumers will be in a position of power.

Ninety-nine Lives

Trendbending is the process of shaping your product or strategy around emerging trends.

FAITH POPCORN

The lifestyle of multiple roles and multiple jobs will become commonplace at an ever-increasing rate. Life will be incredibly complicated—people will be encouraged to maintain health, be ethically aware, have a successful career, raise a family, and much more. With so many goals and so little time, people will streamline their activities. Fast food will be even faster. Services will come into the workplace—dry cleaners, hairdressers, massage therapists, and take-home gourmet meals. People will be able to shop by fax or go drive-through shopping. Consumers will need not just speedier service but more services.

SOS (Save Our Society)

This trend identifies any effort that contributes to making the 1990s our first truly socially responsible decade. The "Decency Decade" will be dedicated to the environment, education, and ethics. The question of the survival of the world is *the* issue. Doing good is no longer an option—it is a must. People will give up short-term personal gain for long-term goals such as a healthy environment. It is no longer enough to just "do no wrong"; people will "do right" and encourage others to do right.

Analyzing Predictions from *The Popcorn Report*
Consider each of Faith Popcorn's predictions. In your journal, respond to the questions below.

- Why do I agree or disagree with the prediction?
- If I agree, how does the prediction make an impact on my life? (Illustrate with an example.)
- If I disagree, how can this prediction be disproved by my life? (Illustrate with an example.)

* * * * * * * * * * * * * * * * * * * *

In essay form, examine the similarities and differences between the predictions from *Megatrends 2000* and *The Popcorn Report*. For example, you may want to compare John Naisbitt's prediction of the triumph of the individual with Faith Popcorn's prediction of egonomics. You may want to obtain copies of the books from the library for further reference.

A C T I V I T Y
Comparing Futurists' Predictions

* * * * * * * * * * * * * * * * * * * *

1 The chart on page 44 shows predictions of where the jobs will be in the year 2000. Using your knowledge of predicted future trends, make a list of the types of jobs that you think will be available in the future as well as the jobs that you think will not be available.

2 How might future trends affect business, industry, education, health, and social institutions?

3 How might future trends affect your career choices?

A C T I V I T Y
Implications for Future Careers

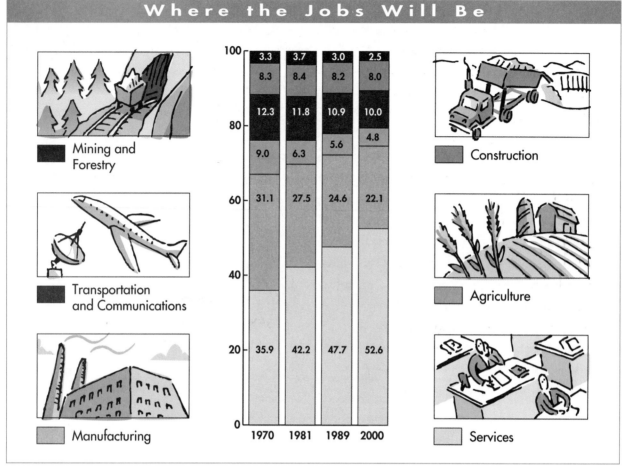

Where the Jobs Will Be

Mining and Forestry

Transportation and Communications

Manufacturing

Construction

Agriculture

Services

	1970	1981	1989	2000
	3.3	3.7	3.0	2.5
	8.3	8.4	8.2	8.0
	12.3	11.8	10.9	10.0
	9.0	6.3	5.6	4.8
	31.1	27.5	24.6	22.1
	35.9	42.2	47.7	52.6

Source: The Wefa Group

CASE STUDY

Home Is Where the Office Is

by Trish Crawford

Bob Bowen thinks it's silly to put on a suit and tie when he's working.

The president of Bowen Office Systems and Services says his employees, "can work in their bathing suits, if they want."

For all he knows, they do. Because Bowen's employees work mostly from home and rarely come into the office.

Bowen, who runs a computer software company from his home, checks in with his three employees each morning by computer. He sees

where they are going and when, which projects they are working on, and how far they have gone. All he doesn't see is them.

"The important thing is that they get the work done," says Bowen, who wears track suits or cords and a sweater when he sits down to work at one of the computers in front of his cozy fireplace.

There is a staff meeting every Monday morning but, after that, Bowen might only see each employee one day of the week.

This is the office-less office.

Technological links between worker and job could one day mean no more commuting (goodbye traffic jams), no more suits (who sees you anyway?), no more costly office towers (they'll all become condos).

This was the world glimpsed decades ago when the full potential of computers and facsimile (or fax) machines was first being understood.

Although we continue to build huge office towers downtown and the workplace revolution didn't happen as quickly as first predicted, we are on the cusp of a major change in our work lives, say computer equipment manufacturers, swamped with requests for home-based equipment.

The pressures for change are coming from two different directions. Due to the declining birth rate of the past 20 years, the service industry will experience increasing worker shortages.

And, with the downtown real estate prices shooting through the sky and even the suburban locations costing the earth, companies will be less and less inclined to erect skyscrapers to house workers for only seven or eight hours a day.

But so far in the technological revolution, what we've got is mostly a hybrid—some employees work from home, some of the time.

Reprinted with permission — The Toronto Star Syndicate.

▼ ▼ ▼

1 List the advantages and disadvantages of working at home for employers and employees.

2 Would you like to work at home? Why or why not?

The Six-Wave Economy

According to Canadian futurist Frank Feather, author of *Canada's Best Careers Guide,* there are six waves in North America's economy. Each wave represents how North Americans earned money to keep the economy healthy in a specific time period or how they will in the future. The first wave was agriculture and resources in the 1880s. The second wave was manufacturing in the early 1900s. In the third wave in the 1950s, the service sector became the largest employer. The fourth wave, or information age, began to rise to supremacy in the 1980s and the information industry is still the predominant employer in the 1990s. The fifth-wave sector, growing fast in the 1990s, is the leisure sector—the travel, tourism, hospitality, recreation, entertainment, and cultural industries. This sector will be the largest employer in North America by about 2020. The sixth-wave sector is outer space, which Feather expects to reach its peak in 2050.

A small percentage of each wave will continue to be part of the next wave of the North American economy. Evidence of the next waves appear as small percentages of the previous waves. For example, agriculture accounted for almost 80 percent of the first wave, but Feather predicts it will be just 2 percent of the sixth wave. Outer-space economy is 2 percent of the fourth wave and is expected to be 20 percent of the sixth wave.

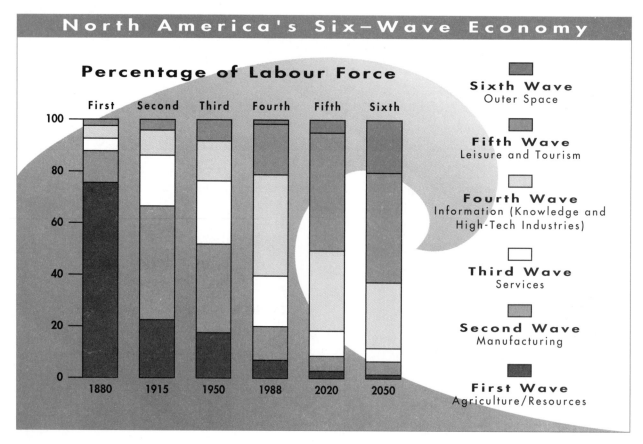

North America's Six–Wave Economy

Percentage of Labour Force

Sixth Wave
Outer Space

Fifth Wave
Leisure and Tourism

Fourth Wave
Information (Knowledge and High-Tech Industries)

Third Wave
Services

Second Wave
Manufacturing

First Wave
Agriculture/Resources

Redrawn from Frank Feather, *Canada's Best Careers Guide* (Aurora: Global Management Bureau, 1990). © 1990 by Frank Feather. Historical data from U.S. Dept. of Labor and Statistics Canada.

ACTIVITY

Creating a Sixth-Wave Business

1 According to the graph, Feather's sixth wave includes some of all the previous waves. The growth area is the outer-space economy. At present, this is almost completely uncharted territory. In this activity, you have the opportunity to be an outer-space pioneer. In small groups, create a company that will prosper in the outer-space industry. You must develop a company name, a logo, and a product or service. Write a full description of your product or service, including uses, size, colour, and materials. As well, determine your typical customer in terms of age, gender, income, family status, and so on.

2 Present your company, logo, and product or service to the class, who will be your prospective customers. Explain why you chose this type of company and product or service. In order to evaluate your presentation, ask your classmates how they like your concept. Ask them to explain why they would or would not buy your product or service.

Your Ideal Future

In your journal, complete the statement below.

- My ideal life in the year 2050 would be...

Demographic Trends

*D*emography, the statistical study of human populations, can help you prepare for future careers as well as future workplace conditions. David Foot, an economist at the University of Toronto, maintains that demographics explain about 75 percent of just about everything, including the future.

One phenomenon that has had one of the greatest demographic impacts on Canada has been the age group labelled the "baby boomers." Boomers are people born in the postwar years between 1947 and 1966. These babies created a huge bulge in the Canadian population. A total of 400 000 new Canadians were born in each of these years, peaking to almost half a million in 1960. This group now comprises one-third of the Canadian population or almost 9 million people, the result of the greatest population growth ever seen in any developed country in this century. This group has dominated and will continue to dominate our population until about the year 2040. The boomers' progress through the stages of life has been the central social and economic fact in Canada for the last five decades. What the boomers want and demand is what the marketplace responds to and provides. For example, tennis clubs thrived when the boomers were in their 20s, while bird-watching will become more popular by the year 2000. Future careers will include those in industries that meet the needs of aging baby boomers, such as health care and leisure.

The graph that follows shows how the 1990 population breaks down by age and the projected population breakdown in Canada in the year 2000.

Population in the Years 1990 and 2000

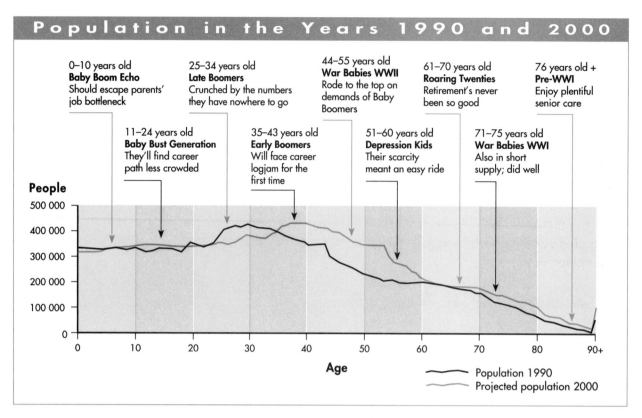

0–10 years old
Baby Boom Echo
Should escape parents'
job bottleneck

11–24 years old
Baby Bust Generation
They'll find career
path less crowded

25–34 years old
Late Boomers
Crunched by the numbers
they have nowhere to go

35–43 years old
Early Boomers
Will face career
logjam for the
first time

44–55 years old
War Babies WWII
Rode to the top on
demands of Baby
Boomers

51–60 years old
Depression Kids
Their scarcity
meant an easy ride

61–70 years old
Roaring Twenties
Retirement's never
been so good

71–75 years old
War Babies WWI
Also in short
supply; did well

76 years old +
Pre-WWI
Enjoy plentiful
senior care

Population 1990
Projected population 2000

Source: Statistics Canada

According to the Ontario Women's Directorate, among the demographic trends challenging Canadians today are:

- *A steady decline in the nation's birth rate.* In the 1950s, there were 28 births for every 1000 Canadians. By 1985, this had dropped to 15 births per 1000.

- *Decreasing fertility rates.* In 1960, Canadian women had an average of 3.9 children. In 1986, this was down to 1.7.

- *A steady increase in the number of senior citizens.* Seniors (aged 65 years and older) made up 10 percent of Canada's population in 1986. By 2011 they will represent 16 percent of the population, and by the year 2036, some 25 percent of Canadians will be 65 or older.

The declining pool of workers, indicated in the graph on page 49, will create skill and labour shortages in key areas of the economy. In a recent survey of Canadian employers, 60 percent reported difficulty recruiting professional, managerial, and technical employees; 42 percent had problems locating skilled tradespeople; and 35 percent had trouble finding good clerical, administrative, and sales staff. Employers will find themselves competing for employees to fill jobs. Not only will organizations be drawing from a smaller pool of workers, but those workers will have more and different obligations apart from their work. Those obligations may well affect the way employees prioritize their work and personal lives. For example, caring for an elderly relative may affect a person's work priorities.

While Canada's pool of workers will decline, the Third World (developing nations) labour force will increase at an enormous rate. In less than two decades, the Third World population will grow by 700 million people. This population explosion may reach crisis proportions, and many of these people will join Canada's labour force through immigration.

More importantly, Canada will need workers with advanced and specialized skills in order to be competitive on a global scale. Individuals can no longer expect to acquire one set of skills that will carry them throughout their working lives. Frequent retraining will be needed to ensure that existing members of the work force keep up with technological developments.

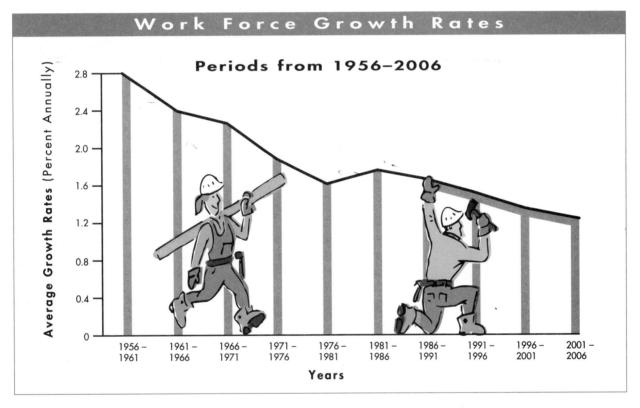

Work Force Growth Rates

Periods from 1956–2006

Average Growth Rates (Percent Annually)

Years

Source: Ontario Women's Directorate

Changing demographics will likely affect the Canadian work force in a number of ways. The book *Work and Family: The Crucial Balance*, published by the Ontario Women's Directorate, outlines the nature of the new work force as follows:

More dual-earner families.

- More mothers and fathers will be combining the responsibilities of child raising with the requirements of their jobs.

- In 1961, only 20 percent of all two-parent families reported both parents working in the paid labour force. By 1986, more than half (53 percent) of all two-parent families were dual earner.

- For many households, having both partners in the paid labour force is an economic imperative. The number of two-parent families below the poverty line would increase by an estimated 78 percent if only one person in the household had paid work.

More heads of single-parent families.

- Between 1977 and 1984, 163 000 more single parents joined the work force. By 1986, labour-force participation for single parents had reached 61.2 percent. While the vast majority of Canadian single-parent families were mother-led (82.2 percent), the proportion of father-led single-parent families is growing.

More women of all ages and at all stages of their lives.

- The enormous influx of women into the paid labour force is perhaps the most striking trend in Canada's demographic profile. Among western democracies Canada ranks behind only Scandinavia in dependence on women in the labour force.

- In 1951, only 23.5 percent of Canadian women worked for pay outside the home. By 1987, this was up to 56.2 percent. The Conference Board of Canada estimates that by 1993, the number of women in the paid labour force could reach 63.1 percent.

- Approximately half of the paid work force will be women. Not only are more women entering the work force, but they are also staying longer than ever before. Women now spend between 34 and 37 years on average in the paid labour force—a term comparable to men.

More women with children, particularly mothers of young children.

- Labour-force participation for women with children under 16 has risen steadily over the past number of years (from 41.6 percent in 1975 to 56.8 percent in 1983). For women with young children, however, the increase has been dramatic. In 1976, fewer than 32 percent of mothers with children under three years of age were in the paid work force. By 1986, one out of every two mothers with children under three were in the labour force, with 66 percent of them working full time.

More men with direct responsibility for family care.

- While historically women have been the primary caregivers, recent surveys and articles show that responsibility for the care of children and elderly relatives is now being shared increasingly by men. Many men are pursuing more balanced lifestyles and exploring work settings and arrangements that enable them to participate fully and directly in family care.

More workers caring for elderly parents or relatives.

- With the aging of the baby-boom generation, the fastest-growing group in Ontario's labour force over the next 12 years will be workers 45 to 54 years of age. Their share of the labour force will rise from 15.9 percent in 1988 to 21.8 percent in the year 2001. Not only will this be the fastest-growing segment of the work force, but also it will be the group sharing much of the responsibility for the care of older family members.

- Right now, two out of five people 30 years of age and older provide some kind of care for elderly relatives. As the parents of baby boomers continue to age, more of their adult children will be combining a job with elder care.

More workers caring for people with disabilities.

- The number of people combining a job with caregiving for a relative or friend with a disability will also increase. A national survey on health and disability showed that out of a population of 2.5 million people (aged 15 and over) with disabilities, only 842 000 were physically independent. Some 400 000 were partially dependent, and 1.1 million were dependent on others. Close to 1 million people had a disability that prevented them from working.

As a result of these changes in the work force, employers will need to demonstrate that they welcome, support, and reward employees and accommodate both work and family priorities. Human-resource policies and programs will be developed to address employee needs and the balance between work and family. For example, some programs that are emerging include day-care centres in the workplace, elder-care centres, working at home, flexible working hours, and parental leaves to look after family members.

ACTIVITY

Charting Your Life Line

Create a life line as shown at the top of page 52, and plot the significant events in your life that have occurred between birth and today (for example, starting school, moving to a new place, or the birth of a sibling). Plot what you think will probably happen to you over the next ten-year period. Include your predicted level of education, type of work, and personal lifestyle (such as whether or not you will be married and where you will live).

Birth   Today   In 10 Years

Paradigms

Knowing the predictions and understanding the demographic trends does not guarantee that people will use this information as they plan their future. Some predictions may be hard for people to accept. The information may conflict with a person's **paradigms,** which are patterns, or models, of acting or thinking. Your ways of doing things and what you believe are your paradigms. Changing to a new way is called a **paradigm shift.**

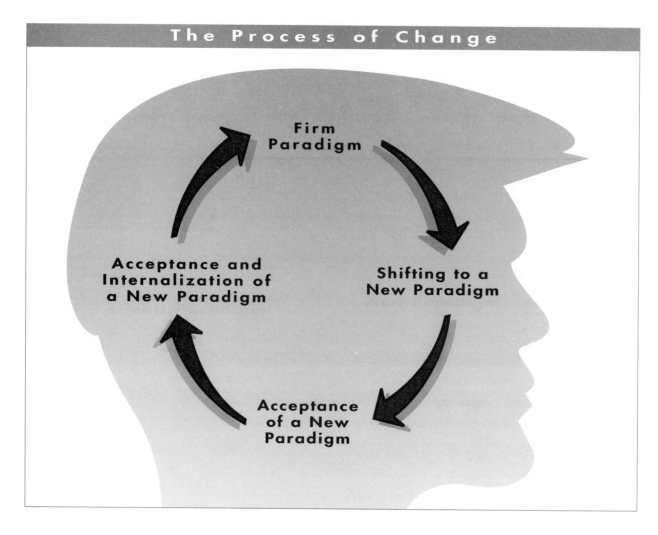

The Process of Change

Firm Paradigm

Shifting to a New Paradigm

Acceptance of a New Paradigm

Acceptance and Internalization of a New Paradigm

For some people, strong beliefs make them feel threatened by new beliefs. When people's beliefs are challenged, they may find that their patterns of thinking change. But resistance to new beliefs is a natural reaction. For example, hundreds of years ago, scientists were persecuted and tortured because they had evidence that proved the Earth is round. Despite the evidence, the belief that the Earth is flat was so entrenched that their persecutors tried to make the scientists deny that the Earth is round. More recent shifts have occurred with the invention of the photo-copier and the digital watch. Kodak turned the inventor of the photo-copier away, but Xerox did not. Swiss watchmakers turned the inventor of the digital watch away, but Japanese watchmakers did not. In both cases, the shift in beliefs required was too great for those who were first approached. Paradigm shifts and resistance to shifts occur in all areas of our lives. For example, past beliefs about the role of women in society are very different from those today.

By reading about predictions and forecasting future events, you can identify predictions with which you agree or disagree. If you disagree with a prediction, consider whether your own paradigm is preventing you from accepting the change.

Nothing in life is to be feared. It is only to be understood.
MADAME CURIE

What Are Your Beliefs?

Consider the aspects of the new work force that you can readily accept. Select two of your strongest beliefs and, in your journal, respond to the questions below.

- Am I prepared to change one of my two strongest beliefs?
- Are there some beliefs I do not want to change? Why am I resisting these changes?
- What prevents me from changing my beliefs?
- What resistance to change in the past proved advantageous to me?

Shifting Paradigms

JASON

Jason was counselled in school to take a keyboarding course, but he never did.

He used to boast that when he started working he would have an administrative assistant to do his typing. After graduation, he did have an assistant. Six months later, the company changed its policy and decided that all employees in Jason's department should have a computer and do their own word processing. Once everyone was fully trained, time would be saved. The assistants were given more administrative duties. Jason joked about how they could give him a computer but he was not going to use it. Courses were offered, but Jason refused to attend them. He was convinced that word processing was not part of his job description.

▼ ▼ ▼

1 Why was Jason unable to accept the change in company policy? What did he believe?

2 What do you think would change Jason's behaviour?

MITSU

Mitsu enjoyed her job as a dispatcher for a trucking company. The work was challenging and feedback from her supervisor was positive. No one saw a need for change. After two years on the job, Mitsu realized that an important change to her procedures could be made. New technology she had read about in a communications trade magazine would help her to be much more efficient. Although it would be a major expense for the company initially, the long-term benefits seemed to be good. Mitsu discussed the new technology with her supervisor, who asked her to prepare a report about how the new technology would improve the dispatch procedures. Mitsu researched and prepared her report, outlining the advantages of the new technology, and made a presentation to her supervisor.

▼ ▼ ▼

1 What other behaviours could Mitsu have demonstrated when she realized a change could be made?

2 Mitsu chose to create change. Think of a situation in your life that may require change. Outline the change and develop a plan to enable you to carry it out.

Make the Connection

CONSIDERING THE FUTURE

1 Research the future of your job at your placement and the industry in which the company is involved. Ask your supervisor for a list of business and trade periodicals that will assist you in your research. The company may also have a library of relevant material.

2 In report form, predict what might occur by the year 2010 in your job and industry. As well, discuss any changes in your job or the industry that have occurred recently due to changing times and needs.

WHAT HAVE YOU LEARNED?

▼ ▼ ▼

1 Explain why you think it is important to analyze futurists' predictions.

2 How can an individual capitalize on a predicted trend?

3 Describe Frank Feather's six-wave economy. Explain why you agree or disagree with his theory.

4 How do the sizes of different age groups in a population affect career opportunities and choices?

5 Identify and explain five ways in which changing demographics affect the work force.

6 Why do you think people tend to resist paradigm shifts?

7 What are the positive effects of paradigm shifts?

CHAPTER 4

CAREER PLANNING

WHAT YOU WILL LEARN

After completing this chapter, you should be able to:

▼ ▼ ▼

- Identify reasons why career planning is important.
- Identify and research your career options.
- Understand the relationship between career choices and personal lifestyle.
- Evaluate business ownership versus working for others.
- Form career goals and a career plan.
- Understand the importance of continually evaluating career options.

TERMS TO REMEMBER

▼ ▼ ▼

career	occupation	occupational research
career planning	job	interview
career goal	lifestyle	apprenticeship
entrepreneurship		volunteer work

Why Plan a Career?

The purpose of planning a career is to develop a satisfying, successful work life. A **career** is a person's entire experience in the work world. **Career planning** is the process of identifying your choices and then forming **career goals** suited to both your individual needs and the realities of the work world. This planning involves examining **occupations**, the fields or areas in which people work, as well as **jobs**, the particular kinds of work people do within an occupation.

Why do people seek a career? What are their reasons for working? A review of Maslow's hierarchy of needs can answer this question—people work to satisfy basic and higher-level needs (such as survival, safety, love and belonging, esteem, and self-fulfillment needs). The basic premise for most people is that they must work for financial reasons. Any job would not be very satisfying, however, if that was the only reason. Since our work lives absorb so much time, personal satisfaction on the job is also important. Based on a 40-hour work week, full-time workers spend about 35 percent of their waking hours at work. It is also important to enjoy work because negative feelings about work can carry over to our personal lives.

In the past, people often chose an occupation, completed the necessary training, and worked within that occupation (and often at the same company) until retirement. Nowadays, people change occupations an average of five or six times in their lives. These changes may be due to technological advances, market demands, or personal reasons. For example, a person may leave a job with a major corporation to pursue his or her own business. Or a particular job may become obsolete when

The major personal concern of Canadian young people—characterized by almost 70 percent of them—is what they are going to do when they finish school.
REGINALD W. BIBBY AND
DONALD C. POSTERSKI

You have got to own your days and name them, each one of them, every one of them.
HUGH GARNER

ROBOTMAN® by Jim Meddick. Reprinted by permission of Newspaper Enterprise Association.

robots can complete the tasks more efficiently. The workplace is changing rapidly, so you too must be able to change. Planning ahead is an essential tool for assisting you with change. Through planning, you will be better able to determine what happens to you and, therefore, be in control.

Forming and attaining career goals involves: identifying career options, researching career options (including research through co-operative education, or work experience, programs), forming career goals, planning ways to attain the goals, and evaluating your progress.

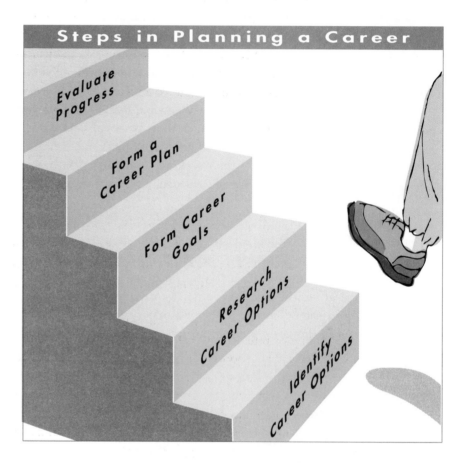

Steps in Planning a Career

Evaluate Progress

Form a Career Plan

Form Career Goals

Research Career Options

Identify Career Options

Why Are You Planning a Career?

In your journal, respond to the questions below.

- What three reasons do I have for working?
- What three reasons do I have for planning a career?

Identifying Career Options

*I*n Chapter 2, you examined who you are and what you are capable of doing. This self-assessment can help you now to determine your career options. When choosing careers, many people decide to adopt the job of a parent or a common job in the community. This kind of path is successful only if you consider how the job suits you and how it will be affected by future trends. Frank Feather has done extensive research into the best growth careers of the 1990s. These are listed on page 60.

In order to identify career options, consider your self-concept, personality, needs, values, interests, and abilities, and future trends and how they affect the work world. Other factors that are important to evaluate are your desired lifestyle and the requirements and benefits of certain types of work. For example, do you want to be able to travel the world? Is having a family important to you? Would you prefer to have your own business or work for others?

Career Choices and Lifestyle

*C*areer choices and **lifestyle**, which is how a person lives in terms of her or his work, habits, pastimes, attitudes, accommodation, and material possessions, are interrelated. How people choose to spend their leisure time each day, as well as on vacations and weekends, can affect career choices. Personal factors that can have an impact on career choices include the desire to travel, pursue education or retraining, have a family, buy a house, enjoy regular sports and cultural events, or be able to pursue a certain hobby or interest. In turn, aspects of a job can limit or provide access to leisure. The amount of money earned, the time spent at the job, and the amount of necessary overtime can influence lifestyle. Ideally, a person should be able to balance career choices with lifestyle. If work takes over, then an individual's personal life will suffer. As well, if a person sacrifices job responsibilities to satisfy personal demands, an employer may take action against the employee.

When looking at possible careers, consider the requirements and benefits of jobs and how they will affect your lifestyle. For example, you should consider:

- Working hours—such as shifts, four 12-hour days, weekends, or nights.
- Location—such as distance from home, the need for public transit, or the need for a car for commuting.
- Travel—such as weekly or monthly travel, time away from family members, and destinations.
- Size of company—such as a large corporation, a small family business, or your own business.
- Work apparel—such as uniforms, safety gear, or business suits.
- Opportunities for advancement.

There is only one success—to be able to spend your life in your own way.

CHRISTOPHER MORLEY

- Opportunities for further education or training to assist with advancement.
- Sample merchandise, discounts, or other employee benefits.

THE 30 BEST GROWTH CAREERS IN THE 1990s

(Ranked by percentage growth, 1987–2000)

TYPE OF OCCUPATION

1	Physicians and surgeons	**17**	Radiology technicians
2	Pharmacists	**18**	Hospital orderlies
3	Nurses	**19**	Denturists/hygienists/assistants
4	Nursing assistants	**20**	Food/beverage service supervisors
5	Audio/speech/physiotherapists		
6	Community college/vocational teachers	**21**	Public relations officers/promoters/agents
7	Osteopaths and chiropractors	**22**	Welfare/community service workers
8	Product and interior designers		
9	Optometrists	**23**	Chefs and cooks
10	Dispensing opticians	**24**	University teachers
11	Food/beverage servers	**25**	Dietitians and nutritionists
12	Bus and transit drivers	**26**	Biologists and related scientists
13	Medical laboratory technicians		
14	Dentists	**27**	Social workers
15	Personnel officers	**28**	Security guards
16	Teachers of exceptional students	**29**	Executives and senior officials
		30	Educational/vocational

From Frank Feather, *Canada's Best Careers Guide* (Aurora: Global Management Bureau, 1990), pp. 87–88. © 1990 by Frank Feather.

Your Career and Lifestyle Choices

In your journal, respond to the questions below.

- What kind of lifestyle is important to me?
- In a job, what would be my ideal working hours, location, opportunities for travel, size of company, apparel, and opportunities for advancement and further education?

How Career Choice Affects Lifestyle

CASE STUDY

Fatima had wanted to be a radio announcer for as long as she could remember. After graduating from a radio and television course at community college, she went to work for a small radio station in a town unfamiliar to her. When she accepted the position she knew that, in radio, opportunities like this were scarce and an entry-level person had to go where there was work. She was just beginning her career and had had no other job offers. Fatima's shift was from midnight to early morning. One technician also worked this shift with her.

1 a Prepare a schedule of what a typical day might be like for Fatima; for example, when she wakes up, eats, works, and so on.

b Explain why you could or could not adapt to this schedule.

2 List the advantages and disadvantages as you see them both for Fatima's career satisfaction and for her resulting lifestyle.

Entrepreneurship

*E*ntrepreneurship is the process of pursuing opportunities or fulfilling needs and wants through innovation or the establishment of a business. Many Canadians have started their own businesses or ventures, and entrepreneurship is a viable career option. An entrepreneur begins by recognizing a market opportunity, want, need, or demand. Many demographic trends can provide opportunities for entrepreneurs (for example, products that appeal to an aging population or individualized services for busy workers with families).

Entrepreneurs are usually hardworking, self-starters, self-disciplined, realistic, and comfortable with a moderate degree of risk. Ideally, the risk is moderate because sound planning has been completed prior to the launch of a venture.

Market research and a business plan should be completed before launching any venture. Statistics show that eight out of ten new businesses will fail, so research and an effective plan are important. Many people begin the process of starting a new business but never actually carry it out. It takes about six to nine months to plan and set up a new business. During this time, an entrepreneur firmly establishes her or his concept and business plan. Then the entrepreneur works to provide the product or service that satisfies a demand.

Entrepreneurship appeals to a certain type of person and is not appropriate for everyone. In a recent survey, 50 percent of people not self-employed at the time said they would prefer to own their own businesses if they had a choice, and 42 percent said they would prefer to work for someone else. Potential entrepreneurs are motivated by a strong desire to be their own bosses and are not discouraged by the prospect of long hours of work or risks. There are several reasons why people are motivated to start their own businesses, including:

- A desire for personal achievement and excellence.
- A need for personal fulfillment by building on an interest or a talent.
- A need to have more control over working conditions, such as type of work, type of co-workers, location, and hours of work.
- A desire to have their earnings equal their efforts.
- A way to supplement income or replace income from a lost job.
- A strong desire to be independent.
- An effort to maintain a family business.

Small opportunities are often the beginning of great enterprises.

DEMOSTHENES

About 7 percent of all new businesses are started by people under 24 years of age.

A C T I V I T Y

Am I an Entrepreneur?

1 Most successful entrepreneurs have similar basic personality characteristics. On a copy of the following quiz provided by your teacher, circle the numbers that apply to you.

	Not at All				A Great Deal
• Are you a self-starter? Entrepreneurs don't need someone else to tell them when to start work on a project.	1	2	3	4	5
• Are you organized and self-disciplined? Entrepreneurs stick to a schedule and are not easily distracted from their work.	1	2	3	4	5
• Do you like being in charge and enjoy having responsibility?	1	2	3	4	5
• Do you have a lot of energy and are you willing to work hard?	1	2	3	4	5

- Are you able to plan, on both a long- and short-term basis?   1 2 3 4 5
- Can you anticipate problems and plan how you will handle these problems if they arise?   1 2 3 4 5
- Are you realistic? Entrepreneurs assess each situation in a practical manner and don't avoid or ignore problems.   1 2 3 4 5
- Are you optimistic and self-confident? Entrepreneurs generally have faith in their own abilities and see others in positive terms.   1 2 3 4 5
- Are you comfortable with a moderate degree of risk? Successful entrepreneurs are not gamblers; they plan carefully and realistically and so eliminate some risk. However, there are always factors that the entrepreneur cannot control and so there is always a moderate degree of risk in going into business for yourself.   1 2 3 4 5

Reprinted with permission from Saskatchewan Education.

2 Add up your numbers to get your score. A score between 35 and 45 indicates you may have the characteristics to be a successful entrepreneur.

3 In small groups, discuss the advantages and disadvantages of entrepreneurship and working for others. Then compare your answers with the other groups.

Journal Entry

Entrepreneurship Versus Working for Others
In your journal, complete one of the statements below.
- I want to be an entrepreneur because…
- I want to work in an established business or organization because…

Profiling Entrepreneurs

CASE STUDY

ANIL LAD

Two years before I launched my venture, I first saw a speaker box for a car stereo. From that moment, I was interested in them. That year, John Chhina (my partner) and I built our very first prototype with some friends. We made the prototype from a couple of house speakers, which was inappropriate because the frequency was wrong. No one liked our first prototype.

We took another chance. Last summer, I experimented with making different styles of speaker boxes with my friends. I learned how to hook them up in a car with the proper connections. That year, John and I took a co-operative education course in school. They were offering an entrepreneurship placement, where you could start your own venture.

Starting off was one of the hardest obstacles we had to overcome because we were not sure if we were committed. We started off by doing market research, which we had done before. We decided to repeat the market research because the trends may have changed. After many attempts to think of a name for our venture, we both decided on the name "Ultimate Tremorz." Our first attempt at a prototype was poor, but we created a cheaper, smaller, and better-built speaker box. Our idea for a venture is unique because people our age can afford the speaker boxes.

As I became an entrepreneur, I noticed a lot of changes in my lifestyle and myself. I am more open to conversation and feel positive about everything. Starting my own business has made me feel differently about myself and made others feel differently about me.

We received our loan money from the government and we are trying to sell our speaker boxes. We used some of the loan money and some of our own money to purchase materials. We get our wood cut at a friend's place because we cannot afford the equipment. But after selling all of the speaker boxes, hopefully we can pay back our loan. Although this is a short-term venture, we will try to pursue it if our sales are good. If our sales are not good, we will try something else. I will always look back with fondness at my first business. It taught me a great deal.

Reprinted by permission of Anil Lad.

LORANE POERSCH

"I don't think of myself as an environmentalist," says 37-year-old Lorane Poersch, "but an everyday sort of person. I'm always on the lookout for good ideas." Two years ago, Poersch decided to do something about the annoying avalanche of junk mail at her door. "I made a hand-lettered sign that said, 'PRESERVE OUR TREES NO FLYERS PLEASE.' And it worked!" Soon friends were asking her to make signs for them, and Poersch realized she had a viable item for her Winnipeg-based Desert Rose Productions Inc., a company she founded in 1984 to develop environmental products.

Next year she expects to distribute 30 000 of the $10 green-and-white signs (made from non-returnable pop bottles) to stores in Winnipeg, Toronto, and LA and through Global ReLeaf, a national forest-establishment program. "I like the idea of using garbage to create something useful."

Before working on the sign, Poersch produced and marketed natural-fibre travel cases carried by such stores as Holt Renfrew and Brettons. Now she's developing a line of recycled plastic products, like rulers and binders for children, who she says are her best supporters.

Every summer Poersch spends several weeks on a windswept arm of Great Bear Lake, NWT, where she helps operate one of Canada's last fly-in fishing lodges. Her office there is a long way from a road or hydro line, let alone a landfill site. "Most of this country is so clean and beautiful," Poersch says. "We owe it to the next generation to keep it that way."

Reprinted from Jake MacDonald, "Lorane Poersch." *enRoute Magazine*, September 1992, p. 18.

▼ ▼ ▼

1 How do the products of these entrepreneurs meet the needs of their market?

2 Who are their potential customers?

3 What abilities and personality traits do these entrepreneurs exhibit?

1 With a partner, study the best growth careers listed on page 60. Categorize them according to three of the trends you studied in Chapter 3—the aging population, specialized or individualistic services, and social responsibility.

2 In Chapter 2, you completed an interest quiz in which you assessed your interests and compared them to a chart of possible jobs (see pages 24–28). Compare these jobs to the ones on Frank Feather's list on page 60.

3 Based on your study of who you are, predicted future trends, your lifestyle needs, and your interest in owning a business or working for others, brainstorm a list of occupations that are appropriate for you. Rank your occupations in order of preference.

4 With a partner, share why you are considering these occupations and what you know about these possible occupations and related jobs at this time.

Researching Career Options

Once you have identified possible occupations, the next step in forming a career plan is to research these options. You may be familiar with some aspects of an occupation, but **occupational research interviews,** in which you interview people in various occupations, will help you to better understand the demands and rewards of these occupations. (See Chapter 8 for more information on how to conduct interviews.) It is important to have an accurate understanding of any occupation in order to determine how appropriate it is for you.

Career information can also be obtained from the following sources:

- *Career centres.* Your community and your board of education may have a career centre that has information on careers as well as tests to help you determine appropriate occupations.
- *Guidance offices.* Your school guidance counsellor can provide you with much career information.
- *Career counsellors.* These people are specially trained in helping others to select the most appropriate occupation. They may work independently or be part of a career centre, and their services may require paying a high fee.
- *Libraries.* Use the library to research occupations that interest you. You can also use libraries to find out what services are available in your area to assist you.
- *Canada Employment Centres.* At these offices you can pick up brochures, study job boards that describe jobs available in your area,

speak with employment officers, and gain information on job-training programs sponsored by the government. Provincial government employment offices will also have valuable information.

- *Post-secondary institutions.* Certain occupations require certain types of education and training such as a degree, diploma, certificate, or licence. Universities and colleges have course calendars that describe all the programs and courses they offer. **Apprenticeships** involve education (usually at a community college) and on-the-job training with people experienced in a particular field. For example, carpenters must apprentice for a number of years. Apprenticeship programs are regulated by provincial governments and conclude with written examinations that lead to licensing.

- *Armed forces.* The armed forces in Canada offer valuable work experience and will assist with education, such as a university program, in exchange for work for a specified period of time.

- *Human resource departments.* Contact these departments in large companies to request information on the opportunities and the range of occupations in a company.

- *Newspapers, magazines, and trade journals.* Job advertisements and publications that focus on a particular occupation can supply information.

- *Parents, relatives, friends, neighbours, and other contacts.* Ask people you know what they do for a living and what qualifications are needed in their fields.

- *Volunteer work and part-time jobs.* Experience an occupation through volunteer work or a part-time job in order to determine whether it is right for you and to learn valuable skills. Helping others through **volunteer work,** work performed for free, can also be personally satisfying.

- *Computer databases.* Databases are available to assist people in making career decisions. Many are available, including *Choices*, an interactive computerized career information system, and *Horizons*, a program that provides information about post-secondary education. These types of programs are available in some schools and Canada Employment Centres. A career or guidance counsellor can provide you with more information.

- *Unions and professional associations.* Some of these have education departments that will provide information on occupations.

CASE STUDY

Making Informed Decisions Through Work Experience

Lesley Maari had always wanted to work with young children. She had enjoyed baby-sitting in the neighbourhood. She was also coach of a children's soccer team and found that role to be very rewarding—the kids loved her and she had fun. Lesley decided that being an early-childhood educator was probably a good career option for her. During Lesley's placement at a day-care centre, she started to doubt her decision. The day started very early—the centre opened at 7 a.m.; she worked this early shift half the time. The second shift ended at 7 p.m. Lesley found that coping with young children for eight hours a day was dramatically different from coaching once a week. The children were both emotionally and physically draining. Lesley came home every night exhausted and irritable, and coaching was beginning to feel like a chore. She also discovered that the pay was low, although basic pay rates were improving. Lesley decided to research other occupations.

▼ ▼ ▼

1 Why did Lesley think she would like to be an early-childhood educator?

2 What factors made her change her mind?

3 What are some other, related occupations she could research that may be suitable?

1 As a class, brainstorm more sources of career information to add to the list on pages 65–66.

2 Once you have completed your list, work in groups to explore what resources are available in your community. For example, one group could visit your school's guidance department and make a list of all the services and resources that are available to students. Some options on the list may not be available in your community; for example, a group exploring the career centre option may need to write or phone for information if the closest centre is too far away to visit.

3 Compile a detailed list of sources of career information and give everyone in the class a copy. Include a brief description of the resources and services offered by each source.

A C T I V I T Y
Sources of Career Information

1 Select two occupations from your list of career options and research them using the list of sources of career information from the previous activity. Compile a thorough description of both occupations.

2 As part of your research, conduct an occupational research interview for one of your two occupations. With a partner, create a list of questions you have about the occupation. Then contact a person in that occupation by telephone to request an occupational research interview. Explain who you are and why you want the interview. During your conversation, write down the company name, the person's name, the interview time, and the address. Be sure to bring a pen and paper to the interview. Write a thank-you letter to the person after your interview. (See Chapter 5 for more information on telephone conversations and Chapter 8 for more information on how to conduct interviews.)

3 After your research, complete a summary similar to the one below for each occupation you researched. Create a file for each occupation, and file the research information you have collected. Continue to collect and file information about the occupations that interest you.

SUMMARY OF OCCUPATIONAL RESEARCH

Occupation:

Entry-level position:
Responsibilities:
Education required:

Supervisory position:
Responsibilities:
Education required:

Management position:
Responsibilities:
Education required:

Top-level position:
Responsibilities:
Education required:

Working conditions:

How the working conditions could change:

Salary or wages and benefits:

Future trends in this occupation:

The impact of technology on this occupation:

Skills I will need for this occupation:

My interests that relate to this occupation:

What I like about this occupation:

What I may not like about this occupation:

Other comments:

Forming Career Goals and a Career Plan

Once you have researched career options, you will need to make a decision about what occupation you wish to pursue and how to pursue it. Analyze the career information you gathered to determine your career goals. To set effective goals, use these guidelines:

- Conceptualize a goal and clearly identify the first few steps that need to be taken toward this goal.
- Believe you can reach your goals.
- Be sure that your goals are attainable in terms of your strengths and abilities.
- Identify the factors affecting your goals that you can control as well as those you cannot control. For example, you may not be able to control whether a job opportunity will be available at a company that interests you, but you can actively seek out an opportunity at that company.
- Set goals that can be measured in some way, such as in time or in quantity. For example, your goal may be to achieve a certain grade level in school or to complete a diploma or degree.
- Be sure that your goals are what you really want, rather than what you think you should want.

People with goals succeed because they know where they're going.
EARL NIGHTINGALE

- Set one goal at a time.
- Make sure that your goals leave as many opportunities as possible open to you. For example, continuing your education after high school will allow you more job opportunities.

Obstacles are what you see when you take your eyes off your goals.
ANONYMOUS

Once you have set your goals, plan how to attain them. To do this, set short-term goals or smaller achievements that lead to your long-term goals. As well, you should identify the challenges that face you and how you can cope with these challenges. A sample career plan follows.

CAREER PLAN FOR JEREMY LANG

CAREER GOAL: HAZARDOUS WASTE MANAGEMENT TECHNICIAN

Goals	Challenges
Short-Term Goals	
▪ Complete my work experience	▪ Maintain a positive relationship with the people at my placement
▪ Take a senior math and physics course	▪ Return to studying
▪ Apply for part-time work at my placement (Smithers Waste Management Co.)	▪ A job may not be available
▪ Volunteer to work for Ecology House	▪ Manage volunteer work and studying
One-Year Goals	
▪ Graduate from high school with a focus on math and science	▪ Graduate with good marks in order to get into college
▪ Apply for community college courses in waste management	▪ Save enough money for college by working part-time and during the summer
	▪ Move to an unfamiliar place to attend college
Three-Year Goals	
▪ Graduate from college	▪ Maintain good marks
▪ Obtain a part-time job while at college	▪ Balance college and work
▪ Continue to take courses relating to waste management	▪ Budget my finances effectively
▪ Take courses on becoming an entrepreneur	
Long-Term Goals	
▪ Contribute to waste management in a unique way	▪ Keep aware of future trends by reading trade magazines and attending seminars
▪ Own my own company	▪ Develop the skills and abilities required to become a successful entrepreneur

WALNUT COVE by Mark Cullum. Reprinted with special permission of King Features Syndicate.

1 In your notebook, create a career plan using the sample on page 70 as a model.

2 Discuss your career goals and plan with a partner. Try to give your partner helpful, friendly advice about her or his career plan.

A C T I V I T Y

Forming Your Career Plan

Evaluating a Career Plan

*O*nce you have formed career goals and a career plan, remember to continue to evaluate and modify your goals. As you progress in your career, there may be many reasons to modify your career plan. In order to secure change, you need to seek out opportunities for yourself. People change their career plans for many reasons; for example:

- A person might review his or her personal goals and determine that they are not currently being met.
- A unique and unexpected opportunity may present itself.
- A spouse may have to relocate.
- A person may need to adapt to a new situation, such as moving to a city with more opportunities or a town with a different occupational focus.
- A person may change occupations due to limited opportunities for advancement.
- A company may close or merge with another company, causing a person to lose his or her job.
- New technology may make a job obsolete.

Present and Future Plans

In your journal, respond to the questions below.

- How will my career plan affect my high school behaviour?
- How will my high school course selections and activities affect my career options?

▼ ▼

LEARNING ABOUT OTHERS' CAREER PLANS

1 In small groups, brainstorm a list of questions you could ask someone about her or his career plans. Some possible questions include:

- Did you plan your career? If so, how closely did you follow this plan?
- What factors influenced your career choices?
- What career advice would you give to students who are about to graduate from high school?

2 Using your questions, interview one person at your placement about her or his career plan.

3 In your groups, compare the results of the interviews. What conclusions can you draw? Share your conclusions with the class.

WHAT HAVE YOU LEARNED?

▼ ▼ ▼

1 Why do you think career planning is important?

2 Explain the relationship between career choice and lifestyle.

3 How will your chosen occupation affect your lifestyle?

4 List five advantages and five disadvantages of owning your own business and of working for others.

5 Summarize in a brief essay why your career plan will succeed. Include challenges and how you will overcome them.

6 Why should you continue to evaluate your career goals and plan?

7 State ten reasons why people might make career changes.

PART 2

DEVELOPING YOUR CAREER SKILLS

*There is a principle at
the heart of life: Life is not what
you find, it is what you create.*

CHARLES TEMPLETON

▼ ▼ ▼

CHAPTER 5

COMMUNICATION

After completing this chapter, you should be able to:

▼ ▼ ▼

- Understand the process of exchanging messages.
- Recognize common barriers to effective communication.
- Assess your communication skills and identify areas that need improvement.
- Practise and improve your listening, speaking, nonverbal communication, telephone, reading, and writing skills.

TERMS TO REMEMBER

▼ ▼ ▼

communication	feedback	nonverbal
sender	communication	communication
medium	barrier	reading
message	listening	writing
receiver	speaking	

The Communication Exchange

Seventy percent of our waking hours are spent on some form of communication.

Communication is the process of exchanging information. Effective communication is basic to every successful business and to every successful employee. When you are searching for a job, you will communicate your skills and abilities to a potential employer. When you are on the job, you will communicate with many people, such as supervisors, co-workers, and the public. Every day you will send, receive, and respond to messages when you practise listening, speaking, reading, writing, and nonverbal communication. It is important to be aware of the value of these skills and the need to continually improve them.

In any communication, each person is a responsible and active part of the process. The **sender** is the person who originates the message. He or she communicates in a **medium**, such as speech, a piece of writing, or a visual display. The **message** is the information that the sender wishes to communicate. For example, a message about an upcoming town fair can be communicated in a variety of ways. Town merchants can remind people about the fair, posters can encourage people to read about the fair, and advertisements can convey the message through the radio and television media. The **receiver** is the person who receives the message by listening, reading, or viewing. **Feedback** is the receiver's response to the message and can take many forms, such as gestures, facial expressions, and spoken or written responses. Feedback can occur at any time during the process of exchanging information.

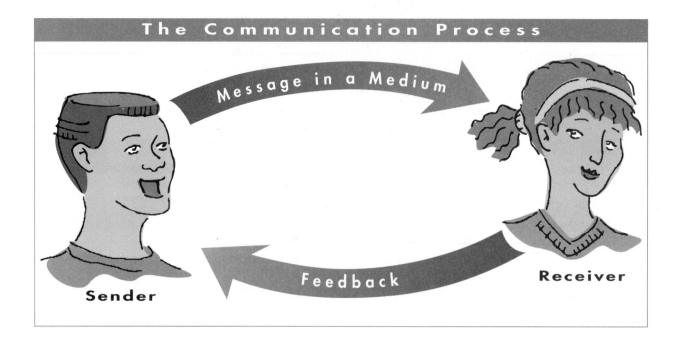

The Communication Process

Message in a Medium

Feedback

Sender   **Receiver**

Avoiding Communication Barriers

*F*requently, messages are misunderstood, even when the sender and receiver are standing right next to each other. A **communication barrier** occurs when the true intent of a message is blocked in some way. The following are common barriers to effective communication and ways to avoid these problems:

- *Distractions.* Sounds and movement may distract a receiver from concentrating on a sender's message. As well, the receiver may have a preconceived idea about the message that blocks understanding. To avoid distractions when you are the receiver, focus on the message regardless of interruptions.
- *Lack of concentration.* Understanding a message is difficult if either the sender or the receiver is not interested in the topic. Concentrate on the message and on showing interest in it, whether you are the sender or the receiver.
- *Amount of information.* Too much information can bore or insult a receiver and too little information can cause frustration and misunderstanding. As a sender, adjust the amount of information you give according to the situation and the receiver. For example, if someone asks you how your day was, you might respond by providing a few highlights. If someone asks you how to operate a piece of equipment, you are more likely to respond with detailed step-by-step instructions.
- *Use of jargon.* Language that is too technical or contains jargon can cause a communication barrier. Technical words or jargon should be used carefully and only when all receivers involved understand the words.
- *Disorganized message.* A disorganized message can result in a communication barrier. Consider your purpose before you communicate a message, and express your message in a sequential, organized manner.
- *Unsuitable language.* Using an inappropriate language level for a situation is another common communication barrier. When speaking or writing, consider your audience in terms of personality, age, and level of ability and experience with the language.
- *Emotional response.* It is often difficult to accurately receive a message if you disagree with the message or if there is a personality conflict between you and the sender. Try not to let personal feelings interfere with communication—respond to the message, not the person sending it.
- *Thinking of a response.* When receiving a message, we are often too busy planning a response to receive the complete message. To avoid a misinterpretation, make sure you understand the entire message before responding.

Language is not simply a reporting device for experience but a defining framework for it.
BENJAMIN WHORF

I know you believe you understand what you think I said, but I am not sure you realize that what you heard is not what I meant.
ANONYMOUS

- *Lack of feedback.* If no feedback is offered, a sender may assume a message is understood. A receiver should provide feedback and ask for clarification when necessary. A sender should seek confirmation that the receiver understood the message.

- *Mixed messages.* A person may send mixed messages when speaking by saying one thing and implying another through tone of voice, gestures, or facial expressions. Be aware of the subtle messages you send.

Reprinted from *The Saturday Evening Post.*

ACTIVITY

Role-Play Organizing a Class Trip

1 Assume that your class has been granted permission to take an educational field trip. In groups of six, role-play planning the trip. Decide when the trip will be taken, where it will be, how the class will get to the destination, how the trip will be funded, and any other details you think of. Determine in private who will play each of the following roles:

Person 1: This person is not a listener. She or he has a personal agenda and keeps interrupting with "Yes, but what about..."

Person 2: This person is just not listening. She or he seems to be off in a dream world and is not really involved in the discussion.

Person 3: This person is very emotional. She or he exclaims and comments about everything that is said.

Person 4: This person enjoys using jargon for its own sake. No constructive input is given—just a lot of technical words without coherence.

Persons 5 and 6: These two people are really trying to organize this trip and come up with as many ideas as possible in spite of the obstacles.

2 The rest of the class observes each role-play. During the action, the observers try to determine who is playing which role.

3 At the completion of each group's role-play, discuss how well the observers identified the roles people played and how the players felt about their roles.

1 Use the communication inventory that follows to evaluate your communication skills. In your notebook, write the number of each statement and respond with Never, Occasionally, Almost Always, or Always.

2 In groups of four, discuss your responses. How are you going to change your Never and Occasionally responses into Almost Always or Always responses?

3 Make a list of class strategies that will help everyone to improve their communication skills.

COMMUNICATION INVENTORY

1 I let others finish speaking before I speak. _____

2 When I listen, I look at the speaker and express interest in the message. _____

3 I speak clearly and directly. _____

4 When I speak, I look at the listener with encouragement. _____

5 I read carefully and review the content of a written piece. _____

6 I write thoughtfully and consider the structure of what I am writing. _____

7 I am more concerned about understanding others than about convincing them that I am right. _____

8 I ask questions to clarify my understanding of a message. _____

9 I make sure that others know I understand them. _____

10 I pay attention to how messages are expressed to help me understand them. _____

11 I am open to new ideas. _____

Communication Challenges

Communication with others is not always easy. Reflect on your communication strengths and weaknesses and, in your journal, complete the statements below.

- Sometimes when I am communicating with someone I get impatient because...
- I deal with my frustration over a misunderstanding by...
- When I try to put myself in the other person's place, I realize that...

From 65 to 75 percent of a manager's working day is spent communicating. Of that, nearly 70 percent is spent listening.

Listening

Surveys have shown that people spend more time listening than on any other communication activity. After all, there is no communication unless a message is received. The average person is only 25 percent efficient in using his or her listening skills, which means that up to 75 percent of the information contained in a message may be lost. The average person, therefore, can greatly increase his or her listening and retention skills with practice. On the job, being able to listen accurately to supervisors, customers, and co-workers is very important. Effective listening can help you to increase your knowledge, broaden your experience, improve your job performance, and develop better language skills.

Some people think that listening and hearing are the same. **Listening** is actively participating in the communication process by attentively receiving and retaining messages, while hearing is passively sensing sounds. The listener's attitude is important, since he or she must *want* to listen to and grasp the meaning of a message.

Use the guidelines that follow to help improve your listening skills.

- *Pay attention.* A person's listening capacity ranges from 400 to 600 words per minute. The average speaking rate is 125 words per minute. The result is that receivers often start thinking about other things rather than listening to a message. When someone is speaking to you, stop whatever you are doing and look at the person. Think about what the person is saying, and ask questions to clarify points.
- *Give feedback.* As a listener, you can improve understanding by sending signals back to the speaker. For example, you can acknowledge that you are listening by nodding your head, and you can encourage further clarification with a quizzical look.

- *Take notes.* Recording the speaker's main points or instructions is often useful. If it is not possible to write, make mental notes. Repeat the message in your own words after the speaker has finished talking to make sure you understand it. Relate the message to your own experience and knowledge.
- *Listen with empathy.* Empathetic listeners learn to just listen with understanding and support without taking on a speaker's problems. Try to put yourself in the speaker's place and make an extra effort to understand his or her point of view.
- *Keep an open mind.* Listen to the message with an open mind. Forget your biases and opinions for the moment and be ready to receive new ideas. Try to listen to the whole message without jumping to any conclusions.
- *Listen critically.* Listen to determine motives and biases and to distinguish fact from opinion. Listen to what the speaker is *not* saying. In other words, listen "between the lines" to what is implied.

A C T I V I T Y

Listening Effectively

1 With a partner, discuss the following question: What is the most important factor in developing a positive relationship with your supervisor? One of you should try to keep the conversation focussed on the topic, while the other responds with totally unrelated statements.

2 As a class, discuss how it feels to make a statement and receive no relevant response from your listener and how it feels to ignore what a person is saying.

3 Join your partner again, and continue your discussion with both of you listening carefully and giving positive feedback to each other.

4 As a class, discuss the differences between the first and second conversations.

Journal Entry

Forming Listening Resolutions

In your journal, complete the statements below.

Now that I have discovered how to improve my listening skills, I will change some of my listening habits.

- I will continue to…
- I will try to…
- I will try not to…

Speaking

*S*peaking refers to expressing a message verbally. Although some jobs require more speaking than others, in many jobs you will need to be able to express yourself verbally to your supervisor, co-workers, customers, and other people. The words you use, the ways in which you put words together, the sound of your voice (in terms of tone, pitch, volume, and tempo), your pronunciation, and your enunciation all affect how well you communicate. Before speaking, think carefully about your choice of words and organize your thoughts. You should be aware of how to use proper English, and you should avoid inappropriate language, such as slang, at work.

Most experts agree that *how* you say something is much more important than *what* you say. Your tone of voice reveals your attitudes and feelings; in the workplace, you should use a pleasant and cheerful tone. Pitch refers to how high or low your voice is. A moderately low voice is ideal in the workplace. Appropriate volume involves making yourself heard without projecting undue force and intensity into your voice. On the other hand, speaking in such a quiet voice that people must strain to hear you is also inappropriate. Tempo is the speed of your speech. When speaking, use pauses to stress major points and to add variety to your tempo. Speak important words more slowly and unimportant words more quickly to contribute to understanding. Don't speak so slowly that you put your listeners to sleep. Try to vary your tone, pitch, volume, and tempo to add interest—avoid speaking in a monotone.

Pronunciation refers to speaking words correctly. Pronunciation is affected by social, cultural, and regional influences. An accent is an example of how these differences influence speech. Use a dictionary to learn the most common pronunciations of words. Sound out people's names or ask for the proper pronunciation of their names.

Enunciation refers to speaking words distinctly. Poor enunciation results from running words together, leaving out letters and syllables, adding letters and syllables, or mumbling. Speak clearly by enunciating each letter, syllable, and word.

A major part of speaking is being aware of the receiver. Look at your listener while you speak and avoid distracting mannerisms, such as clearing your throat repeatedly or playing with objects. Remember to give the listener an opportunity to respond to your message. Watch for signs of disinterest, and try to alleviate boredom by providing more interest. Use people's names or titles (Mr., Mrs., Miss, Ms., Dr., and so on) in formal speaking situations.

Part of speaking skills is knowing how to prepare and give a speech. You can apply many of the same guidelines to preparing for a difficult conversation, such as asking your supervisor for a raise. When preparing a speech, consider your purpose and subject. For example, are you trying to entertain, inform, or convince your audience? What is your main topic or focus? Once you know why you are going to talk and what you are going to talk about, consider the audience, the occasion, the length of the speech, and how you can capture the audience's interest. Know your audience in detail in terms of age, experience, language level, interests, and so on. Decide how much or how little information to supply. It may be helpful to prepare an outline of your speech that includes the scope of your subject and your notes in point form. When it is time to give your speech, try not to be nervous. If you are fully prepared, you have no reason to be nervous. Remember to speak effectively by maintaining eye contact, avoiding distracting mannerisms, and staying on topic.

With a partner, role-play these challenging communication situations. Try to determine the best way to convey your message in speech.

1 A fellow worker who has been very helpful and friendly to you approaches and asks you to help with unpacking a shipment of new materials. You are in the middle of an important assignment for your supervisor and unpacking shipments is not your job.

2 Your supervisor has asked you at the last minute to work an extra two hours. You have another commitment that you really do not want to change.

3 You are late for work because you forgot to set your alarm before you went to bed last night. The first person you see as you walk in the door is your supervisor.

A C T I V I T Y

Role-Playing Verbal Situations

Nonverbal Communication

When you speak, you send two types of messages: spoken ones and unspoken ones. Messages that are not expressed in words are forms of **nonverbal communication,** or body language. For example, if your supervisor says, "Please complete this project on time," you may assume that the message is to meet the deadline for the project. But if the message is accompanied by a frown or a frustrated facial expression, your supervisor may be implying additional messages, such as "You often miss deadlines" and "I am frustrated with your failure to meet deadlines." Learning to use and interpret nonverbal communication can help you to send and receive verbal messages more effectively. As well, by watching the nonverbal communication of a receiver, you can better adapt your message to suit the receiver.

Nonverbal communication greatly contributes to the meaning of messages through facial expressions, gestures, posture, body movements, attire, and grooming. For example, shrugging your shoulders may indicate that you have lost interest in a subject. An upright posture may indicate that you are confident and in control. However, nonverbal communication does not reveal the whole message. Interpret body language

The impact of a spoken message is 7 percent verbal (word meanings), 38 percent vocal (tone of voice), and 55 percent physical (facial expression and body position).

in relation to the subject matter and the situation. Cultural and environmental differences must also be considered when interpreting nonverbal messages. For example, people from some cultures require less personal space than others.

In order to determine the appropriate attire and grooming for a situation, consider who will be your receivers. For example, when dressing for the workplace, you should dress in a similar manner to others at that workplace. Observe employees of a company and read company manuals to determine proper dress and grooming. Be aware that many businesses prefer conservative dress. Your clothing should be clean, pressed, and in good repair. When grooming for the workplace, remember that a lack of cleanliness is offensive to most people. Be sure that your skin, teeth, breath, hands, and fingernails are as clean as possible. Try to make the best impression you can through your attire and grooming.

A C T I V I T Y

How Can You Encourage Speakers?

1 In small groups, list the forms of nonverbal communication from the examples below that you could use to encourage a speaker. Make a second list of the forms of nonverbal communication that would have a negative effect on the speaker.

- Smiling
- Sitting forward
- Maintaining eye contact
- Looking at your watch
- Fiddling with something
- Folding your arms
- Narrowing your eyes
- Looking delighted
- Bouncing your leg
- Raising your eyebrows

- Nodding your head
- Looking away
- Frowning
- Rolling your eyes
- Scowling
- Sighing
- Puffing your cheeks
- Tapping your fingers
- Slumping in your seat
- Not moving

2 Add to your lists any other types of nonverbal communication that you have observed.

A C T I V I T Y

Role-Playing Without Words

1 With a partner, prepare a silent role-play in which messages are conveyed through nonverbal communication only. Here are some suggestions for role-plays:
- It is an employee's first day at a new job. The supervisor is showing the employee around and explaining the daily routine.
- A person who just got laid off runs into a friend who just found a new job.
- A person really wants to buy a new car from a car salesperson but feels the price is too high.

2 Perform your silent role-play for the class. After the role-play, ask the class to describe the messages that were conveyed through nonverbal communication.

Messages Without Words

In your journal, complete the statements below.

- When I feel bored with a discussion, I usually...
- When I feel annoyed with someone, I usually...
- When I am excited and trying to communicate my thoughts, I always...
- When a stranger asks me for directions, I try to...
- When I am trying to convince someone that I am right, I...

Never Start With a Joke...

by Janice Turner

He's known as The Camel Man and he commands thousands of dollars for his words.

Ted Mouradian, realtor turned professional speaker, goes absolutely nowhere without his beloved mascot Humphrey.

His licence plates boast Camel 1, even his wristwatch bears the beast.

So what's the attachment?

"I wanted to be a little different," he says. "I can do a camel smile that just blows people away," he confides.

A stuffed toy camel seemed like a natural companion during his straight-from-the heart motivational talks.

The St. Catharines entrepreneur bills himself as an expert in "relationship management" with keynote addresses entitled Life's Too Short, It's O.K. To Be Me, Service with a Smile and (for the real estate crowd) Don't be a Listless Lister.

Mouradian, 44, delivered his first paid speech back in 1984, quit the real estate business two years later, and like others on the talk circuit, now entertains and inspires the masses full-time.

What's wrong? You still don't get the camel?

Mouradian explains: "When all the other beasts of burden fall by the wayside and they don't finish the job, the camel's the only creature that starts the job and finishes; no matter how bad the weather is, how tough the terrain is, the camel is always reliable. That's the first thing we should be as human beings—reliable."

Get it?

The camel, Mouradian waxes on, may not be the prettiest creature, but it's adaptable. Treat the camel right, give it respect, and it will always come through.

Message? It doesn't matter who you are—colour or creed—everyone has the right to go through life with dignity, he says.

The camel is important, too, because it doesn't destroy things in its path. The creature's padded feet bend rather than break the grass beneath.

Mouradian has brought his motivation-with-a-beast to a host of audiences, from cattle ranchers to dairy folk.

"You have to entertain people before you can get your message across," he says.

He has a collection of more than 70 camels, all shapes and sizes, "none live, yet" that people have given him over the years.

Mouradian puts himself in the mid-fee bracket, charging $1500 to $3000 per engagement, expenses extra.

He's one of only a few hundred people in Canada who can actually make a comfortable living talking full-time.

Twenty-five thousand dollars a pop celebrity gabbers they are not. But they couldn't imagine doing anything else.

"None of us think of ourselves as having a real job," quips Steve Schklar, president of 60 or so member Ontario Speakers Association, a chapter of the U.S.-based National Speakers Association.

"It takes discipline, confidence, tenacity" and flexibility—you have to adjust quickly to your market and the audience in front of you.

"It can be a tough way to make a living. You're always trying to sell yourself, to distinguish yourself."

You can be the greatest speaker in the world, but if nobody's there to listen, so what?

Business presentation guru Peter Urs Bender stresses the importance of body language and dress.

Style is just as important as content. Words alone account for only a small part of the message we communicate, he says.

Among his tips:

Love your body. If you're a bit overweight, adore your body anyway.

Stand and sit to your tallest. Never slouch.

Move slowly, deliberately, and gracefully. Shoulders back. Chest out. Chin up. Smile.

Power dressing?

Opt for dark (timeless and reassuring) suits or dresses, plain white shirts or blouses (purity and trustworthiness), red (power) ties or scarves, dark shoes (down to earth) freshly polished, discreetly worn jewellery (yet big earrings for women), and a black pen.

Bender's tips on delivery:

Get rid of the podium and get in front of your group.

Never start with a joke.

If you're wearing a blazer, have it buttoned to begin with and unbutton it sometime during the address.

Keep your hands out of your pockets, it's a sign of nervousness or, at best, indifference.

Don't point at people and keep your hands open, not clenched.

Tailor your message.

If he's speaking to a group of jewellers, for example, he's not going to tell them chunky jewellery is a no-no—"they'd throw me out"—but rather he'll suggest they "dress down."

Large earrings for women are one thing (confidence, presence), but pass on the holiday decoration type.

On being nervous: "It's not just okay but highly suggested."

More critically—end on time.

Swiss-born Bender has been sharing the secrets of power presentations for more than a decade and does up to 100 engagements a year.

The key to making it in this biz? You have to have a niche, he says. You can't claim to be an expert at everything.

"Speaking is easy, the getting (work) is tough," he says.

"Every speaker thinks they're great. I haven't met one who doesn't. But how many really are?"

Not nearly enough, he suspects.

Bender says once established (by the fourth year things start to look really good) a speaker can make a darn good living, "but it's a lonely job."

You're selling yourself as much as, if not more than, your topic, he says.

His motto: "If you do what you've always done, you'll get what you've always gotten."

Right.

If you laugh, people will be attracted to you, offers Valerie Kates, self-proclaimed humorologist.

"We spend so much time trying to be perfect, we miss out on all the funniness that's around us and in us," she says.

One of her favourite cartoons is of a man with his feet up on his desk. The caption says: I'm unwinding on company time because that's when I got wound up.

Kates advocates more humour in the workplace. It's hard to argue. But pay to hear that? You bet. Up to $3000 a shot.

With arms waving, Kates, 31, can get a group of suited men and women in a staid convention hall pulling faces, swaying to their own version of "Singing in the Rain," all with utter glee.

"They love it because they've never had permission to do that kind of thing," she says.

The one-time theatre performer who's working on her Ph.D. has been speaking professionally for about the last four years.

With a masters degree in adult education, Kates started out by doing workshops for teachers on how to bring humour into the classroom.

She easily lands dozens of appearances a year in front of groups as varied as the Ontario Golf Superintendents Association and the Packaging Association of Canada, from curling enthusiasts to big league chartered accountants.

Her mission: to help organizations develop a "comic vision," to see humour in their own profession.

Need more?

Funny business is laughter between 9 and 5. Strengthening the bottom line means strengthening people from the inside out...Laughter brings perspective. Laughter builds trust. Being human is funny, very funny.

Indeed.

_____

Reprinted with permission—The Toronto Star Syndicate.

▼ ▼ ▼

1 a In what ways do professional speakers use humour to entertain their audiences?

b Why, in the author's opinion, is humour valuable?

2 What would be appropriate dress when speaking to the following audiences:

a A group of government representatives,

b A class of grade 1 students,

c Fashion consultants,

d Your classmates?

3 How can you sell your message when you speak to a group of people?

4 What are the differences in your speech when you are at home, with friends at school, and with fellow workers?

5 List six points that you would like to make about the positive aspects of working at your placement and prepare a short speech for your class.

Telephone Procedures

Telephone interaction in the workplace is as important as face-to-face interaction. Since telephone communications rely totally on voice, how quickly you respond to messages, what you say, and how you say it are extremely important. During a business call, you need to remember that your voice creates an impression on the listener. Try to sound natural, pleasant, clear, and interesting. Although some callers may be unpleasant or even rude, it is important to treat everyone with understanding and courtesy. When calling an organization for any purpose, always be polite. Ask for the person with whom you wish to speak, or, if you do not know the person's name, ask for him or her by job title.

Following certain procedures is essential when you meet the public through the telephone as part of your job. Remember that you are representing your employer. When answering a telephone call:

- Answer the phone promptly. A caller will becoming increasingly impatient and angry if left waiting.
- Identify the company and yourself immediately.
- Find out the caller's name and purpose for the call. Assist the caller yourself if you can, or, if necessary, transfer her or him to the appropriate person. If this person is not available, write down the necessary information on a telephone message pad.
- Close the conversation courteously.

MESSAGE FOR

M r *Sealey*

M s *S Moran*

OF *Tel Kel*

PHONE NO. *555-5151*

TELEPHONED	X	RETURNED YOUR CALL	
CALLED TO SEE YOU		PLEASE CALL	
WANTS TO SEE YOU		WILL CALL AGAIN	X

MESSAGE *Wants to talk to you about damage to a recent shipment.*

DATE *Aug 27*   TIME *2:30 p.m.*

RECEIVED BY *B.P.*

L13-99915
RECYCLED PAPER   GRAND & TOY

Courtesy Grand & Toy.

ACTIVITY

*Role-Playing
Telephone Conversations*

1 With a partner, role-play telephone conversations that might occur in the situations below. Use copies of the telephone conversation checklist provided by your teacher to evaluate each role-play.

   a Make an appointment for a job interview.

   b Reserve a table at a restaurant for a business lunch.

   c Order supplies for a business.

2 With a partner, role-play telephone conversations that involve a message for a third person in the situations below. Use a telephone message pad provided by your teacher to record the messages. Use copies of the telephone conversation checklist provided by your teacher to evaluate each role-play.

   a Make a date for a committee meeting.

   b Remind someone of an appointment.

   c Inform a supervisor of an absence.

   d Request a repair person to come in.

TELEPHONE CONVERSATION CHECKLIST

1 Answered call promptly. ____

2 Answered by identifying the company and self. ____

3 Greeted caller pleasantly. ____

4 Spoke clearly and confidently. ____

5 Treated caller with respect and courtesy. ____

6 Obtained needed information. ____

7 Wrote down necessary information, asking for proper spelling of name. ____

8 Did not make the caller wait unnecessarily. ____

9 Answered questions discreetly. ____

10 Helped the caller as much as possible. ____

11 Kept any caller who was on hold informed. ____

12 Spoke clearly and at an appropriate volume. ____

13 Spoke at an appropriate pace. ____

14 Used appropriate language. ____

In Canada, we make a world-record 27 billion calls a year on 17 million telephones—in other words, 1100 calls per person.

Reading

Reading is the mental process of receiving and comprehending a written message. At work, you may need to read instructions, memos, reports, invoices, and forms. Effective workers use different styles of reading for different materials. For example, detailed instructions and research reports should be read slowly and carefully. A company newsletter, on the other hand, could be skimmed quickly, and you may choose to read only the articles that interest you.

To effectively use your reading time, follow these guidelines:

- *Preview the material.* Read over the first and last paragraphs as well as the headings. With a general idea of the content, you can determine your purpose for reading.
- *Consider your purpose for reading.* For example, to gain detailed information or to skim for interest.
- *Read silently.* Reading time and comprehension are slowed down when you read aloud.
- *Recall.* Immediately after reading a section, visualize or repeat to yourself the content of the section. Associate it with a part of your experiences before continuing to read.
- *Improve your vocabulary.* Try to determine the meaning of a word you do not know from the context, and consult a dictionary when necessary.

Sixty-two percent of Canadians aged 16 to 69 can do most daily reading without difficulty.

Reading is to the mind what exercise is to the body.
SIR RICHARD STEELE

Illiteracy in the Workplace

CASE STUDY

For 13 years, Ruby held a production-line job at a large bottling plant in Winnipeg. She enjoyed the job, her co-workers, and the steady income. But early last year, the company installed new machinery—a change that required Ruby to read a technical manual. Ruby is one of thousands of Canadian workers who face limited job prospects due to poor reading skills. When she first heard about the new machinery, Ruby considered asking for a transfer to another department where she would not need to read. But her employer recognized the need for education and training and offered a training program for Ruby and others like her to upgrade their skills. From the employer's perspective, it is advantageous to provide employees with further training since workers with weak reading skills require more time and supervision to finish assigned tasks than co-workers who can comprehend manuals and memos.

▼ ▼ ▼

1 As a class, discuss ways to combat the problem of illiteracy in Canada.

2 In small groups, investigate the availability of literacy programs in your area and present a report to the class in the form of a news broadcast.

3 Design a poster with no words to describe how to perform a simple task you do at your placement.

Writing

Writing is the act of putting a message into words on paper. A large variety of written documents are necessary for the successful operation of an organization. Ineffective written messages do not achieve results and very often cause confusion, lost business, and frustration.

At your placement, you may be required to complete forms and write memos, letters, directions, or announcements. Memos, or interoffice memorandums, are messages between two or more people within a company. For example, a manager may issue a memo to all staff about new company safety policies. Letters are correspondence between two or more people in different companies or between companies and the public. Although memos tend to be less formal than letters, good writing practices should be used for all written communications.

Successful writers follow these guidelines:

- *Consider the purpose for writing.* Purposes for writing include informing, making or responding to a request, confirming, inquiring, complaining, selling, or promoting. Once you know your purpose for writing, the appropriate tone and level of language to use will become clear. For example, if you are writing to make an inquiry into a particular product or service, your tone should be courteous and your language concise.

Approximately 3 million Canadians cannot read, write, or use numbers well enough to meet the literacy demands of everyday life. Of this number, 1 million can hardly read or write at all.

- *Select a format.* There are many forms of written communication, but in business most written messages are in the form of memos, letters, and reports. For the proper format of a memo and a letter, see pages 94–95.
- *Consider the audience.* Before writing, consider who will be reading the message, why they will be reading it, and what they already know about the topic. For example, a supervisor will address the owner of the company and the employees he or she supervises in different ways.
- *Consider the structure.* Outline the content of your message by listing the main points. Then arrange the points in logical order. Any message should have an introduction, a body, and a conclusion.
- *Write clearly.* Avoid unnecessary expressions, such as "due to the fact that," "all things considered," and "in spite of everything." Include only the information that is relevant to the reader, and include all necessary information.
- *Check for accuracy.* Proofread your written messages for spelling, grammar, and content errors.

The fascinating thing about writing is that it's a way of transforming the things you've experienced; it's like being able to live twice.

Jacques Godbout

- - - - - - - - - - -

A c t i v i t y
Writing Workplace Messages

1 Assume you are a supervisor. Write a memo to your employees announcing the hiring of a new employee. Be sure to include all the details that they will want to know.

2 Assume you want to know about a particular product or service of an organization. Write a letter outlining what you want to know.

SUPPLY COMPANY
381 Main Street
Fredericton, New Brunswick
E3B 6J7

Memorandum

To:　　　Ms. Hardings, President
From:　　Amud Alomor, Supervisor
Subject:　Flooding in the stockroom
Date:　　September 8, 19—

On Saturday evening, a broken pipe caused a section of the stockroom to be flooded. The drying and reorganization of supplies caused a delay in our deliveries. As of today, we are back on schedule, although two working days were lost due to clean-up operations.

I will contact you with a full damage report within the week. As well, I intend to thoroughly investigate the cause of this accident in order to ensure it will not happen again.

AA

Sample interoffice memorandum

SUPPLY COMPANY
381 Main Street
Fredericton, New Brunswick
E3B 6J7

September 15, 19—

Mr. Mikelanas
Clean-All Limited
22 Frankel Avenue
Fredericton, New Brunswick
E3B 5F7

Dear Mr. Mikelanas:

My main purpose in writing is to let you know that I have never seen such a
thorough clean-up and efficient handling of equipment. Your staff is certainly
efficient and courteous.

Please find enclosed a cheque in the amount of $107.64 in payment of your
cleaning services. Thank you for your prompt attention to our needs.

Sincerely,

Amud Alomor

Amud Alomor
Supervisor

AA/kn

Sample block letter with standard punctuation

Make the Connection

▼ ▼

COMMUNICATION AT YOUR PLACEMENT

1 Watch people interact at your placement. In small groups, list the ways in which information is transmitted at your placement. Discuss the positive listening, speaking, and nonverbal communication that you observed among employees.

2 With the permission of your supervisor, collect samples of written communication at your placement. Consider messages such as policy statements, form letters, order forms, and annual reports. With your group, create a chart like the one below and assess the written materials you collected.

3 Form conclusions about the effectiveness of communication at your placement. Describe ten ways in which communication at your placement could be improved.

WRITTEN MATERIAL	PURPOSE	FORMAT	AUDIENCE	STRUCTURE	CLARITY	ACCURACY

WHAT HAVE YOU LEARNED?

▼ ▼ ▼

1 What are the various ways in which people communicate in the workplace?

2 Describe the process of communication using an example of an effective exchange of information.

3 Describe a situation in which a communication barrier prevented a message from being received.

a How was the communication process interrupted?
b How could this communication barrier be overcome?

4 How does nonverbal communication affect what a person says and how a person listens?

5 What unique challenges does communication by telephone present?

6 List five guidelines for communication that are important for success in a co-operative education, or work experience, program.

7 List five occupations that involve a lot of speaking and writing.

CHAPTER 6

FINDING EMPLOYMENT

WHAT YOU WILL LEARN

After completing this chapter, you should be able to:

▼ ▼ ▼

- Identify a variety of ways to locate job opportunities.
- Understand how to find jobs in the hidden job market.
- Recognize the importance of developing a network.
- Understand how to handle the stress of a job search.

TERMS TO REMEMBER

▼ ▼ ▼

job search

personal contacts

professional
   contacts

employment
   agency

Employment
   and Immigration
   Canada

job lead

hidden job
   market

referral

network

Ways to Find Employment

Studies show that today's young people will likely change occupations about six times throughout their lives. Therefore, being able to find a job is essential. The challenges are not only to know your career goals and to develop a plan, but to be able to achieve your goals and satisfy your plan by finding the jobs you want. Knowing how to find employment, or conduct a **job search**, involves knowing where to find employment and how to promote your qualifications to show employers that you have the skills they need.

The diagram below shows how most jobs are found. **Personal contacts**, such as relatives or friends, and **professional contacts**, people you know within an occupation, are the most common sources for finding jobs. In fact, unadvertised openings account for about 75 percent of all jobs. Only about 26 percent of all workers get their jobs from newspaper advertisements and employment agencies. Leads from contacts and direct contact with employers are more successful job-search techniques.

How Most Jobs Are Found

Direct contact with employers and leads from people you know

Job advertisements

Agencies

Others

63.3%   13.9%   12.2%   10.6%

PERSONAL AND PROFESSIONAL CONTACTS

A simple way to find a job is to talk to family members and friends who may have some knowledge of jobs in an occupation that interests you. As well, you can directly contact local employers or people you know in an occupation to see if there are any suitable jobs available. Before you contact anyone, prepare a list of people who might be able to provide you with information about jobs. In terms of employers, try to find out the names of the people who would supervise the positions by telephoning the organizations and asking their receptionists. Then contact these people by telephone or in person. It may be more appropriate to contact a family member or friend in person and an employer by telephone. When contacting people about possible jobs, clearly state your name, briefly outline your career goals, and ask them whether they know of any jobs that might be suitable. Even if no jobs are currently available, you may learn about other opportunities. More information on how to develop contacts follows later in this chapter.

JOB ADVERTISEMENTS

About 50 percent of all job seekers use newspaper ads as sources of job leads, but only about 14 percent of all jobs are obtained through these ads. In spite of these figures, job ads in newspapers and trade magazines are valuable sources of information. They indicate the types of openings that are available in a particular occupation and geographic area. They also give an indication of the levels of education and training employers are looking for and the salaries they are willing to pay. When looking for a job by using advertisements, follow these guidelines:

- Read the entire help-wanted section. Sometimes interesting jobs are listed in unexpected places.
- Circle all interesting ads.
- Note the types of employers hiring people with your skills.
- Respond to ads that contain sufficient information, such as the company name and address and a clear description of the position and required qualifications.

EMPLOYMENT AGENCIES

Some employers use employment agencies to find job candidates. An **employment agency** is an organization that helps people find jobs and employers find people. People who are searching for jobs register with an employment agency, and then the agency tries to match the people to the jobs available. Employment agencies may advertise a job in a newspaper or trade magazine. A fee is charged for the agency's services, which is usually a percentage of the new employee's salary when hired. The fee may be paid either by the employer or by the person who takes the job. If you choose to register with an agency, you may have to sign a contract that outlines who pays the fee, the amount of the fee, and so on. Before signing any contract, be sure you read and understand it thoroughly. If you are unsure about any part of the contract, do not sign it. Ask for a copy to take with you, and seek the advice of someone you know.

About 4 percent of all jobs are available at any given time due to retirements, deaths, resignations, firings, promotions, transfers, and sickness and maternity leaves.
EMPLOYMENT AND
IMMIGRATION CANADA

GOVERNMENT EMPLOYMENT CENTRES

Canada Employment Centres are operated by **Employment and Immigration Canada** across the country. Their services are free, and anyone can register with a centre. The centres offer listings of available jobs and the help of job counsellors, but they do not usually arrange interviews for you. A job seeker usually contacts an employer directly. Some provincial and territorial governments also offer employment services.

THE *YELLOW PAGES*

A good source of potential employers in your area is the *Yellow Pages*, which lists companies by the products or services they offer. You can make an excellent list of employers to contact by considering products or services related to your chosen occupation and then finding the companies in the *Yellow Pages* that offer those products or services.

SCHOOLS

Many high schools, colleges, and universities offer job information and career counselling to both students and the general public.

Two-thirds of all employees work in small organizations of under 25 people. Most of the new jobs created in the future will be in small organizations.

"WE'LL DO THE BEST WE CAN, MR. AVERY . . . WHAT TIME DO YOU LIKE TO GET UP?"

Reprinted from *The Saturday Evening Post*.

There are many more ways to find employment. For example, volunteer work, part-time jobs, summer jobs, or temporary work can all lead to full-time jobs. Thinking creatively when looking for a job is important. Remember, though, that finding a job is a job in itself—it requires perseverance and dedication. In the chart that follows, four characteristics of a full-time job are compared to four characteristics of the job search.

In a lifetime, the average individual spends 70 000 hours working. Considering the importance of work, looking for work is a full-time job in itself and the more time you spend looking for a job, the greater your chances are of getting one.

EMPLOYMENT AND
IMMIGRATION CANADA

FULL-TIME JOB	JOB SEARCH
• Responsibilities determined by the demands of the job	• Responsibilities set by yourself
• Be at work on time every day	• Set out early to look for a job every day
• Work the required hours per week (usually about 40 hours)	• Look for work 40 hours a week
• Report to a supervisor	• Be your own boss

Read the help-wanted section of a local newspaper and choose five advertisements that appeal to you. Then answer these questions:

1 What characteristics attract you to certain ads?

2 List the key words that appear in these ads, such as "team player" or "stable employment history." These words indicate the characteristics that employers are looking for in an employee. Explain why you think these words are appropriate.

3 List the specific educational, work experience, and personal requirements outlined in each ad.

4 What rewards for suitable employees are listed in each ad?

A C T I V I T Y
Analyzing Job Advertisements

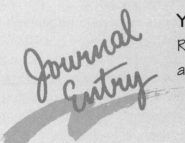

Your Perfect Job
Reflect on your ideal job. Then, in your journal, create a job advertisement for it.

Searching for Jobs

TIRE PLANT CLOSES

A tire plant closed in a small town due to shifting business trends. Forty-five people in a town of 2000 became unemployed; many of them had worked at the plant for over 25 years. Marla Bryant was one of those people. She joined the company when she was 19 years old, and in 31 years she was never late and rarely away. She worked with a positive attitude at various unskilled jobs around the factory. The severance pay and pension were generous, but at the age of 50, Marla does not want to stop working—she wonders what she will do all day. She likes working, being with people, and feeling useful.

MARCO RETURNS TO WORK

Marco Capponne is a young man of 26 who has been out of the work force for four years. He has been taking care of his two children, who are both under the age of four. It was important to him and Fran, his wife, that one of them stay home with the children for as long as possible. Fran has a full-time job as a real estate appraiser during the day. They decided that Marco would try to find a job during the evenings and weekends in order to save on day-care costs. Then Fran could look after the children in the evening while Marco is at work. Marco is trained as a a legal assistant and has two years of experience in this occupation. He should be able to find a job that uses his research and computer skills and office experience.

▼ ▼ ▼

Look through the help-wanted section of a newspaper and find jobs for Marla and Marco. Discuss your choices as a class. Be prepared to:

1 Explain why you think certain jobs are suitable for them.

2 Suggest what each of them could do to increase their chances of finding a job.

3 List sources other than the newspaper that they might use to find suitable jobs.

Finding Unadvertised Jobs

Job leads, or information about possible job openings, from job advertisements, employment agencies, and Canada Employment Centres are easy to find. Since this information is so readily available, there is usually a lot of competition for these jobs. Jobs that are not advertised or available through employment agencies are part of the **hidden job market.** These jobs require more time and effort to find, so there is less competition for them. For example, if you contact an employer directly to inquire about a possible job opening and you are granted an interview, you are most likely one of only a few candidates being interviewed.

Many employers prefer not to advertise because of the high number of responses they receive. Reading hundreds of résumés and interviewing a large number of applicants is time-consuming and, therefore, expensive. Training interviewers is also expensive. For these reasons, an employer will often hire someone who has been recommended by a friend or business associate. Some employers are more comfortable hiring a person who is known to them in some way.

Advertising is expensive and frequently generates far too many applicants to interview. About 80 percent of job opportunities are not advertised.
EMPLOYMENT AND
IMMIGRATION CANADA

The most effective method of finding jobs in the hidden job market is to apply directly to employers. Do not assume that there must be an advertised job opening before you can approach an employer—many employers are willing to speak to job seekers even when no job openings exist. They know that they will need good employees in the future when someone quits or retires or when the company expands.

There are many opportunities to make direct contact with employers before and during your job search. Never turn down an opportunity to make a contact. One way to develop contacts is by phoning employers who may be interested in hiring you. Before making a call, you need to know the name of the appropriate person to speak to. Perhaps the supervisor of a department or the owner of the business is the appropriate contact. If you do not know the person's name, phone the organization and ask for the name of the person who supervises the department you are interested in. Then ask for the person. Tell him or her you are looking for a job and would like to talk briefly. Even if the person has no job openings, there may be one in the future. The flowchart on page 104 illustrates how to conduct this type of telephone call.

Don't wait for your ship to come in. Swim out to it.
ANONYMOUS

Getting an interview is the main goal of calling. However, there are three additional goals: getting information about when a job may be available, getting information about other employers with possible openings, and getting a **referral.** A referral is a lead to another specific company or person. When you contact this company or person, you should state who you were referred by. A referral gives you a slight advantage in that the person you are contacting may be encouraged by the referral to grant you an interview.

On the Telephone

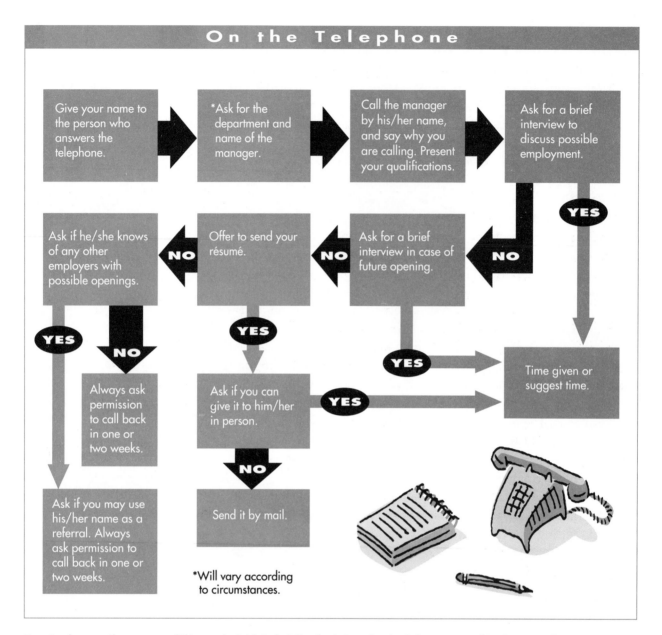

Give your name to the person who answers the telephone.

➤ *Ask for the department and name of the manager.

➤ Call the manager by his/her name, and say why you are calling. Present your qualifications.

➤ Ask for a brief interview to discuss possible employment.

YES

Ask if he/she knows of any other employers with possible openings.

NO Offer to send your résumé.

NO Ask for a brief interview in case of future opening.

NO

YES **NO**

Always ask permission to call back in one or two weeks.

YES Ask if you can give it to him/her in person.

YES Time given or suggest time.

YES

Ask if you may use his/her name as a referral. Always ask permission to call back in one or two weeks.

NO Send it by mail.

*Will vary according to circumstances.

From *People to see, Places to go, and Things to do: A Job Seeker's Handbook.* Reproduced with the permission of Employment and Immigration Canada and Supply & Services Canada, 1993.

Getting a Job

by Janis Foord

In a high school marketing and advertising class, Karen found she had a special talent for, and interest in, advertising. She didn't know enough to be sure of its long-term appeal, she only knew she liked "the way it felt."

Before leaving school, Karen wisely made sure she took keyboarding, information management, and some accounting courses.

Upon graduation, Karen blitzed all the ad agencies in her city. In each case, her message was the same: "I will do anything." She was offered several positions in other industries but turned them down.

Finally, one day she received a call from an advertising agency she'd had an interview with a month earlier. They needed a junior receptionist/mail clerk, "was she interested?" She started the following Monday.

Within a few months Karen knew she had found her environment. She loved the high-energy atmosphere, the deadlines, the wild people. After consulting with the personnel manager she enrolled in an evening class offering basic copywriting training.

A year passed. Karen's interest had been noticed and appreciated in her company. She was willing to do any task. She was the one who often stayed if a presentation had to be out the next morning. She loved it.

She asked for an interview with the office manager. Showing him some of her assignments, she told of her ongoing interest and her

classes. A promise was made to her that when the next junior copywriting position came available, she would be considered for it.

That was the real beginning. Karen continued her evening classes. Branching out, she took an advanced copywriting course. Her promotion came through. Some two and a half years after she joined the company, Karen was made a full copywriter. A year after that she became a Group Creative Chief.

Today, five years have passed. Karen is Creative Director with a smaller West Coast agency. She wanted the all-round involvement of a small agency and she also wanted to live in the West.

All her goals and dreams are steadily being realized. Having started slowly and steadily, paid her dues, and worked hard, Karen is exactly where she wanted to be.

From *Get to Work* by Janis Foord. Used by permission of the Canadian Publishers, McClelland & Stewart, Toronto.

▼ ▼ ▼

1 Describe how Karen developed the job leads for her positions as junior receptionist/mail clerk and copywriter.

2 Imagine you are a career counsellor. Write a letter giving advice to a person you know who is looking for a job.

Perseverance

In your journal, reflect on how the quote below relates to the job search and write about your understanding of perseverance. Give examples of occasions when you or someone you know persevered and, thus, attained a personal goal.

Perseverance is a great element of success. If you only knock long enough and loud enough at the gate, you are sure to wake up somebody.

Henry Wadsworth Longfellow

Networking

If you ask two people for the names of two contacts and then you ask each of those four people for two contacts, and so on, you will have a network of 1024 people to help you after only the tenth level.

A **network** is a group of personal and professional contacts. Networking is the process you use to contact these people. For example, you might ask a neighbour if he or she knows about any job openings. The neighbour may in turn ask a variety of people—his or her network—about job opportunities. The larger the network, the greater the opportunity of finding a job opening.

There are probably more people ready to network with you than you can imagine. Many groups of people can help, such as:

- Friends
- Relatives
- Former employers
- Classmates
- Members of clubs or sports teams
- Neighbours
- Friends of parents

- Former co-workers
- Former classmates
- Friends' parents
- People who provide products (e.g., clerks or salespeople)
- People who provide services (e.g., mechanics or hairstylists)

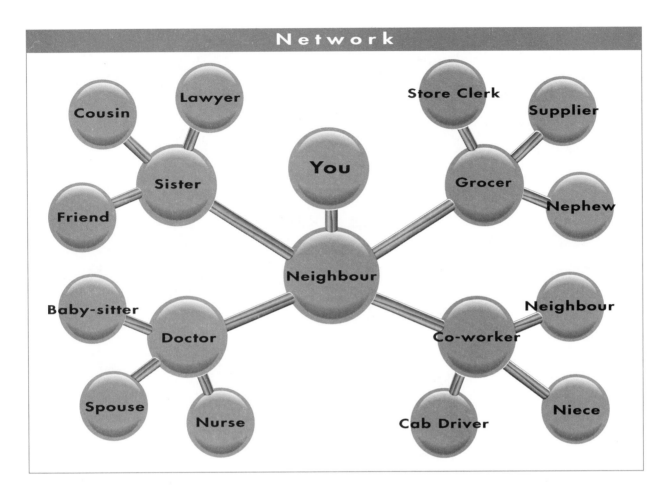

As soon as you begin to develop a network and a list of job leads, you will need to organize and keep track of the information. It may be as simple as keeping a list of contacts and job leads or as detailed as organizing a set of job-lead forms or cards. Keeping careful records saves time and keeps you on the job of finding a job.

COMPANY	CONTACT	ADDRESS	TELEPHONE
BP Printing	Al Smith	862 North Ave.	555-3872
Graphic Source	Sonja Weiss	42 Central St.	555-0037
Plus Printing	Jill Marz	52 St. Mary Blvd.	555-3242

> **Job Lead**
>
> **Job Title:** *Graphic Designer*
>
> **Source of Information:** *Advertisement in the magazine The Ink Spot*
>
> **Contact Person:** *Sonja Weiss*
>
> **Phone:** *555-0037*
>
> **Company Name:** *Graphic Source*
>
> **Company Address:** *42 Central St.*
>
> **Interview Date/Time:** *10:00 a.m., December 2*
>
> **Interview Location:** *as above*
>
> **Interviewer's Name:** *Sonja Weiss*
>
> **Notes:** *No position available. Much useful information. Call in six months to maintain contact and check for a job opening.*

From *People to see, Places to go, and Things to do: A Job Seeker's Handbook.* Reproduced with the permission of Employment and Immigration Canada and Supply & Services Canada, 1993.

ACTIVITY
Listing Your Contacts

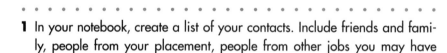

1 In your notebook, create a list of your contacts. Include friends and family, people from your placement, people from other jobs you may have had, and so on—refer to the list of possible contacts on page 106.

2 Using copies of the job-lead form provided by your teacher, fill out the forms for five of your most important contacts and create a file of job leads. Maintain this file as you progress through your career.

Stress and the Job Search

*E*veryone feels stress at one time or another. Stress can be positive and give you extra energy and stamina. However, the stress associated with the job search can be negative. Fear of the unknown often causes stress in job seekers. They may wonder: Will I get a good lead today? Will my interview go well? Is a hiring team looking at my résumé right now? Doubts can be a problem: Should I have taken engineering? Should I be staying here or moving to a place with a wider job market? Is my suit too conservative or my hair too long?

Learning to control this stress is difficult. Recognizing it, however, is a big step toward controlling it. Here are four hints for managing the stress of a job search:

- *Set a daily routine and stick to it.* Plan your daily chores, job search, and leisure activities. This will lessen your sense of unstructured time.

- *Recognize that finding a job is a job.* This will add purpose to each day as well as reinforce the structure of each day.
- *Be aware of the value of good health.* Stress manifests itself in many ways—insomnia, headaches, poor digestion, forgetfulness, irritability, and depression are a few of the symptoms. These symptoms are aggravated when you do not eat properly, sleep regular hours, and get moderate exercise.
- *Be positive.* Tell yourself positive things so that your self-concept will be strengthened and negative stress will be decreased. The important thing is to remain optimistic.

Praising Yourself

In your journal, list your personal and professional attributes. Then write yourself a letter outlining your potential as an employee.

1 Read a book or an article or watch a television show or movie about a person who is out of work and looking for a job. Outline the sequence of events in the story and determine how the events affected the stress level of the person.

2 In small groups, compare your findings. What similarities and differences are evident? What conclusions can you draw about how the stress of a job search can affect a person? Brainstorm suggestions for handling stress and share them with the rest of the class.

A C T I V I T Y
The Effects of Stress

▼ ▼

HOW DID PEOPLE FIND THEIR JOBS?

1 List the names of ten people at your placement or other people you know who are employed in a chart like the one below. Beside each name, list the person's job. Contact these people and ask them how they got their jobs. Ask them to be specific.

2 In small groups, discuss how the people you contacted obtained their jobs, and rank the most commonly used ways of finding a job in order from most popular to least popular.

NAME	JOB	HOW FOUND
Jay Lee	Telephone installer	Direct contact with employer
Benji Wisnicki	Graphic designer	College bulletin board
Noni Bell	Administrative assistant	Job advertisement in *The Daily Bugle*

WHAT HAVE YOU LEARNED?

▼ ▼ ▼

1 List methods for finding employment.

2 If you were looking for a job in your community, which job-search methods do you think would be most successful? Why?

3 Describe how to discover jobs in the hidden job market.

4 a What is a network?

b Describe how to develop a network.

5 What suggestions would you give to a young person who is looking for her or his first part-time job?

6 a Why might a job search be stressful?

b Describe ways of coping with this stress.

CHAPTER 7

RÉSUMÉS, COVERING LETTERS, AND APPLICATION FORMS

WHAT YOU WILL LEARN

After completing this chapter, you should be able to:

▼ ▼ ▼

- Gather and organize the information required to complete résumés, covering letters, and application forms.
- Recognize the purpose and function of a résumé.
- Choose a résumé style that best suits your needs and write a résumé.
- Recognize the purpose and function of a covering letter and write a covering letter.
- Recognize the purpose and function of an application form and complete an application form.
- Understand your rights when completing application forms.

TERMS TO REMEMBER

▼ ▼ ▼

Social Insurance Number (SIN)	résumé	combination résumé
	chronological résumé	covering letter
reference	functional résumé	application form

Gathering Information

Luck is what happens when preparation meets opportunity.

E. LETTERMAN

The beginning of the job-search process encourages you to reflect on what you have done and examine how your past may influence your future. An initial step in the process is gathering precise information (such as the details of previous jobs) in order to complete a résumé, a covering letter, or an application form. The same data is usually required whether you are applying for a part-time or full-time position. Gather and organize the information that is described in the sections that follow. All of this information may not be necessary to include in your résumé, letter, or application form, but you should have it available in case it is required.

CAREER GOALS

Although career goals are not required in order to apply for a job, you should have a clear idea of your goals. (See Chapter 4 for more information about forming career goals.) A one-sentence career goal is often included in a résumé. The employer can then determine how your career goal fits with the needs of the organization. You may need to word your goal slightly differently on each résumé submission to relate to specific jobs you apply for.

PERSONAL INFORMATION

Personal information includes your name, current address, and telephone (and fax) number. Remember that these details must be accurate since, for example, an incorrect telephone number could result in a lost opportunity. Other personal information is sometimes required by an employer, such as date of birth, citizenship, ability to drive, or languages spoken. These types of information need only be supplied to an employer when they relate to the position for which you are applying.

A **Social Insurance Number (SIN)** is a nine-digit number used by the federal government to identify people for purposes such as income taxation. Everyone in Canada must have a SIN in order to be employed. Although it is not necessary to give your SIN to anyone until you have been hired, make sure that you have one before applying for a job. You can obtain a SIN by visiting your local Canada Employment Centre and completing a form like the one on page 113. Be sure to take your birth certificate with you.

EDUCATION

This category includes your educational background and training. List the name and address of every secondary school, business and technical school, college, and university you have attended or are currently attending. Also note the grade completed and the diploma, degree, certificate, or licence you received. Remember to include any extra courses or seminars you have taken to expand your working knowledge of a field.

Employment and **Emploi et**
Immigration Canada **Immigration Canada**

PROTECTED WHEN COMPLETED - A

APPLICATION FOR A :

- ☒ FIRST SOCIAL INSURANCE NUMBER CARD
- ☐ REPLACEMENT CARD (fee of $ 10.00 must be paid)
- ☐ CHANGE OF NAME(S) ON CARD
- ☐ CHANGE OF DATE OF BIRTH ONLY (no card will be issued)

DO NOT WRITE IN THIS AREA

YOUR APPLICATION WILL BE RETURNED IF NOT ACCOMPANIED BY THE REQUIRED DOCUMENTS (see instruction sheet for details)

INFORMATION CONCERNING THE APPLICANT. PLEASE PRINT CLEARLY.

| 1 | NAME TO BE SHOWN ON CARD ▶ | FIRST NAME Mei | MIDDLE NAME (if wanted on card) Lynn | PRESENT FAMILY NAME Kong |

| 2 | DATE OF BIRTH ▶ | D M Y 0,6 1,0 — | 3 | SEX ▶ ☐ M ☒ F | ☐ TWIN |

| 4 | MOTHER'S FULL NAME AT HER BIRTH Lynn Anne Wu ☐ UNKNOWN | 5 | FATHER'S FULL NAME AT HIS BIRTH Xiang Fu Kong ☐ UNKNOWN |

| 6 | PLACE OF BIRTH ▶ | CITY, TOWN OR VILLAGE Halifax | PROVINCE Nova Scotia | COUNTRY Canada |

| 7 | FAMILY NAME AT BIRTH Kong | 8 | OTHER FAMILY NAME(S) PREVIOUSLY USED |

| 9 | HAVE YOU EVER BEFORE APPLIED FOR OR RECEIVED A SOCIAL INSURANCE NUMBER ▶ ☒ NO ☐ YES | 10 | IF "YES", WRITE YOUR NUMBER HERE ▶ | ☐ DON'T KNOW |

| 11 | STATUS IN CANADA ▶ ☒ CANADIAN CITIZEN ☐ REGISTERED INDIAN ☐ PERMANENT RESIDENT ☐ OTHER | 12 | AREA CODE TELEPHONE NO. 9,0,2 5,5,5 1,2,3,4 |

| 13 | ADDRESS WHERE YOU WANT YOUR SIN CARD TO BE MAILED | NUMBER AND STREET 45 Vimy Avenue | APARTMENT |
| | | CITY, TOWN OR VILLAGE Halifax | PROVINCE Nova Scotia | POSTAL CODE B,3,M 4,C,5 |

| 14 | (IF YOU ARE UNDER 12 YEARS OF AGE, YOUR PARENT/GUARDIAN MUST SIGN AND INDICATE HIS/HER RELATIONSHIP. IF "X" IS USED AS A SIGNATURE, HAVE 2 WITNESSES SIGN HERE) APPLICANT'S SIGNATURE ▶ | DATE ▶ May 12, 19_ |

INFORMATION COLLECTED ON THIS FORM IS USED FOR THE PURPOSE OF ISSUING SOCIAL INSURANCE NUMBERS. ITS COLLECTION IS AUTHORIZED BY THE UNEMPLOYMENT INSURANCE ACT. FOR MORE DETAILS ON THE USES AND RIGHTS CONCERNING INSPECTION AND CORRECTION OF THE INFORMATION. REFER TO THE PERSONAL INFORMATION INDEX, BANK NO EIC PPU 390, AVAILABLE AT CANADA EMPLOYMENT CENTRES AND POST OFFICES.

IT IS AN OFFENCE TO KNOWINGLY APPLY FOR MORE THAN ONE SOCIAL INSURANCE NUMBER. YOU ARE NOT PERMITTED TO GIVE OR LEND YOUR CARD TO ANYONE.

DO NOT WRITE BELOW. FOR LOCAL OFFICE USE ONLY

| A | ALL NAMES AS SHOWN ON PRIMARY DOCUMENT | FAMILY NAME |

| B | DATE OF BIRTH AS SHOWN ON PRIMARY DOCUMENT D M Y | C | DOCUMENT(S) SEEN PRIMARY DOCUMENT | SUPPORTING DOCUMENT |

| D | EMERGENCY SIN REASON | E | FEE PAID IF REPLACEMENT CARD AMOUNT $ RECEIPT NO | CERTIFICATION STAMP |

| F | REMARKS | | |

NAS 2120 (12-91) B

(FRANÇAIS AU VERSO)

Canadä

EMPLOYMENT

List the names, addresses, and telephone numbers of all the jobs you have had for which you were paid. As well, list volunteer work and work experience gained through school programs. Be sure to include the supervisors' names, periods of employment, types of businesses, job titles, reasons for leaving, and responsibilities for each position.

SKILLS

Three types of skills apply to résumés and application forms: technical skills, which are practical skills that are learned, such as the use of specific equipment, computer programs, and languages; self-management skills, which are personal skills, such as organizing and communicating; and transferable skills, which can be applied to many situations, such as mathematical ability. Both technical and self-management skills can be transferable skills. (See Chapter 2, pages 27–31, for more information on skills.)

ACTIVITIES AND INTERESTS

Chance favours the prepared mind.
LOUIS PASTEUR

These may or may not be included in a résumé or an application form. Although your activities and interests allow a potential employer to gain some insight into your personality, they should clearly relate to the position for which you are applying. For instance, if you are applying for a job as program director of a day camp, you may want to list the sports you take part in.

REFERENCES

A **reference** is a person who recommends you to a potential employer. People who are acting as references should know something about your skills, personality traits, experience, and education. You should select references who can be contacted easily and who will respond quickly and positively. Your references might include former employers, teachers, or people for whom you have done volunteer work. Using family members as references is not an acceptable practice.

Contact people in advance and ask them if they are willing to act as references for you. Make them aware of your plans—you might send them supportive material, such as a résumé and a list of the companies you have applied to. When contacting references, ask them what they would say about you to a potential employer. Obtain the correct spelling of their names and job titles, and make sure you have their correct addresses and telephone numbers.

Once all the necessary information has been collected, you will be ready to write your résumé or complete an application form.

A C T I V I T Y

Creating a Personal Information Sheet

1 Organize all the information about yourself under the following headings: career goals, personal information, education, employment, skills, activities and interests, and references. Consider the information you collected about yourself in Chapter 2.

2 Check the information thoroughly for proper spelling and accuracy.

3 Exchange your personal information sheet with a partner. Check that all the necessary information is included, clarify any vague or inaccurate information, and consider whether or not the information indicates what the person intended.

4 Provide constructive feedback on your partner's personal information sheet.

Evaluating Your Personal Information

In your journal, complete the statements below.

- If I could highlight only one accomplishment in my life, it would be...

- If my references are contacted and asked to make three statements about me, I am sure that they will say I am...

- I feel positive about my employment information because...

Résumés

A résumé is a summary of your education, employment history, and accomplishments. It is sometimes called a personal data sheet or curriculum vitae. The purpose of a résumé is to summarize aspects of you that are relevant to an employer. It is often sent with a covering letter to a potential employer in order to generate interest and an interview. The résumé must hold the reader's attention and create a positive, lasting impression of the writer.

A résumé is only one or two pages in length and should be neat, complete, and concise. When preparing to write a résumé, consider your past experiences and accomplishments in terms of how they can benefit an employer. You should be able to prove every statement by using a specific recent example. As well, consider the unique advantages you can offer an employer. In your résumé, you must convince her or him that you can physically and mentally do the job, that you have the required knowledge, skills, and attitudes, and that you are genuinely interested in the job. Ultimately, the purpose of a résumé, like every aspect of a job search, is to help you find a job you enjoy.

Résumés can serve several different functions during the job-search process:

- *Inventory.* The résumé is an inventory of your experiences. It can help you to clarify your value as an employee and prepare yourself for the job-search process.
- *Summary.* A résumé offers a valuable summary to an employer. At a glance, a potential employer can evaluate whether you should be interviewed.
- *Interview outline.* At a job interview, the résumé can be used as a reference for questions by the interviewer and for comments by the interviewee.
- *Review.* The résumé can be used by a potential employer to review candidates who have been interviewed and it can be filed for future reference.

Résumés are a useful part of a job search because they are an easy way to contact many people cheaply and efficiently. But using a résumé to find a job can have certain drawbacks. Consider how many résumés may be sent in response to a single job advertisement in a newspaper. If an employer receives 200 résumés in response to an ad, how much time will he or she spend reading each one? Most employers will only quickly glance at a résumé to determine the appropriateness of a candidate for a job. Therefore, your résumé must be extremely effective and appealing in order to stand out from the crowd.

Employers Scan Résumé for Clues to Attitudes

by Janis Foord Kirk

"What do employers look for on a résumé?"

It's a question that comes up often—understandably. People write résumés to please and attract employers.

Those looking for work can spend hours trying to figure out what words to use; how to best describe their background, training, and experience; how to hit the right note. The goal, always, is to convince the employer to grant an interview.

So, what do employers look for? It's almost impossible to answer that question with any certainty. Employers are individuals. Like all of us, they have subjective views on lots of topics, résumés being one of them. What appeals to one, doesn't necessarily appeal to another.

Recently, we asked several employers and personnel specialists, many of whom are currently recruiting, "What attracts you to one résumé over another?" It wasn't a scientific sampling. Everyone surveyed admitted to having their own biases.

Nonetheless, there does seem to be a consensus on the main points. If you're currently trying to write, or re-write, a résumé that doesn't seem to be working for you, pay attention to the views of the people who do the hiring.

Résumés today should be clear, concise, and brief, they said.

"Two pages—maximum; anything over that is getting too long," said David Peters, a human resources manager with Royal Trust. "It doesn't matter how long you've been working. I don't really care, frankly, about the stuff you did in 1972."

"If you're in the 20th year of your career and you feel you must note it, make a brief chronological laundry list as an addendum," Peters adds.

Most of those surveyed agreed on another point: don't bother attaching references to your résumé. A simple notation at the end—references available on request—is adequate.

"Quality" is what Judith Kidd looks for when scanning résumés to decide whom to interview.

"If there's a spelling mistake, it goes to the bottom," says Kidd, manager of human resources for one of Canada's largest law firms, McCarthy Tetrault. "If (the résumé) is addressed to a particular individual, the name must be spelled correctly. It's the detail, and the care they've taken. If they don't care about that, are they going to care about our clients?"

One professional, who asked not to be identified, cautioned against using a résumé that's "so slick it was obviously written by someone else." A recruiter for a major firm in the retail service sector, she had this to say: "There are a lot of professionally written résumés around right now. They make it practically impossible to conclude whether or not the person fits the job opening."

Résumés of this sort open with "one page of accomplishments or point-form notes that say: 'I did this, or I did that' " she said. "But they don't tell me about their work experience or how long they worked at any particular place. You can tell by looking at it that the person who sent it didn't write it."

Above all, the information on a résumé must be easily accessible to the reader, says David Peters. It's a simple factor of time.

"It's not unusual these days to sit and go through 200 or 300 résumés at a time," Peters says. "You can't afford to spend ten minutes going over each résumé. If you haven't told me in the first minute and a half what it is you do, I'm not going to bother looking for it."

The best résumés, Peters says, offer "a concise representation of a career in reverse chronological order."

Under each job "list major responsibilities and accomplishments in bullet, point form rather than paragraph," he suggests. "A résumé stands out if it has a lot of white space—almost like a good ad—with clearly blocked, easy to read, short sentences that give nothing but information."

And be sure, Peters adds, to "stay away from heavy adjectives and superfluous information."

Several of the people mentioned the importance of the covering letter. But no one put as much emphasis on it as Ira Travers, executive vice-president and general manager of Cal-Abco, a distributor for the microcomputer industry.

"I spend more time reading the covering letter than I do the actual résumé," Travers said. "The résumé tells me where they've been in the past. The covering letter tells me what kind of person they are.

"I read a lot into the psychology of the letter," he explains. "You can find out levels of sincerity, levels of sensitivity, and how concerned people are about doing the job you want them to do. If it's a form letter, I generally don't even bother to read the rest of the application."

Overall, in any job application, Travers looks for "sincere comments" he says. "And, I look for things that are tailored towards our industry." The people he eventually interviews are those "who've done some research and who can talk with some industry knowledge."

The message is clear. When employers review résumés they're searching for clues. Not only about your skills and experience but about your personality, your attitude, and your work habits.

© Janis Foord Kirk, 1991. Reprinted by permission.

▼ ▼ ▼

1 **Each of the Canadian employers and personnel specialists interviewed described what they felt to be key aspects of a good résumé. Which five key aspects of a résumé do you consider important? Explain why you chose each aspect.**

2 **a Explain the importance of attitude in a résumé.**
  b How can you exhibit a positive attitude in your résumé?

3 **Using the article as a reference, write a letter of advice to a younger person who is looking for a part-time job.**

4 **If you had to fit your résumé on an index card instead of on a regular sheet of paper, what would you write? Why?**

FREQUENTLY ASKED QUESTIONS ABOUT RÉSUMÉS

Should my age be on my résumé?

A person's age (as well as marital status, race, height, mass, and so on) is usually not included on a résumé unless it is relevant to the job.

Should I include a photograph of myself?

Most human-resources managers agree that they are interested in the appearance of potential employees but that including a photograph is not a businesslike approach. In an interview, you will have the opportunity to present yourself visually.

Why do most applicants write "References available on request" at the end of their résumés, instead of including the actual references?

Writing "References available on request" on a résumé is an accepted practice today. References are not usually needed until a potential employee has successfully completed an interview. Before going to an interview, prepare a neatly typed sheet of three or four references in case the interviewer asks for them.

Do I have to include my Social Insurance Number on my résumé?

No. This information is only required when a person becomes an employee of a company.

Collecting information for a résumé is time-consuming and labour-intensive. Do I really need a résumé to get a job?

Some people believe that the emphasis on résumé writing is misplaced, while others believe that no one can get a job without one. Most employers do require a résumé, though. A résumé also helps to organize your goals, thoughts, and facts. As well, it is better to prepare a résumé than to find yourself without one when it is required.

Can I handwrite my résumé?

Although some employers may prefer a handwritten résumé, it is not a common practice. Ideally, a résumé should be neatly keyed using a word processor so that it can be easily modified for each job. The layout should be spacious, pleasing, and easy to follow.

What kind of paper should I use?

Résumés are usually printed on letter-sized paper without lines. White, off-white, or grey paper is acceptable; other colours are usually avoided. Remember, though, that there are exceptions to every rule. No one style or format can guarantee success.

Writing a Résumé

Errors in spelling, grammar, and punctuation can cause your résumé to be dismissed. Make sure your résumé is error-free.

When writing a résumé, keep the audience (an employer), purpose (to obtain an interview), and the position for which you are applying in mind. Direct your writing to appeal to an employer so that she or he will grant you an interview.

These guidelines can help you write a résumé:

- Use verbs to indicate action and continued growth and improvement. For example, use words such as "developed," "enriched," "demonstrated," and "gained" when describing job responsibilities and skills.
- Spell out words in full; for example, use "Street" not "St." and "telephone" not "phone."
- Reword sentences to avoid using the word "I," where possible.
- Include enough relevant information to clearly demonstrate skills and abilities without being wordy.
- Exhibit a positive attitude.
- Present yourself in the best possible way. For example, a job description for a salesclerk might include the following: "Developed an ability to effectively serve the public in a courteous manner."
- Ensure there are no spelling, grammar, or punctuation errors.

A single résumé format can never please all potential employers. The question is: Will the employers you are interested in like your résumé?

There are three common ways of organizing the information in a résumé. Most people prefer a **chronological résumé**, where the information is outlined from the most recent to the least recent. The **functional résumé**, which highlights transferable skills, is also common. A third format is the **combination résumé**, which uses aspects of both the chronological and the functional résumé. When choosing a résumé format, consider how you can best show the employer who you are and how you can benefit the organization. The purpose is not only to show that you are capable of doing the job, but also that you are the *best* candidate for the job.

The chronological résumé describes the historical sequence of job experience and education. It illustrates the development of the applicant through job title, responsibilities, and other concrete accomplishments.

The functional résumé is used by people who are well on the way to having the skills required for the job and who have focussed career plans. This type of résumé describes the tasks that the person did in a job, and it is usually tailored to each job applied for. The functional résumé is usually used by people who have years of experience in many jobs. Some employers do not like this style because it leaves out details of the applicant's past work and educational experience—this can make it look like the applicant has something to hide.

The combination résumé stresses skills as well as providing some details of past employment. It is useful to relate past experiences and skills to a specific goal. Education, dates of employment, and personal information (such as nonwork-related interests) may or may not be included. This résumé format is the best choice for someone with extensive experience or an interrupted employment history.

In the samples that follow, the person has used the two most common résumé styles: the chronological and the combination résumé.

CHRONOLOGICAL RÉSUMÉ

Chris Hood
19 Stoney Road
Mountain View, Alberta
T6Y 1B4
Home: (403) 555-1234
Business: (403) 555-4321

Career Goal	To gain experience as a manager in a retail setting.
Skills	• Working knowledge of word processing and spreadsheet software • Training in leadership roles • Spoken and written knowledge of English and French

Education

1990–1993
Conestoga College, 19 Black Road,
Red Deer, Alberta T5M 1S4
• Obtained a diploma in Business Administration with
emphasis on management

1986–1990
Mountain View Secondary School, 35 Rocky Street,
Mountain View, Alberta T6Y 1B4
• Received the Senior Student Achievement Award
• Courses included Consumer Studies, Computers, and French

Work Experience

1990–present
Manager: Conestoga College Store, 212 Centre Avenue,
Red Deer, Alberta T5M 1S2
• Hired as a cashier and promoted to manager in 1991
• Responsibilities included inventory control,
purchasing, and scheduling shifts

1986–1990
Clerk: Mountain View Hardware, 16 Narrow Path,
Mountain View, Alberta T6Y 1B3
• Duties involved shipping and receiving as well as
general clean-up

1988–1990
Volunteer: Mountain View Hospital, 6 Neighbour Way,
Mountain View, Alberta T6Y 1B3
• Assisted in the gift shop
• Helped on outings for disabled patients

Activities and Interests
• Swimming instructor and lifeguard qualifications
• CPR training
• Hiking and skiing

References   Available on request.

Combination Résumé

Chris Hood
19 Stoney Road
Mountain View, Alberta
T6Y 1B4
Home: (403) 555-1234
Business: (403) 555-4321

Career Goal   To gain experience as a manager in a retail setting.

Skills

Administration   As Manager of the Conestoga College Store, I supervise a staff of twelve full-time and part-time cashiers and warehouse staff. I oversee all aspects of inventory control, purchasing, and shift scheduling. As well, my educational training has prepared me to adapt quickly, identify and solve problems, and develop new ideas.

Customer Relations   Throughout my educational and work experience, I have continued to provide quality service through considerate and attentive interaction with customers.

Communication   I am able to clearly communicate with customers, suppliers, staff, and management. I have developed both my written and spoken skills in French and have a working knowledge of word processing and spreadsheet software.

Experience

1990–present   Manager: Conestoga College Store, 212 Centre Avenue, Red Deer, Alberta T5M 1S2

1986–1990   Clerk: Mountain View Hardware, 16 Narrow Path, Mountain View, Alberta T6Y 1B3

1988–1990   Volunteer: Mountain View Hospital, 6 Neighbour Way, Mountain View, Alberta T6Y 1B3

Education

1990–1993   Conestoga College, 19 Black Road, Red Deer, Alberta T5M 1S4
- Obtained a diploma in Business Administration with emphasis on management

1986–1990   Mountain View Secondary School, 35 Rocky Street, Mountain View, Alberta T6Y 1B4
- Received the Senior Student Achievement Award
- Courses included Consumer Studies, Computers, and French

Activities and Interests
- Swimming instructor and lifeguard qualifications
- CPR training
- Hiking and skiing

References   Available on request.

1 In groups of four, discuss the advantages and disadvantages of chronological, functional, and combination résumés. Create a chart like the one below to compare the three résumé formats.

	CHRONOLOGICAL	**FUNCTIONAL**	**COMBINATION**
Advantages			
Disadvantages			

2 Prepare your résumé for a prospective employer using one of the formats.

3 Ask the people in your group to assess your résumé using a copy of the résumé checklist provided by your teacher.

4 Revise your résumé based on the comments you receive.

RÉSUMÉ CHECKLIST		
Item	**Check if Answer Is Yes**	**Suggestions for Improvements**
Is the résumé clear? Does it provide a "picture" of the writer's qualifications?		
Is all personal information relevant to the job?		
Is all the necessary information included?		
Does the résumé include positive self-evaluation?		
Is the language clear and understandable?		
Does the résumé emphasize benefits for a potential employer?		
Does the résumé make the reader want to continue to read it?		

Item	Check if Answer Is Yes	Suggestions for Improvements
Is the layout appealing? Do strong points stand out?		
Do the sentences begin with action words?		
Is the résumé brief, to the point, and neat?		
Is the length appropriate?		
Is the résumé free of spelling and grammatical errors?		
If you were a potential employer, would you grant an interview based on this résumé?		

Covering Letters

A **covering letter** is a letter that accompanies your résumé when you respond to an advertisement, follow up on a job lead, or just want to indicate interest in a company. The purpose of the covering letter is to introduce yourself and your résumé and to get an interview.

A covering letter should be addressed to a specific person. If necessary, phone the organization to which you are applying to find the appropriate person, such as the manager of a particular department, the manager of the human resources department, or the owner of a small business. The receptionist or the human resources department can usually give you the person's name, title, correct mailing address, and any other information you may need. If you cannot discover the name of the contact person or if you are unsure of his or her gender, begin your letter with "To Whom It May Concern" or "Dear Sir/Madam."

A covering letter should also be neatly typed, free of errors, and follow the correct format (see page 95 for the proper format of a letter). Be sure to include your name and full address, the date, the name and title of your contact person, and the full address of the company.

In the first paragraph, clearly explain your purpose for writing, which is to apply for a job. State the job for which you are applying and how you learned about the position. If you are replying to a job advertisement, explain where you saw the ad.

In the second paragraph, explain why the person should want you as an employee. Refer to your résumé, highlighting the major qualifications that relate to the position for which you are applying and how they can benefit the employer. Include any special experience or training you have.

In the concluding paragraph, express your enthusiasm and appreciation for the person's attention to your application, and request a personal interview.

Three sample covering letters follow on pages 125–127. Each is for a different situation and each will be sent with a résumé. The first letter is from an applicant who has no job lead, the second is a response to a job ad, and the third is from someone who found a lead through a friend.

Dear Mr. Persynick:

Please accept this letter and résumé as an indication of my interest in working with the Tall Trees Research Centre as a field technician.

I am very impressed with the work your organization has been doing in the area of forest management. The article that appeared in the September 18 *Cedartown Herald* about your success in controlling the spread of tent caterpillars in northern British Columbia was most interesting. As a recent graduate of Cedartown Collegiate Institute who has experience in chemical spraying as well as supervisory experience, I would welcome the opportunity to join your team.

Next month, I will be visiting British Columbia and would be pleased to arrange a meeting with you to discuss my suitability for the position. I will call you on Tuesday, March 4, to see what date would be convenient for you. I can be reached at (519) 555-1726 during the day.

Thank you for taking the time to consider my application. I look forward to speaking with you.

Sincerely,

Dear Jacqueline Blanche:

I am writing to apply for the position of Executive Assistant as advertised in the June 6 edition of *The Calgary Herald*.

Your advertisement states that you are looking for someone who can handle a variety of administrative duties and who has a working knowledge of word processing and spreadsheet applications. I have recently graduated from secondary school where I took several business courses. As part of my school experience, I participated in a work experience program with a local engineering firm where I had a variety of responsibilities. I am familiar with several computer programs, including word processing and spreadsheet software. I am confident that my skills would be an asset to your company.

I look forward to hearing from you so that we may arrange a mutually convenient time to meet and discuss my qualifications further. Thank you for your consideration.

Sincerely,

ACTIVITY

Writing Covering Letters

1 Look through the newspaper and choose a job advertisement that appeals to you.

2 Write a covering letter to apply for this job, outlining your suitability for the position. (Refer to the sample covering letters on pages 125–127.)

3 Exchange advertisements with a partner and write a covering letter for his or her advertisement.

4 Compare the similarities and differences between your covering letters.

Dear Ms. Wong:

Recently, I heard through Robert Piroux of your department that a change in the products you are carrying has created a need for more sales staff. I would like to be considered for the position of sales representative and have enclosed my résumé for your consideration.

Since graduating from university, I have worked with the companies Computer Pitstop and Computers Our Way as a sales representative. My communication skills and knowledge of computer equipment and software are excellent, and I have consistently met or exceeded sales targets throughout my three years in this field.

I would appreciate a personal interview at your earliest convenience to discuss how my skills can benefit your organization. I will call you on Monday, December 7, to arrange a suitable date. Thank you for taking the time to read my résumé.

Sincerely,

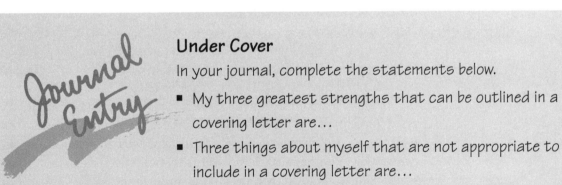

Under Cover

In your journal, complete the statements below.

- My three greatest strengths that can be outlined in a covering letter are...
- Three things about myself that are not appropriate to include in a covering letter are...

Application Forms

Focus your résumé, covering letter, and application form to the needs of the employer. List the experience and qualifications you have that match the employer's requirements.

When applying for a job, you may need to complete an **application form,** which is a request for employment. The purpose of an application form is to help a potential employer to evaluate the fitness of an applicant for a job. The form usually includes sections for personal data, employment history, educational background, and so on. When you are applying for a job, be sure to take along all the information you will need and a pen to complete an application form, even if you have your résumé with you. Use the following guidelines to complete application forms:

- Read the form before filling it out.
- Follow the instructions carefully. Should you "Print" or "Print in ink"? Are certain sections "For office use only"? Do you write above or below the lines? Employers want to know that you can follow simple instructions.
- Complete the application form neatly, accurately, and thoroughly. Ensure that you use proper spelling, grammar, and punctuation.
- Focus your responses on the requirements of the employer.
- If a question does not apply to you, fill the space after it with a short dash or N/A (meaning "not applicable") to indicate that you have read the question, not missed it.

The purpose of a résumé or an application form is to be invited to an interview. Whether or not you get hired depends on the interview.

Hiring decisions should be based on an applicant's ability to do the job, rather than on factors that are unrelated to job performance. In Canada, the federal and provincial human rights commissions prohibit job discrimination based on race, ancestry, place of origin, colour, citizenship, gender, sexual orientation, criminal record, marital status, disabilities, and more, except where these are relevant to a job. For example, questions about physical strength are allowed when a job involves a lot of heavy lifting or requires stamina. (See Chapter 10 for more details.) Therefore, an application form must not violate these laws. Questions on an application form that directly or indirectly indicate discriminatory employment practices are illegal according to human rights legislation. (See the Guide to Screening and Selection in Employment in Chapter 8, pages 147–149.) For example, an application form may include a question asking if you are willing to relocate, but it may not ask if you have plans to have children.

If an application form requests information that is discriminatory, you may choose to put a short dash or N/A in the space for the answer. You may be asked to explain why you did not answer the question. If so, respond by indicating that the answer to that question has no bearing on your ability to successfully carry out the duties of the job. For example, if you do not answer a question that asks for your date of birth and the employer asks why, you might reply with "I did not answer that because my age has no relation to my ability to do this job."

The sample application form that follows was published by a provincial human rights commission. Notice the sensitivity in the questions concerning citizenship and age. As well, notice the lack of questions concerning marital status, gender, race, colour, place of origin, and so on.

SAMPLE APPLICATION FOR EMPLOYMENT

Position being applied for	Date available to begin work
Manager	November 1, 19—

PERSONAL DATA

Last name	Given name(s)	Social insurance number
Hood	Chris Thomas	1│2│3│–│4│5│6│–│7│8│9

Address	Street	Apt. no.	Home telephone no.
19 Stoney Road		—	(403) 555-1234

City	Province	Postal code	Business telephone no.
Mountain View	Alberta	T6Y 1B4	(403) 555-4321

Are you legally eligible to work in Canada? ☑ Yes ☐ No
Are you between 18 and 65 years of age? ☑ Yes ☐ No

Are you willing to re-locate?	Preferred location
☑ Yes ☐ No	Southern Ontario

To determine your qualification for employment, please provide below and on the reverse, information related to your academic and other achievements including volunteer work as well as employment history. Additional information may be attached on a separate sheet.

EDUCATION

SECONDARY SCHOOL	BUSINESS, TRADE, OR TECHNICAL SCHOOL	
	Name of course	Length of course
Highest grade or level completed Grade 12	—	—
Type of certificate or diploma received Advanced level diploma	Licence, certificate or diploma awarded? ☐ Yes ☐ No	

COMMUNITY COLLEGE		UNIVERSITY		
Name of program	Length of program	Length of course	Degree awarded	☐ Pass
Business Administration	3 years	—	☐ Yes ☐ No	☐ Honours
Diploma received? ☑ Yes ☐ No		Major subject —		
Other courses, workshops, seminars —		Licences, certificates, degrees —		

WORK-RELATED SKILLS

Describe any of your work-related skills, experience, or training that relate to the position being applied for.

I have working knowledge of computer software as well as spoken and written knowledge of English and French. I am highly skilled in customer relations and administration.

EMPLOYMENT

Name and address of present/last employer	**Present/last job title** Manager
Conestoga College Bookstore	**Period of employment** From 1990 To present — **Present/last salary** $25 000/year
212 Centre Avenue	
Red Deer, Alberta	**Name of supervisor** Efra MacDonald — **Telephone no.** (403) 555-4321
T5M 1S2	
Type of business College store	**Reason for leaving** To gain experience in another aspect of retail management.

Duties/responsibilities
Responsibilities include inventory control, purchasing, scheduling of shifts, and supervising staff.

Name and address of previous employer	**Previous job title** Clerk
Mountain View Hardware	**Period of employment** From 1986 To 1990 — **Final Salary** $10/hour
16 Narrow Path	
Mountain View, Alberta	**Name of supervisor** Deniz Oner — **Telephone no.** (403) 555-2211
T6Y 1B3	
Type of business Hardware store	**Reason for leaving** To attend college

Duties/responsibilities
Duties involved shipping and receiving as well as general clean-up.

Name and address of previous employer	**Previous job title** Volunteer
Mountain View Hospital	**Period of employment** From 1988 To 1990 — **Final salary** unpaid
6 Neighbour Way	
Mountain View, Alberta	**Name of supervisor** Lisa Raslawski — **Telephone no.** (403) 555-1122
T6Y 1B3	
Type of business Hospital	**Reason for leaving** To attend college

Duties/responsibilities
Duties included assisting in the gift shop and helping on outings for disabled patients.

For employment references, may we approach:
Your present/last employer? ☑ Yes ☐ No
Your former employer(s)? ☑ Yes ☐ No
List references if different than above on a separate sheet.

Activities (civic, athletic, etc.)
Swimming instructor, lifeguard qualifications, CPR training, and hiking and skiing.

I hereby declare that the foregoing information is true and complete to my knowledge. I understand that a false statement may disqualify me from employment or cause my dismissal.

Have you attached an additional sheet?
☐ Yes ☑ No

Chris Hood
Signature

Oct. 16, 19—
Date

"Human Rights: Employment Application Forms and Interviews," Ontario Human Rights Commission, Toronto.

CASE STUDY

Maria's Dilemma

When Maria sat down to complete the application form from a local sporting goods store, she was surprised to see requests for information that seemed irrelevant to the job. There were questions about religion, age, and place of origin on the application form. Maria knew that these questions were illegal. On the other hand, she felt that if she did not answer them the employer might think she had something to hide. As she sat there, she thought of her physical education teacher, who had provided the job lead. She thought about the items she had already planned to buy with her wages if she got the job.

▼ ▼ ▼

1 In small groups, debate this statement: "People should not compromise their rights in order to get a job."

2 Write an ending for this case study.

---

1 With your partner, make a list of questions to evaluate a properly completed application form.

2 Complete a copy of the application form on pages 129–130 provided by your teacher for a job that interests you. For example, you may apply for a job as a social worker.

3 Evaluate your partner's application form according to your list of questions.

4 Provide feedback to your partner about her or his completed application form.

A C T I V I T Y
Completing Application Forms

Improving Your Qualifications

In your journal, complete the statements below.

- The areas in which I want to gain more qualifications or experiences are...

- I am now going to work toward adding these qualifications or experiences to my résumé and application forms by...

Make the Connection

▼ ▼

WHAT DO EMPLOYERS PREFER?

1 Ask your supervisor for the names of one or two people at your placement who are involved in hiring. Make an appointment with one of these people to discuss résumés, covering letters, and application forms.

2 Before the meeting, prepare a list of questions to ask. For instance:

- Does the person require application forms or résumés and covering letters?
- Which résumé format does she or he prefer?
- How much content is relevant in a résumé?
- Should a résumé be mailed or hand delivered?

Think of any other questions you would like to ask.

3 As a class, analyze the information gathered to form conclusions about what employers prefer in terms of résumés, covering letters, and application forms.

WHAT HAVE YOU LEARNED?

▼ ▼ ▼

1 What information about applicants do employers need, and how do they obtain it?

2 In what ways do résumés and covering letters help applicants and employers?

3 a Explain the similarities and differences among the three résumé formats.

b Which format is most suitable for you, and why?

4 a Give five suggestions for completing application forms properly.

b Explain why each of your suggestions is important.

5 What do you think are the advantages and disadvantages of a résumé and a covering letter as opposed to an application form?

6 What questions are inappropriate and illegal on an application form?

INTERVIEWS

After completing this chapter, you should be able to:

▼ ▼ ▼

- Identify the purpose of an interview and the roles of the interviewer and the interviewee.
- Prepare for an interview.
- Understand the interview process, including the greeting, exchange, parting, and follow-up.
- Describe the process of acceptance and negotiation of a job offer.
- Recognize the rights of an interviewee.

▼ ▼ ▼

interview	greeting	wages
job interview	exchange	job benefits
human resources	parting	negotiate
department	follow-up	raise
screen	thank-you letter	salary review
portfolio	salary	

What Is an Interview?

An **interview** is a meeting between two or more people. Interviews can have different purposes, including occupational research interviews and job interviews. The purpose of an occupational research interview is to gain information about a particular job or occupation. The purpose of a **job interview** is to match a job seeker to a particular job. The interviewer may consist of a single person, a few people, or even a panel of people. For the purposes of this chapter, it is assumed that there is only one interviewer.

An interview requires an interviewee to be prepared for anything, to respond to any tactic, and to cope with the outcome. Both the interviewer and the interviewee influence the interaction, however—interviews do not have to be controlled by the interviewer alone. The interviewer has influence since he or she decides whether to offer the job to the interviewee. But the interviewee, as a potential job candidate, may have skills, experience, and attitudes that are desirable to the employer.

The interviewer assesses the interviewee's suitability for the job. He or she also assesses how well the interviewee handles pressure, since an interview can be quite stressful. A good interviewer will prepare an agenda for the interview in order to address concerns such as the following:

Only about 15 percent of all companies or organizations have human resources departments.

- Does the candidate have the necessary skills and experience for the position?
- Why did the candidate apply for this job at this company?
- What are the candidate's self-concept, personality, and values?
- Would the candidate be able to relate well to other employees?

The interviewer may be the owner of the organization, the manager or supervisor to whom the candidate would report if hired, or a member of the human resources department. In smaller companies, which create about two-thirds of all new jobs, the owner or a supervisor will likely conduct the interview. In large companies, a member of the **human resources department**—which assists with staff concerns such as hiring, benefits, and labour negotiations—may **screen** job candidates for a supervisor. In the screening process, a member of the human resources department assesses job candidates in a first round of interviews and then asks the most appropriate candidates to return for a second interview with the job supervisor.

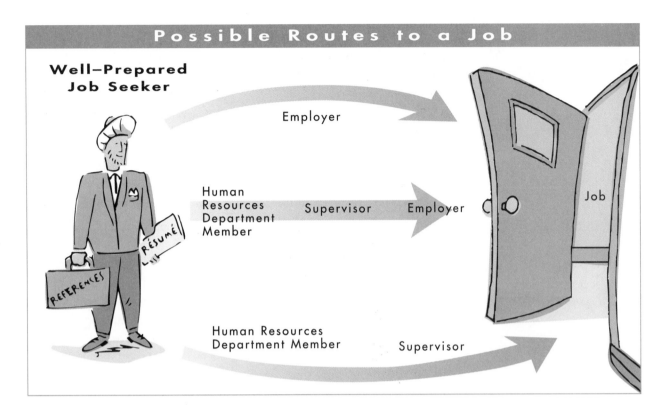

Possible Routes to a Job

Well–Prepared Job Seeker

Employer

Human Resources Department Member → Supervisor → Employer

Job

Human Resources Department Member → Supervisor

Factors That Affect an Interview

The interviewer may have personal or professional concerns that are unrelated to, but still affect, the interview. For example, an interviewer may want to simplify her or his own job by finding the right person, or the interviewer may be more concerned about a family dilemma at home than about the interview. In other words, the person interviewing may not be a *good* interviewer. As well, the interviewer, like the interviewee, will probably have fears and anxieties about the interview and its outcome. The interviewer may wonder if the successful candidate will have the necessary skills, have a sense of humour, be responsible, and be satisfied with the position. Or the interviewer may wonder if the candidate will be absent from work often, leave the company after a short period of time, have difficulty getting along with others, work slowly and inefficiently, take no initiative, or be dishonest.

An interviewee should follow the interviewer's lead to a certain extent. For example, the interviewee should wait until the interviewer offers a seat before sitting. The interviewee should try to find out whether the job and the organization are appropriate for her or him. Interviewees should try to discover:

- What skills the job involves and whether they possess or want to learn them.
- Whether or not the job is suitable in terms of their values, interests, skills, and goals.

- Whether or not they would fit in with the type of people with whom they would be working.

If the job seems suitable, the interviewee must prove to the interviewer that she or he is the best person for the job.

Preparing for an Interview

*I*nterviews can be obtained in many ways, such as by responding to a job advertisement, contacting people who may have positions available, and networking. Once you have obtained an interview, you must prepare for it. This preparation should include the following:

Before your interview, ask yourself the following questions:

- *Have I chosen suitable clothing?*
- *Are my clothes clean and wrinkle-free?*
- *Are my shoes clean and in good repair?*
- *Is my hair tidy?*
- *Are my papers in a neat briefcase, folder, or envelope?*
- *Am I smiling and acting with confidence?*

1 Research the company or organization as thoroughly as possible. You may want to know more about its products or services, the size of the organization, opportunities for advancement, employer expectations, the hierarchical structure, and so on. Friends, family, and other contacts may be able to provide information. The library is also a valuable source of information—there are many magazines and books that are specific to an industry. These may include articles and advertisements that will give you clues about the industry. If you responded to a job advertisement, it may provide clues on how to behave, what to expect, and what kinds of questions to ask at the interview. For example, if an ad states, "High-energy, friendly individuals should apply," you would want to behave in an enthusiastic, friendly manner during the interview. If you obtained an interview through a contact, he or she may have valuable information. From this research, develop a list of questions to ask the interviewer about the job and company. Showing interest in an employer and the industry demonstrates your enthusiasm and commitment.

2 Prepare a two-minute oral summary of your career goals, skills, experience, education, and strengths to present at the interview. Your summary should be influenced by your research on the company. Include examples from your past experience to back up your statements about your qualifications.

3 Be sure you know where the interview is, how long it takes to get there, and what route to take. You may even want to do a trial run in advance, especially if you are using public transit. Ideally, arrive a few minutes early for the interview—never be late. If you are going to be late due to car trouble or some other unexpected delay, call the interviewer to explain what has happened and to let her or him know what time you will arrive. Perhaps you will need to set a new time or date for the interview.

4 Gather together what you need to take to the interview. You may want to take along your résumé or personal information sheet, a list of references, and even examples of your work, such as samples of writing or projects you have done. For example, artists usually bring a **portfolio**, a collection of their work, to an interview.

5 Your clothes should be appropriate to the work environment. For example, in a business office people typically wear more formal clothing than people who work in an automobile repair shop. Your clothes should always be clean and neat. If you are not sure what to wear, ask someone in the industry or go to a similar place of business and observe what people are wearing. You should be well-groomed, freshly bathed, and neatly dressed.

A C T I V I T Y

Interviewee Expectations

1 In small groups, discuss the issues that you think may concern a job candidate. Then brainstorm a list of questions to ask an interviewer that would address these concerns. Some possible questions are:

- How many employees does the company have?
- Does the company have plans for expansion?
- How does the work of this department fit in with the work of the other departments?
- What are your expectations of the person you will hire for the position?
- What do you consider to be the most important duties of the position?

2 Compare your concerns and questions with those of the other groups. Combine the lists of questions to create a comprehensive list.

CASE STUDY

Overcoming Stress

Jennifer Morra felt frustrated enough to cry. She finally had been offered an interview with the human resources manager at ACME Designs. Her training at the local art college as well as several summers working with an interior design company in Winnipeg had prepared her for this opening at ACME. But as she had put the finishing touches on a computer-graphics project that she intended to add to her portfolio for the interview, a system error occurred and her work was suddenly erased. Although she did not need the project for the interview, Jennifer was crushed.

She had two hours left before the interview. When she tried to read over her notes for the interview, she felt panicked and exhausted.

▼ ▼ ▼

1 How can Jennifer prepare for a positive interview in her remaining hours? Make a list of suggestions in order of priority.

2 Continue to tell the story: explain what happens in the two hours before the interview.

Preparing for an Interview

When you are facing an upcoming interview, complete the statements below in your journal.

- During the interview, I will try to remember...
- I will not worry because...
- If I feel nervous during the interview, I will...
- This interview will be a positive experience because...

The Stages of an Interview

An interview consists of the greeting, exchange, parting, and follow-up. When you arrive at the workplace, you may have to approach a receptionist first. Remember that you are being appraised from the moment you arrive. Tell the receptionist your name and the name of the person you wish to see. The **greeting** is the initial contact between you and the interviewer. Since first impressions can be lasting impressions, this initial contact is important. There are four elements of a successful greeting:

1 Stand upright with confidence and smile.

2 Make direct eye contact to show that you are self-assured and friendly.

3 Introduce yourself and offer to shake hands (with your right hand).

4 Shake hands firmly.

The **exchange** is the longest part of an interview, during which the job, the company or organization, and your experience and skills are discussed. During the exchange, practise effective nonverbal communication as well as effective listening and speaking (follow the guidelines for effective communication outlined in Chapter 5). Remember to maintain eye contact and good posture throughout the interview. Do not slouch or use excessive gestures. Express interest in the interviewer, the job, and the company through your nonverbal communication by sitting forward and looking enthusiastic. Your attitude is important during the entire interview. Remember that you are not begging for a job but determining whether the job is right for you.

You never get a second chance to make a first impression.
Anonymous

An interviewer may ask questions that relate to the industry or type of work, which is why it is important to do research before the interview. The interviewer may also ask questions about your skills, career goals, work experience, education, and interests and activities. The purpose of these questions is to determine whether you are the best person for the job and what you will be like if hired. When responding to questions, concentrate on how your past experiences will benefit the company. Avoid speaking for more than two minutes when responding to a question. Try to create a feeling of trust, and express confidence in the fact that you will be hired. Some common questions asked by interviewers and suggested ways to respond are presented below.

Although you should follow the lead of the interviewer, you should have a mental list of questions you want to ask. Interviewers may offer you the opportunity to ask questions or express opinions. Avoid asking or saying anything personal or controversial.

Quick Ways to Relax Before and During an Interview

- *Talk yourself up. Use positive "self-talk," such as "I am competent" and "I will get this job."*
- *Avoid stimulants. Caffeine blocks adenosine, your body's natural tension reliever. Limit your intake of coffee, tea, cola, and chocolate.*
- *Treat yourself. Buy your favourite magazine or stop at a favourite quiet spot before the interview.*
- *Focus on communication. Observe and participate in the interview process. Enjoy the well-earned opportunity to talk about yourself.*

QUESTIONS FREQUENTLY ASKED BY INTERVIEWERS

Tell me about yourself.
Respond with the two-minute summary you prepared. You may want to begin with a brief personal history and then outline your career goals, skills, experience, education, and strengths. Conclude with a positive statement about your attitude toward work.

Why do you want this job?
Treat this question with great care and be specific. Perhaps the job offers an opportunity to put previous training into practice in a new setting, allows you to expand your knowledge, or presents new challenges.

How did you get along with your former co-workers?
Discuss your flexibility and your respect for the rights of others as well as your ability to work as part of a team or independently.

Were you often absent from your last job?
Absenteeism is a major concern of employers. Stress your good attendance record and the importance you place on always being at work. If you were often absent from a previous job, briefly explain why and indicate that it is no longer an issue. Don't lie— a reference check to your former employer will turn up a poor attendance record.

What is your greatest weakness?
This question actually provides an opportunity to talk about your strengths. Briefly mention a weakness, but stress its positive aspect. For example, "At times I may not respond well to too much supervision because I have lots of ideas and like to take initiative."

After the interview, take time to assess your performance. Ask yourself the following questions:

- *Was I prepared? Did I know enough about the company and the job?*
- *Did I present myself well?*
- *Did I take advantage of every opportunity to sell my skills?*
- *Did I appear relaxed and confident?*

As the interview draws closer to the **parting,** or final stage of the interview, you will want to know when a hiring decision will be made or when a second interview may occur. Ask something like, "When can I expect to hear from you?" The way in which you depart from an interview can affect your image as much as the greeting. Leave in a confident, positive manner. Once again, smile, make direct eye contact, and appear self-assured and friendly. Your parting statement is the last opportunity you have to promote yourself. You might say, "Thank you for your time. The position sounds very interesting, and I hope that I will be able to offer you the benefit of my skills and experience," or, "Thank you for your time. I would be very interested in applying my skills to help your company achieve its goals." Offer to shake hands again, and remember to say goodbye to the receptionist.

The step that is most often overlooked in an interview is the **follow-up.** Immediately after the interview, you should write and mail a **thank-you letter** while the interview is still fresh in your mind. Express appreciation for the interviewer's time and for the opportunity to learn more about the company. Then highlight your strengths once again and express interest in the position. This simple gesture can help the interviewer to remember the interview and you more easily, especially if he or she is conducting many interviews for a position. It also shows courtesy. You might use the sample thank-you letter below as a guide. (See page 95 for the proper formatting of a letter.)

Dear Ms. Warrick:

I would like to thank you for the time you spent with me during my visit to CMB Enterprises yesterday. I enjoyed learning about your organization and the exciting opportunities available.

As I expressed during the interview, my past sales experience has taught me how to work independently and effectively organize a business. I hope I will have the opportunity to use these skills to fulfill the needs of CMB Enterprises.

Thank you again for your time and attention. I look forward to hearing from you soon.

Sincerely,

If you do not hear from the company, call after about one week to find out whether a hiring decision has been made or a second round of interviews has begun. Whatever the response, be careful to answer graciously and without getting defensive or angry—there will be other interviews.

Five common interview questions appear on page 139. There are many more possible questions, such as those below. In your notebook, list any other questions you can think of and write suggestions for responding to these questions as well as to the ones below. For each question, consider whether the intent is to learn more about the self-management skills, the technical skills, or the interests of the job candidate.

1 What led you to choose this occupation?

2 What types of experience did you gain in your most recent job?

3 What do you know about our company?

4 What are your greatest strengths?

5 Do you prefer working with others or by yourself?

6 What are your hobbies and interests?

7 Where do you see yourself in five years?

Reflecting on Your Past

In his book *What Color Is Your Parachute?* Richard N. Bolles says that no employer cares about your past and that what appears to be a question about your past is really about your future. In your journal, respond to the question below.

How do the following experiences from my past reflect my future?

- My earliest memory
- My first hero or heroine
- The best advice I ever received

When You're Being Interviewed You Should Ask Questions, Too

by Janis Foord Kirk

You may find this hard to believe, but some people actually enjoy job interviews. I met one recently.

"They're a great test of my communication abilities," he observed.

Most of us are a little less enthusiastic. There's something daunting about sitting across from a stranger whose job it is to probe your psyche and question your abilities.

Still, when you're looking for work, there's no way around it. Jobs are simply not granted without an interview, sometimes a whole series of interviews.

Generally, job interviews follow a pattern. They begin with a few minutes of "ice-breaker" conversation designed to put you at ease. Next, you get some information about the job that's vacant and the company. Then, with a question like, "why don't you tell me about yourself," the real probing begins.

Interviewers question you in an effort to gain an understanding of your strengths and weaknesses, why you left (or are wanting to leave) your last (current) job, your goals and plans for the future, how ambitious you are, what you know about their organization, and why you feel qualified to do the job in question.

The more involved you are in the interview, the more positive it will be.

People who interview a lot say they leave some meetings feeling energized and others feeling drained. Most draining are those interviews that follow a straight format: A question is asked, the person being interviewed answers it and waits for the next question.

This isn't advisable. Ask your own questions. Take some responsibility for the flow of information.

Say you're asked to describe some of your strengths. Do so fully, then counter: "Perhaps you could tell me some of the strengths a person would need to do this job."

The best response to the request, "tell me something about yourself" is a two-minute summary of your background and training. End that, too, with your own question, something like: "What in my background relates to this position?" The interviewer will feel obliged to answer the question and you'll gain valuable insight into the job and your suitability for it.

Once the interviewer has probed to his or her satisfaction, the focus changes. You'll get an indication of this when you hear, "Do you have any further questions?" If you've been asking your own questions throughout, many of your queries will have been answered. If not, it's your turn to start probing.

You'll want to know why the position is vacant, who your boss would be, what he/she is like, what kind of person works best under his/her direction, the kind of people you'd work with (or supervise), some of the issues the person hired needs to address immediately, and what opportunities exist.

You'll also want to know about salary, benefits, and vacations. If that information hasn't been offered, ask about it toward the end of the interview. If a second interview seems likely, you may be wise to leave those questions until then.

Once your questions have been answered fully, the interview draws to a close, hopefully in a way that lets you know when you can expect to hear from the employer. Be sure to get a clear idea of just when that will be. Then, if you don't hear, check back.

If you're interested in the job and feel you're qualified, don't leave an interview without making that point clear. It's your final chance to sell yourself.

Not all interviews follow a predictable pattern. A few days ago, I heard of an employer who ushered a prospective office manager into his office, offered her a chair, sat down himself, and said: "So, ask me questions."

Being prepared for interviews, whether they are highly structured or come at you from left field, is key.

Write down answers to the questions you're likely to be asked. Practise giving those answers to a friend or into a tape recorder. And write down all the questions you need answers for.

The more prepared you are, the more you'll feel in control. Who knows, you might even come to enjoy interviews.

▼ ▼ ▼

1 What do you consider to be the main elements of a successful interview?

2 If an interviewer is assessing two candidates with similar skills, how do you think she or he will decide who will be offered the job?

3 How would you respond to the following statements and questions?

a "Why don't you tell me about yourself."

b "Do you have any further questions?"

c "So, ask me questions."

Accepting the Hiring Decision

Ultimately, you will either be offered a job or will continue searching for an appropriate position. A major part of the job search is learning how to think positively. You may not find a job that suits you immediately. Whatever the outcome, consider every interview as valuable practice. You may even want to telephone the interviewer to ask for feedback. Some interviewers will not wish to respond, while others will clearly outline your strengths and weaknesses and offer suggestions for improvement. You may want to write a letter to acknowledge the rejection and to request a referral or another job lead. As well, you may want to role-play interviewing with friends or even arrange occupational research interviews for practice. Any interview is a valuable experience, even if it does not result in a job.

If you receive a job offer, either verbally or in writing, it is customary to answer within a day or two. If the offer is verbal ask for it in writing, including the rate of pay in terms of **salary** (a fixed sum, usually paid every two weeks or monthly) or **wages** (an hourly, daily, or weekly rate of pay), as well as the benefits and vacation time. **Job benefits** are certain advantages offered to an employee that can greatly increase the value of a job, such as discounts on company merchandise, a company car, health insurance, and retirement savings programs. You may want to give your response to the offer verbally, but it is a good idea to put it in writing.

Another aspect of accepting a job offer is negotiation. Job candidates **negotiate,** or bargain, with an employer for salary or wages, benefits, and vacation time. You may also want to negotiate when **raises** (pay increases) or **salary reviews** (regular evaluations of your salary) will occur. Knowing *when* to negotiate is important. The diagram below shows when and when not to negotiate with an employer. If the employer is not yet aware of your value, negotiation is inappropriate and even harmful. When an employer is sure that you are right for a job is the ideal time. Once you have accepted a job offer, negotiation becomes more difficult. In order to negotiate, try to discover the salary range for the position during the interview (you should also have researched pay levels for similar jobs before the interview) and research the typical benefits offered within the industry.

You don't get what you deserve, you get what you negotiate.

ANONYMOUS

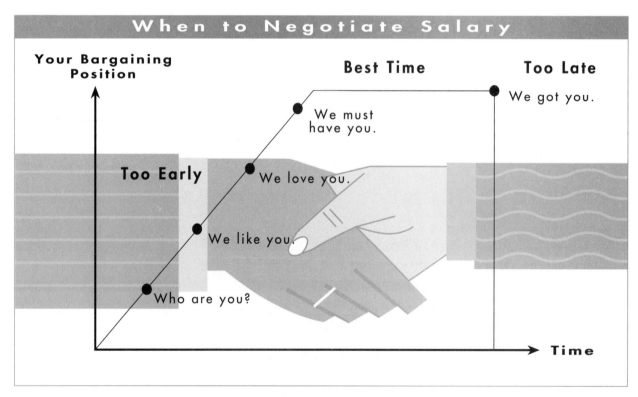

When to Negotiate Salary

Your Bargaining Position

Too Early

Best Time

Too Late

We got you.

We must have you.

We love you.

We like you.

Who are you?

Time

1 In groups of three, role-play an interview. One person is the interviewee, one is the interviewer, and one is an observer. Determine the type of job and employer together. Interviewers should consider their personalities before the role-play—they may have difficult attitudes or perceptions that the interviewees will have to overcome. Interviewees should consider the employer's needs and how to communicate the necessary information to get hired. Both the interviewee and the interviewer should prepare for the interview, including listing possible questions. Some examples are provided below.

Interviewer Questions

- What experiences qualify you for this position?
- What do you know about our company?
- What do you consider to be your greatest strength?
- What have you learned from your mistakes?
- Do you have any questions you want to ask me?

Interviewee Questions

- What would a typical day be like in your business?
- What are the main responsibilities of this position?
- How many people will I be working with and to whom will I be responsible?
- What opportunities for advancement exist within your company?

2 During the interview, the observer takes notes and completes a copy of the interview checklist provided by your teacher. This checklist appears on page 146. (*Note:* If you have access to video equipment, the observer can record the role-play.)

3 After the role-play, the interviewer and interviewee also assess the interview using the interview checklist.

4 Based on feedback from all members of the group, repeat the role-play with variations or repeat segments of the interview that caused the interviewee difficulty.

5 Perform the role-play at least two more times, allowing each member of the group an opportunity to be an interviewee, interviewer, and observer.

6 After the interviews, the interviewees should write thank-you letters to their interviewers.

INTERVIEW CHECKLIST

Before the interview, the interviewee:

- Arrived slightly early. ____
- Was courteous to the receptionist. ____
- Had résumé and other necessary items. ____
- Dressed appropriately and was well-groomed. ____

During the greeting, the interviewee:

- Knew and used the interviewer's name. ____
- Shook hands firmly. ____
- Waited to be invited to sit. ____

During the interview, the interviewee:

- Sat up straight and appeared self-assured. ____
- Maintained eye contact. ____
- Used a pleasant tone of voice. ____
- Used expressive, fluent speech. ____
- Did not use slang. ____
- Showed knowledge of and interest in the company. ____
- Explained work experience briefly and clearly. ____
- Asked pertinent questions about the company. ____
- Asked for clarification about the job. ____
- Demonstrated a confident, positive attitude. ____

Following the interview, the interviewee:

- Left suitable paperwork (résumé or application form). ____
- Thanked the interviewer and shook hands firmly. ____
- Was courteous to the receptionist. ____

Reflecting on Interviews

After each interview you attend, complete the statements below in your journal.

- The interviewer seemed interested when I talked about...
- Next time I would like to include information about my strengths and experience in...
- Before my next interview, I must remember to...
- I benefitted from today's interview because...

Interviewee Rights

According to the Canadian Human Rights Act, "Every individual should have an equal opportunity with other individuals to make for himself or herself the life that he or she is able and wishes to have, consistent with his or her duties and obligations as a member of society." Accordingly, discrimination against job candidates is illegal. Discrimination may be much more subtle than blatant examples of personal prejudice. Some employers may bar certain people through procedures and policies. Everyone should be aware of her or his rights and how to handle situations that involve discrimination. Instances of discrimination can be reported and legal action can be taken against discriminators—tolerating discrimination only helps to perpetuate the problem. (See Chapter 10 for more information.)

The guidelines on pages 147–149 have been developed for employers to use in selecting and interviewing employees. During an interview, you may be asked a discriminatory question. For example, in an effort to establish your availability for weekend work, the interviewer may ask a question about family obligations. This is an unacceptable question. Rather than respond to the question, respond with the hours you would be available for work (see the Family Status row in the chart that follows).

A GUIDE TO SCREENING AND SELECTION IN EMPLOYMENT

Subject	Avoid Asking	Preferred	Comment
Name	About name change, whether it was changed by court order, marriage, or other reason Maiden name Christian name		If needed for a reference, to check on previously held jobs or on educational credentials, ask after selection
Address	For addresses outside Canada	Ask place and duration of current or recent addresses	
Age	For birth certificate, baptismal records, or about age in general Age or birth date	Ask applicants if they have reached age (minimum or maximum) for work as defined by law	If precise age required for benefit plans or other legitimate purposes, it can be determined after selection

Subject	Avoid Asking	Preferred	Comment
Sex	Mr./Mrs./Miss/Ms.		Any applicants can be addressed during interviews or in correspond-ence without using courtesy titles such as Mr./Mrs./Miss
	Males or females to fill in different or coded applications		
	If male or female on applications		
	About pregnancy, childbirth, or child-care arrangements Includes asking if birth control is used or childbearing plans	Can ask applicant if the attendance requirements or minimum service commitment can be met	
Marital Status	Whether applicant is single, married, divorced, engaged, separated, widowed, or living common-law		If transfer or travel is part of the job, the applicant can be asked if this would cause a problem
	Whether an applicant's spouse is subject to transfer	Ask whether there are any known circumstances that might prevent completion of a minimum service commitment, for example	Information on dependents for benefits can be determined after selection
	About spouse's employment		
Family Status	Number of children or dependents	If the applicant would be able to work the hours required and, where applicable, if the applicant would be able to work overtime	Contacts for emergencies and/or details on dependents can be determined after selection
	About arrangements for child care		
National or Ethnic Origin	About birthplace, nationality of ancestors, spouse, or other relatives	Since those who are entitled to work in Canada must be citizens, landed immigrants, or holders of valid work permits, applicants can be asked if they are legally entitled to work in Canada	Documentation of eligibility to work (i.e., papers, visas, etc.) can be requested after selection
	Whether born in Canada		
	If naturalized or landed immigrant		
	For proof of citizenship		
Military Service	About military service in other countries	Inquiry about Canadian military service where employment preference is given to veterans, by law	
Language	Mother tongue	Ask if applicant understands, reads, writes, or speaks languages that are required for job	Testing or scoring applicants for language proficiency is not permitted unless fluency is job-related
	Where language skills obtained		
Race or Colour	Any inquiry that indicates race or colour, including colour of eyes, skin, or hair		Information required for security clearances or similar purposes can be obtained after selection
Photographs	For photo to be attached to applications or sent to interviewer before interview		Photos for security passes or company files can be taken after selection

Subject	Avoid Asking	Preferred	Comment
Religion	About religious affiliation, church membership, frequency of church attendance		Employers are to reasonably accommodate religious needs of workers
	If applicant will work a specific religious holiday	Explain the required work shifts, asking if such a schedule poses problems for applicant	
	For references from clergy or religious leader		
Height and Weight (Mass)			No inquiry unless there is evidence that they are bona fide occupational requirements
Disability	For listing of all disabilities, limitations, or health problems	Ask if applicant has any condition that could affect ability to do the job	A disability is only relevant to job ability if it: — Threatens the safety or property of others — Prevents the applicant from safe and adequate job performance even if reasonable efforts were made to accommodate the disability
	Whether applicant drinks or uses drugs	Ask if applicant has any condition that should be considered in selection	
	Whether applicant has ever received psychiatric care or been hospitalized for emotional problems		
Medical Information	If currently under physician's care		Medical exams should be preferably conducted after selection and only if an employee's condition is related to the job duties. Offers of employment can be made conditional on successful completion of a medical
	Name of family doctor		
	If receiving counselling or therapy		
Affiliations	For list of club or organizational memberships	Membership in professional associations or occupational groups can be asked if a job requirement	Applicants can decline to list any affiliation that might indicate a prohibited ground
Pardoned Conviction	Whether an applicant has ever been convicted	If bonding is a job requirement, ask if applicant is eligible	Inquiries about criminal record/convictions—even those that have been pardoned— are discouraged unless related to job duties
	If an applicant has ever been arrested		
	If applicant has a criminal record		
References			The same restrictions that apply to questions asked of applicants apply when asking for employment references

Source: Canadian Human Rights Commission

1 With a partner, use the chart on pages 147–149 to create role-plays involving an interviewer who is asking inappropriate questions and an interviewee who is responding appropriately to these questions.

2 Perform your role-play for the class. After your role-play, ask your classmates how well they think the interviewee responded to the questions.

Make the Connection

ROUTES TO A JOB

1 After you have become familiar with your placement, inquire about the typical interviewing process. Perhaps as a student you did not follow the same routine as a person seeking a permanent position.

2 Use a diagram to illustrate the usual route to a job at your placement.

3 As a class, compare the results to determine the most typical routes to a job.

WHAT HAVE YOU LEARNED?

▼ ▼ ▼

1 What do the interviewer and the interviewee expect to discover in an interview?

2 Describe the steps involved in preparing for an interview.

3 a Identify the four parts of an interview.
   b How can you make each part of the interview successful?

4 Why do you think a positive attitude is important during the job search?

5 When is the best time to negotiate salary or wages, and why?

6 Provide two examples of questions that interviewers should avoid asking and strategies for responding to these questions.

PART 3

QUALITY OF WORK LIFE

*Nothing is too small
to know, and nothing is
too big to attempt.*

SIR WILLIAM VAN HORNE

CHAPTER 9

Negotiation and Labour Legislation

What You Will Learn

After completing this chapter, you should be able to:

▼ ▼ ▼

- Recognize the benefits to employees of collective action.
- Identify the types of unions and appreciate why unions first developed.
- Understand how a union is formed and negotiation and grievance procedures.
- Understand the benefits of labour legislation.

Terms to Remember

▼ ▼ ▼

collective action	conciliation	lockout
labour union	strike	court injunction
craft union	walkout	strike insurance
industrial union	sitdown strike	arbitration
certification	slowdown	grievance procedure
collective bargaining	work-to-rule	shop steward
collective agreement	wildcat strike	chief steward
ratify	picket	Canada Labour Code

Working Together

*F*or many of the activities throughout this text, you have worked co-operatively in small groups with other students. The ability to success-fully work as part of a team is a valuable skill in any occupation. Employees often work together as a team to negotiate better working conditions for all workers. When part of any group, each member should:

- Contribute ideas.
- Ensure that everyone understands the objectives.
- Stay on task.
- Listen actively.
- Summarize information for better understanding.
- Ask relevant and appropriate questions.
- Seek information and opinions from others.
- Follow directions.

Taking part in group negotiating and problem solving helps to increase your understanding of differences among people. An effective group can usually accomplish more than individuals working in isola-tion. The power of working together is evident when people collectively solve problems to create change. For example, employers and employees can work together to encourage greater safety precautions in the work-place. **Collective action** can be informal, such as co-workers organizing a recycling program, or formal, as organizing associations, federations, guilds, or unions. When a group of people work together, there can be positive gains for everyone concerned.

A member of an informal group can choose to join or withdraw from the group easily. Before joining or withdrawing from a group, consider the long-term effects. For example, are the group's goals and values sim-ilar to your own? Would any personal gain be short- or long-term? Can you choose to withdraw easily? Will you need the group again in the future? Would they accept you back? Ultimately, the choice of joining or not joining a group is up to you. But by working together, a group can often reach solutions that are acceptable to all members.

A C T I V I T Y

Strength in Numbers

1 On your own, read a book or watch a television show or movie about an event that requires people to act collectively; for example, circulating a peti-tion, playing on a sports team, or working as a family to improve relations.

2 Outline the events and then determine the gains of the action, the costs of the action, and how the action affected others. Create a chart showing the gains, costs, and effects for each event.

3 In small groups, compare charts. What similarities and differences are evi-dent in the results? What conclusions can you draw about how collective action is portrayed in the media?

Form groups of three. One person is the referee and the other two people are wheat farmers. The farmers sit back to back while the referee reads the instructions below.[1]

> Each year you have the following two options: you may grow as much wheat as you can, or you may limit production and grow only a portion of what your land could actually yield. How much you are able to sell your wheat for will depend on how much wheat is available in the marketplace. Generally, the more wheat available the lower will be the price per bushel, and thus you will make less money on your sale. You will get a chance to make decisions over a number of years. Now it is time to make your first decision. Write down your designation as either Farmer 1 or Farmer 2 and whether you are going to produce as much as you can or whether you will limit production. Submit your decision to the referee (who represents the marketplace).

The referee takes these decisions and, on the basis of the following chart, determines how much each farmer will receive. The referee then writes the result for each farmer and provides them with the outcomes of their decisions. He or she then asks for the decision for the next year. This process continues for ten years.

REFEREE'S CHART

- Farmer 1 and Farmer 2 both limit production. Each receives $10 000 for the sale of the wheat.
- Farmer 1 limits production and Farmer 2 produces at full capacity. Farmer 1 receives $2000; Farmer 2 receives $15 000.
- Farmer 1 produces at full capacity and Farmer 2 limits production. Farmer 1 receives $15 000; Farmer 2 receives $2000.
- Both farmers produce to full capacity. Both receive $5000 on the sale of their wheat.

Discuss your results as a class. How do they compare? The farmers should share how they felt during the game and how they reacted to the responses of the other farmers. During the discussion, answer the following questions:

1 How can a farmer maximize short-term gains?

2 How can a farmer maximize long-term gains?

3 Compare the maximum short-term and long-term gains. Which option will best benefit both farmers over a long period of time?

4 List three examples of collective action in which short-term benefits are possible if an individual acts in isolation at the expense of others.

---

[1] From Roger I. Simon, Don Dippo, and Arleen Schenke, *Learning Work*, pp. 130–131. © The Ontario Institute for Studies in Education, 1991. Published by OISE Press, an imprint of Greenwood Publishing Group, Inc., Westport, CT. Reprinted with permission.

What Is a Union?

A labour union is a formal group of workers who practise a similar craft or are employed in a similar industry. Its purpose is to improve the economic and social conditions of workers through collective bargaining with an employer and through negotiations with governments. Through these activities, unions indirectly improve working conditions for all people.

Union members can achieve more by acting collectively rather than as individuals. Once workers become members of a union, each member has equal rights and an equal voice in decision making. The union members meet frequently and through voting determine the policies of the union, the objectives in negotiations with management and government, and what they will accept as the outcomes of negotiations.

A union within a company or an organization can be a closed shop, an open shop, a union shop, or an agency shop. Unions encourage closed shops, in which all employees must be union members and must pay union dues (unless an employee was hired before the union was organized). Closed shops are rare because the responsibility of hiring is transferred from management to the union. Management usually prefers open shops, in which employees are free to choose whether or not to join the union. In a union shop, management may hire non-union employees, but after a period of time these employees must join the union. In an agency shop, the employees choose whether or not to join the union. All employees in an agency shop must pay union dues even if they are not union members, because they still receive the benefits of an organized union. The agency shop was introduced by Mr. Justice Ivan Rand to settle a major strike in 1945 and has become the most common arrangement in industrial workplaces.

There are three types of unions: craft unions, industrial unions, and associations that have evolved into unions. A **craft union** is a union of tradespeople, such as carpenters, printers, or electricians. As well as negotiating conditions with employers, craft unions help members find employment and apprenticeships. An apprentice learns a craft by working with experienced people in the field for a period of time. An **industrial union** is a union whose members include everyone who works for a particular employer regardless of individual skills or occupations; for instance, everyone who has a non-management position at an automobile manufacturing plant. Professional associations that have evolved into unions include teaching and nursing federations.

The History of Unions

Employees did not always have the right to be represented by a union. In the past, the law considered collective negotiating of wages a criminal and civil restraint of trade. In 1872, the Trade Union Act provided an opportunity for unions to register and escape criminal

Workers have found that by banding together they can increase their bargaining power with an employer.

Canadian Labour Congress

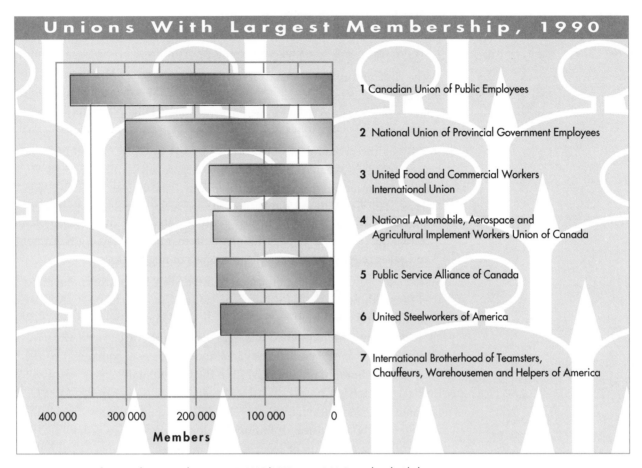

Unions With Largest Membership, 1990

1 Canadian Union of Public Employees

2 National Union of Provincial Government Employees

3 United Food and Commercial Workers International Union

4 National Automobile, Aerospace and Agricultural Implement Workers Union of Canada

5 Public Service Alliance of Canada

6 United Steelworkers of America

7 International Brotherhood of Teamsters, Chauffeurs, Warehousemen and Helpers of America

400 000   300 000   200 000   100 000   0

Members

From Statistics Canada, *Canada Year Book,* cat. no. 11-402E/1992, page 144. Reproduced with the permission of the Minister of Supply and Services Canada, 1992.

prosecution. This was the first time that the concept of a union was acknowledged as something other than a criminal activity, but the Trade Union Act did not protect unions. The conditions of registration were so oppressive that not a single union in Canada made use of this law. Not until the 1930s did union activity cease to be in technical violation of civil restraint of trade.

Unions first formed to help improve working conditions for all workers, including increased wages, safer working practices, the abolishment of child labour, and a shorter work week. In a 1919 study of why there was so much unrest among Canadian workers, the following main reasons were identified:

- Many Canadians were unemployed or were afraid of losing their jobs.
- Living costs were high, and workers wanted higher pay.
- Workers wanted a shorter work day.
- Some employers would not allow workers to organize unions. Some employers refused to deal with the unions that were organized.
- Some employers joined together with others to bargain as a group.
- Canadian workers did not trust the government.
- Poor housing and a shortage of housing for workers existed.

In 1879, the average Canadian worker worked 63 hours a week; today, the average worker works 39 hours a week.

- Freedom of speech for the press was restricted.
- The display of wealth by the rich made workers resentful.
- There was a lack of equal education opportunities.

The first unions were mostly craft unions in major cities. Some craft unions existed before 1815 in the Maritime provinces, but the first recorded union was formed in 1827 by printers in Quebec City. Later in the nineteenth century, Canadian labour organizations began to develop more rapidly as the economy improved and unions in Great Britain and the United States prospered. Initially, unions organized locally, but in 1873, the first national craft union, the Canadian Labour Union (CLU), was formed. The CLU attempted to discourage labour practices that were unfair, encourage union organization and political support of unions, and provide funds for striking members.

In 1881, the Knights of Labour, an industrial union based in the United States, entered Canada to gain union membership and support. Its intent was to organize workers by industry, without regard to their skills or occupations. In 1886, the Trades and Labour Congress of Canada (TLC) succeeded the CLU and encompassed the Knights of Labour. The TLC was an association of craft unions in Canada that was equivalent to the American Federation of Labor (AFL) in the United States.

In the late 1800s, about 35 percent of Canadian child labourers were injured at work and 4 percent were killed. Many more died from work-related illnesses.

Local unions in Canada and the United States were rapidly forming national and international unions. The AFL, through its Canadian affiliates, forced the expulsion of national unions, which were considered to be duplicates or rivals of international unions. The AFL did this by refusing to recognize a national union where an international union existed. In 1902, the TLC excluded the Knights of Labour and other national unions that rivalled international unions. The expelled unions formed the National Trades and Labour Congress of Canada, which was renamed the Canadian Federation of Labour (CFL) in 1908.

The number of industrial workers expanded rapidly in the early 1900s, and many industrial unions were formed to represent them. In 1927, a number of national unions united to form the All-Canadian Congress of Labour (ACCL), which represented Canadian industrial unions. A debate raged in Canada and the United States as to whether unions should be organized by craft or by industry. Several unions in the AFL and TLC broke away to form the Congress of Industrial Organizations (CIO), because they felt that all workers were entitled to representation and the only way to achieve this was to organize industrial unions. The AFL and TLC felt that only skilled workers should be organized, and they should be organized into unions by craft. The industrial unions formed the Canadian Congress of Labour (CCL) in 1940. In 1956, the TLC and CCL joined to become the Canadian Labour Congress (CLC). Today, unions continue to have a significant influence on Canadian government and labour policies.

Why Were Unions Formed?

CASE STUDY

A hundred years ago, children didn't go to school very often or for very long, unless their parents were rich. They might get as far as grade three, or "third book," learning how to add and subtract, how to read simple things, and how to sign their names. After that, most of them left school and got jobs to help support their families. They worked in mines or mills or factories, ten or twelve hours a day, for as little as twenty-five cents.

No matter what your job, it was dangerous. There were no safety rules, no protective clothing or goggles or hard hats, no safeguards on machinery. Thousands of working men, women, and children lost their health, their limbs, their eyes, and too often their lives. Here's a true story of one of those children:

My name is John Gale. I'm seventeen, and I haven't had steady work for five years now. Nobody wants to hire on a fellow like me, who's missing his right arm. I'm a hard worker, too. Leastways I was. I had a good job over in the sawmill on the bay. My dad got me in there before I was eleven, and I was making twenty-five cents a day. I worked at the circular saw, the two-footer, taking away the rough ends of the planks as they got trimmed. To this day I'm not sure what happened, but my arm got caught in the big cog-wheel that drives the machines and chewed it up like it was a sausage. I fainted dead away, right there in the sawdust. It happened just after the noon dinner whistle, but we had a good boss and I got paid for the whole day. Anyhow, I'm not as bad off as some. It wasn't two months later that another boy at the mill got both his arms and his legs taken off.

_____

Excerpts from Claire Mackay, *Pay Cheques and Picket Lines: All About Unions in Canada*, pp. 10–12. Copyright © 1987 by Claire Mackay. Reprinted by permission of Kids Can Press Ltd., Toronto, Canada.

▼ ▼ ▼

1 In small groups, discuss your reactions to this case study.

2 Imagine you are a newspaper reporter living 100 years ago. Write an article about why union activities should be permitted by law.

The Struggle of Unions

In your journal, list as many different reasons as you can to explain why unions were formed. Then respond to the question below.

■ Imagine it is 130 years ago and you have been arrested for participating in union-related activities. How do you feel before you are brought before the court?

How a Union Is Formed

A union can be formed in two ways. An employer can voluntarily recognize a union as the representative of its employees, or a group of employees can approach a Labour Relations Board for **certification,** or formal recognition.

Voluntary recognition of a union by an employer is rare. Most unions start with a group of employees contacting a national or international union to request help in organizing a union. The employees then start a membership drive in secrecy so that the employer does not know what is happening. Employees meet after working hours and off company property to encourage others to join the union. Employees who want to join sign union cards and pay an initiation fee and, later, regular union dues. Once a majority of employees have joined, they contact the Labour Relations Board in writing. If the board certifies the union, both the union and the employer are required by law to negotiate in good faith. The labour relations acts define in detail what bargaining in good faith means. Failure to do this on the part of either the union or management can result in criminal prosecution.

The certification procedure is as follows:

Union membership represented 36.2 percent of Canada's non-agricultural paid labour force in 1990.
Statistics Canada

1 The union applies in writing to the Labour Relations Board for certification.

2 The board determines who is eligible to be represented by the union. For example, in a plant that includes skilled workers, office staff, and management, the office staff and management may not be eligible for representation.

3 The board normally goes into the workplace and conducts a secret vote to determine whether or not a union is really wanted. A union can only be certified if a majority of the workers vote for it. If a majority of workers have signed union cards, a union can be certified without a vote.

4 Based on the percentage of eligible employees who voted for the union, the board may reject the application or certify the union. If the majority of eligible employees voted for the union, the board will certify the union.

During the certification process, both management and labour sometimes use illegal tactics called unfair labour practices. For example, management sometimes attempts to illegally block certification in order to keep production costs low and profits high. Unfair management labour practices include:

- Interfering with the process of organizing a union.
- Interfering with contributions to or administration of a union.
- Discriminating against union sympathizers.

Unfair union labour practices include:

- Interfering with employees who do not want to participate in union activities.

- Discriminating against employees who do not want to participate in union activities.
- Coercing employees into joining the union.

- - - - - - - - - - - - - - - -

Create a role-play in which a group of workers rally to form a union, present their reasons for wanting the union to management, and prepare their reasons for the Labour Relations Board. Divide the class into workers, management, and members of the Labour Relations Board. Determine who will be the leaders or spokespeople for each group. You must also determine the occupations of the workers, the type of company, the workers' reasons for wanting a union, and management's position on union organization.

- - - - - - - - - - - - - - - -

A C T I V I T Y

Role-Play Forming a Union

Negotiation

Once a union is certified, it gives written notice to the employer of its desire to participate in **collective bargaining**, or negotiation. The union elects representatives to negotiate with management on its behalf. The two parties must meet within a specified period of time unless both agree to extend the deadline. The purpose of collective bargaining is to negotiate a **collective agreement**, or labour contract. Unions negotiate for more than just wages, and most contracts have certain standard clauses. Based on Labour Canada surveys of contracts covering 500 workers or more, unions negotiate for the following:

In our society, workers must exchange their knowledge, skills, and labour for the money they need to live. This means that workers and employers negotiate to gain a fair exchange.

CANADIAN LABOUR CONGRESS

- Grievance procedures
- Defined work standards
- Accident insurance
- Fair representation
- Shift premiums
- Jury duty pay
- Shorter work week
- Dental care
- Training and retraining
- Legal aid plans
- Wage increases
- Paid vacations
- Health and safety committees
- Skills upgrading
- Health and safety programs

- Sickness and accident benefits
- Technological change protection
- Relocation allowances
- Early retirement
- Employment standards
- Rotation of premium time
- Medicare protection
- Eye care
- Job security
- Life insurance benefits
- Seniority benefits
- Overtime rates
- Moving allowances
- Employment assistance programs

- Long-term disability benefits
- Job classification
- Protective equipment
- Bereavement pay
- Cost of living clauses
- Paid leaves of absence
- Extended health care
- Severance pay
- Uniform pay scales
- Pension plans
- Rest periods
- Call-in pay
- Supplemental unemployment insurance benefits
- Promotion opportunities

Courtesy Canadian Labour Congress

If the union and management successfully negotiate a contract, the union members vote on whether or not to approve, or **ratify**, it. A ratified contract must then be administered by the union and management. If a contract is not ratified by the union, the union may continue to negotiate or it may hold a strike vote to determine whether or not the majority of its members want to strike. A successful strike vote does not allow workers to stop working immediately. Both parties must go through a process of conciliation before any such action is legal. During the **conciliation** process, the union and management must accept the assistance of a government-appointed conciliation officer to help settle the dispute. The conciliation officer does not have the right to impose a settlement on either party; she or he only makes recommendations in order to help the two sides work together. If conciliation fails, the union and management may use certain bargaining tactics to pressure the other party. These tactics are legal only after conciliation has failed.

BARGAINING TACTICS

Union members may use the following tactics when conciliation fails:

Strike: Employees temporarily refuse to continue working.

Walkout: Employees leave their work stations.

Sitdown Strike: Employees remain at their work stations but refuse to work.

Slowdown: Employees remain at their work stations but deliberately work slowly.

Work-to-Rule: Employees follow the regulations in their collective agreement to the letter, thus causing work to slow down.

Wildcat Strike: Employees strike without official consent of the union.

Picket: Striking employees display signs to discourage replacement workers from entering the workplace and to inform the public about the situation.

Management may use the following tactics when conciliation fails:

Lockout: Management refuses to let employees into the workplace.

Court Injunction: Management requests a court injunction, or order, to prevent union members from taking some sort of action or to limit the number of picketers allowed at a company entrance at one time, for instance.

Hire Replacement Workers: Management hires temporary employees during a strike so that production is not affected.

"Maybe it's time for mothers to unionize."

THE FAMILY CIRCUS ® by Bil Keane. Reprinted with special permission of King Features Syndicate.

The purpose of union bargaining tactics is to cause the employer financial loss and therefore encourage management to accept union demands. During a strike, the union pays its striking members from a strike fund, which each member contributes to regularly through union dues. Strike pay is rarely more than one-quarter of normal pay and includes no benefits. In some areas, essential workers, such as police officers and hospital staff, are refused the right to strike. Other unions can help by providing financial assistance and picketers or by boycotting, or refusing to purchase, the company's product or service.

The purposes of management bargaining tactics are to avoid lost production and to cause financial loss for union members so that they will accept management demands. Management may make regular payments for **strike insurance**. It then receives payments in the event of a strike. Again, both sides must refrain from using unfair labour practices. If the public interest is threatened, the government may interfere in order to settle a dispute.

If union and management bargaining tactics are unsuccessful, the dispute goes to **arbitration**, which means the dispute is settled by a third party, or arbitrator. The appointed arbitrator is usually a retired judge or professor who is acceptable to both parties. He or she listens to both parties and makes a decision that may not be disputed by either side. The

Canada's most famous strike was the Winnipeg General Strike of 1919 when 22 000 workers from a wide variety of trades walked out mainly for better wages.

STATISTICS CANADA

cost of the arbitrator is shared by the union and management. Labour relations laws enforce the inclusion of an arbitration clause in all collective agreements.

1 As a class, read over the list of job benefits on page 161 and define the terms with which you are familiar.

2 Make a list of the terms no one can define. Divide those terms among small groups to research. Each group then presents its definitions to the rest of the class.

3 With your group, rank what you think are the top ten benefits in order of importance. Compare rankings with other groups. Which items cause the most disagreement? Why?

1 Study a strike that is taking place in your community or province. Watch television news broadcasts and clip newspaper and magazine articles about the strike.

2 Write a news article about the strike vote, the issues, the picket lines, the negotiations, and the final settlement. Consider why the settlement was fair or unfair to both sides and how the strike affected the public.

Grievance Procedures

Every collective agreement includes a **grievance procedure** to settle disputes between management and the union. A grievance is an alleged violation of a collective agreement. Although grievance procedures vary, a grievance may be resolved as follows: An employee with a grievance first approaches her or his immediate superior to resolve the dispute. If this action is unsuccessful, the employee approaches a **shop steward,** who is an employee and unpaid union representative in a shop, or section, of a workplace. The shop steward is allowed to use working hours to resolve such disputes. She or he will apply in writing to the immediate superior of the employee to resolve the situation. If the situation is still unresolved, the **chief steward**—an employee and unpaid union representative for a workplace who is above all the shop stewards—will attempt to approach management. If the dispute is not settled, management and a union grievance committee meet to resolve the dispute. If necessary, an arbitrator is appointed to settle the dispute.

Individual Rights During a Strike

Most companies that are unionized have both union and non-union employees. In the event of a strike, the non-union employees have the right to work while the union employees are on strike. Non-union employees must cross the picket line to go to work—in fact, non-union employees cannot legally respect the picket line. Legally, picketers cannot block the entrance to a workplace, and they must keep moving across the entrance at all times. Usually, workers and management have an understanding that a vehicle can be stopped from entering the work premises for a period of two minutes, although technically this is not a legal practice. Picketers may not delay an individual who is on foot for any period of time. This situation can cause much tension between the striking and non-striking employees.

Customers and suppliers of the company are also placed in an awkward situation. Although they have the right to continue to conduct business with the company, some may choose to support the strikers by boycotting the company. This decision is up to the individual or company.

Crossing the Picket Line

In your journal, respond to the questions below.

What would I do and how would I feel in a strike if I were:

- A striking worker who is replaced by a temporary worker?
- Unemployed and given the opportunity to be a replacement worker?

1 As a class, create a list of at least five questions you would like to ask a union representative.

2 Invite a local union representative to speak to your class.

3 After the presentation, write a class letter to the speaker about what you have learned.

A C T I V I T Y

Union Representatives

Labour Legislation

*L*abour legislation outlines the rights and responsibilities of employers, unions, union employees, and non-union employees. The Constitution Act of 1867 determined how the legislative powers would be divided between the federal and provincial governments. In terms of labour, the federal government has authority over certain industries, federal employees, and works that benefit all or part of Canada (as opposed to works for one province or territory only). Because provincial and territorial governments form laws concerning civil rights, labour legislation is largely a provincial or territorial matter.

The federal government enforces the **Canada Labour Code,** which is labour legislation that applies to employees of industries under federal authority, such as those involved in air transport, radio and television broadcasting, banking, and telecommunications. The code includes basic employment and industrial relations standards. The employment standards section requires employers to:

Labour legislation outlines the rights of employees and employers.

- Limit the maximum working hours to 8 hours a day and 40 hours a week.
- Pay an employee one and a half times the regular pay for overtime.
- Pay a specific hourly minimum wage for workers aged 17 and over.
- Pay a specific hourly minimum wage for workers aged 16 and under.
- Provide a minimum of two weeks' vacation with vacation pay of 4 percent of the employee's regular yearly pay after each completed year of employment. If an employee leaves the organization before the year is over, the employer pays the vacation pay for the percentage of the year completed.
- Provide a general holiday with pay on 9 specified days a year, such as New Year's Day, Victoria Day, Labour Day, and other civic holidays.

The industrial relations section of the Canada Labour Code requires industries under federal authority to allow employees to organize unions and bargain collectively. Both management and union representatives must bargain in good faith; that is, honestly and fairly. As well, an arbitration clause must be included in all collective agreements. Unfair labour practices are forbidden, and government conciliation officers are provided to help settle disputes. The Canada Labour Relations Board administers this section of the code.

The federal Fair Wages and Hours of Labour Act requires that wages paid to employees be consistent with wages in that line of work and no less than that outlined in the Canada Labour Code. The maximum hours of labour are the same as those specified in the Canada Labour Code. The Canadian Human Rights Act outlines fair employment practices and requires equal pay for work of equal value with no discrimination on the basis of sex, race, religion, colour, origin, or ethnic background (this legislation will be examined in detail in Chapter 10).

The federal government also administers Unemployment Insurance (UI) and the Canada Pension Plan (CPP). The Unemployment Insurance

Act requires that every employee and employer contribute to Unemployment Insurance with the exception of people who are self-employed, people over 65 years of age, and some part-time employees. Employee UI contributions are deducted from paycheques. Employers are required to pay a higher rate in their UI contributions. The federal government also contributes to the UI fund, and all contributions are adjusted yearly. Employment and Immigration Canada administers Unemployment Insurance.

An unemployed person who has contributed to the UI fund for a specific period of time can apply to receive money for a specified number of weeks when her or his employment is terminated. This person must continue to seek employment while collecting UI. If UI expires before the person is able to find work, social assistance is available. UI also assists people who are temporarily unable to work due to pregnancy or illness.

The Canada Pension Plan, which started in 1965, requires payments from employees and employers, who make equal contributions, and from self-employed people. Contributions must be made by most workers between the ages of 18 and 70. Quebec, which has its own Quebec Pension Plan, does not participate in this program. A worker becomes eligible for the pension at the age of 65. CPP provides pensions to retired workers, surviving spouses, disabled workers, children of disabled people, children of deceased workers, and disabled surviving spouses. CPP will also contribute a lump sum to a deceased worker's estate.

The provinces and territories have legislation that affects:

- Working hours
- Minimum wages
- A weekly day of rest
- Annual paid vacations
- The minimum age for employment
- Fair employment practices
- Equal pay for work of equal value
- Notice of dismissal
- General holidays
- Physical conditions of workplaces
- Apprenticeships and training programs
- Wage payment and collection
- Labour–management relations
- Workers' compensation
- Parental benefits
- Other areas

Labour relations acts vary from province to province (or territory), but in general they ensure the rights of employees to organize unions and negotiate labour contracts. What constitutes unfair labour practices during union organization and collective bargaining is outlined, as well as union certification procedures. Conciliation officers are provided by governments to help settle disputes, and arbitration is ensured. The charts that follow show the federal, provincial, and territorial policies for hours of work, vacation time, and overtime rates.

HOURS OF WORK

JURISDICTION	LEGAL MAXIMUM AT REGULAR RATE		UNION CONTRACTS[1]
	Per Day	Per Week	Percentage That Do Better Than Legislation
Federal	8 hours	40 hours	97%
Alberta	8 hours	44 hours	82%
British Columbia	8 hours	44 hours	83%
Manitoba	8 hours	40 hours	41%
New Brunswick	Not specified	44 hours	97%
Newfoundland	Not specified	44 hours[2]	85%
Nova Scotia	Not specified	48 hours	62%
Ontario	8 hours	48 hours	72%
Prince Edward Island	Not specified	48 hours	80%
Quebec	Not specified	44 hours	90%
Saskatchewan	8 hours	40 hours	43%
Northwest Territories	8 hours	44 hours	50%
Yukon	8 hours	40 hours	100%

[1] Based on Labour Canada surveys of contracts covering 500 workers or more
[2] 8 h/day or 40 h/week for shop assistants

Courtesy Canadian Labour Congress

VACATION

JURISDICTION	LEGAL MINIMUM	UNION CONTRACTS	
		Percentage That Do Better	Maximum With Long Service
Federal	2 weeks or 4% of annual pay; 3 weeks or 6% after 6 years	100%	7 weeks or more
Alberta	2 weeks at regular pay	71%	7 weeks or more
British Columbia	2 weeks or 4% of annual pay 3 weeks or 6% after 5 years	70%	7 weeks
Manitoba	2 weeks at regular pay; 3 weeks after 5 years	69%	7 weeks
New Brunswick	2 weeks or 4% of annual pay	79%	6 weeks
Newfoundland	2 weeks or 4% of annual pay	50%	4–5 weeks
Nova Scotia	2 weeks or 4% of annual pay	56%	7 weeks
Ontario	2 weeks or 4% of annual pay	67%	7 weeks
Prince Edward Island	2 weeks or 4% of annual pay	80%	5 weeks
Quebec	2 weeks or 4% of annual pay 3 weeks or 6% after 10 years	66%	8 weeks
Saskatchewan	3 weeks or 3⁄52 of annual pay 4 weeks or 4⁄52 after 10 years	46%	7 weeks
Northwest Territories	2 weeks or 4% of annual pay 3 weeks or 6% after 5 years	100%	6 weeks
Yukon	2 weeks or 4% of annual pay	100%	7 weeks

Courtesy Canadian Labour Congress

OVERTIME RATES

JURISDICTION	AFTER	LEGAL MINIMUM OVERTIME RATE
Federal	8 h/day or 40 h/week	1½ times regular pay
Alberta	8 h/day or 44 h/week	1½ times regular pay
British Columbia	8 h/day or 40 h/week 11 h/day or 48 h/week	1½ times regular pay 2 times regular pay
Manitoba	8 h/day or 40 h/week	1½ times regular pay
New Brunswick	44 h/week	$6.00 per hour
Newfoundland	44 h/week	$6.00 per hour
Nova Scotia	48 h/week	1½ times regular pay
Ontario	44 h/week	1½ times regular pay
Prince Edward Island	48 h/week	$6.00 per hour ($4.88 under age 18)
Quebec	44 h/week	1½ times regular pay
Saskatchewan	8 h/day or 40 h/week	1½ times regular pay
Northwest Territories	8 h/day or 44 h/week	1½ times regular pay
Yukon	8 h/day or 40 h/week	1½ times regular pay

Courtesy Canadian Labour Congress

ACTIVITY

Researching Labour Legislation

1 With a partner, phone the appropriate government labour departments (such as your local branch of Employment Standards or Employment and Immigration Canada) or ministry of labour to request current information on Unemployment Insurance, Canada Pension Plan, minimum wages, and so on. Use the blue pages in the telephone book to locate the offices in your area.

2 Create a chart that outlines your findings, and compare your chart with another group's to check the accuracy of your information. Keep a file of the information and update it as you learn about any changes to labour legislation.

In groups of six, organize a debate on one of the statements below. Three members of your group prepare the arguments that support the statement, while the other three prepare the arguments against the statement. The two groups of three must work out of hearing distance from each other. A spokesperson from each side presents the initial argument. Once the initial arguments are presented, the other group members may participate in the debate.

1 When negotiating wages, unions should not ask for more than what the employer can afford.

2 During a public-service strike, such as a transit strike, unions represent the public.

3 Because of unions, wages and working conditions have greatly improved for all workers.

4 We needed unions in the past, but they are no longer necessary.

5 Every member is democratically represented in a union. Members work together to form policies, negotiate contracts, and determine when to strike, if necessary.

Maternity Leave

by Janice Turner

CASE STUDY

Some companies consider a pregnant employee "disloyal," while others, discounting the myth that a mother-to-be is less committed to her job, give their staff generous maternity leave benefits, and welcome them back.

Ellen Richards was thrilled to be pregnant for a second time. Her employer, however, was less than enthused.

"I was told to limit my contact with the public to phone and fax. Being pregnant was something they didn't want associated with the organization."

Richards, a pseudonym, had been with the company for six years. She had taken five weeks off after the birth of her first child. When she returned she was given her old job back.

This time, however, she told her employers that she would be taking the full 25 weeks of unpaid pregnancy leave she was entitled to under provincial law.

It was then that Richards—not yet 30— became a nonperson.

"It was like, 'You've done it again,'" says Richards. "They asked me if I really intended to take all the time (available). Then they reminded me that (under law) they were obliged to offer me a job, but not necessarily my job. It was clear that if I took what I had a right to take, I would be seriously jeopardizing my career."

After she confirmed she'd be taking full maternity leave, all of her most challenging assignments were handed over to other workers.

"All of the best assignments suddenly disappeared," she says.

Richards was called by the personnel department and told, verbally, that it was probably a good time to consider another career. Perhaps full-time motherhood was more her style?

"They wondered if I realized that a maternity leave was a great inconvenience to them."

Through it all Richards says she didn't know whether to laugh or to cry. But she needed the work.

In contrast to Richards, Cathy Head isn't spending her pregnancy leave on pins and needles, fretting about the future. A Bell Canada employee of 14 years, Head is enjoying her third maternity leave with the comfort of knowing she'll be welcomed back on her return.

Bell allows women to take two additional weeks of leave, over and above what the law permits.

It also provides a supplementary pregnancy allowance for 15 weeks. For Head, it means an extra $73.50 a week on top of unemployment insurance benefits, if she goes back to Bell for at least six months.

It's a pleasure, she says, to work for a company that respects a woman's decision to have both children *and* a career.

"I've never felt punished because I chose to have a child," she says. "I've continued to be upgradeable and promotable."

Head will return to work in June, not so much for the money—not much is left after child-care costs—but because she finds her work rewarding. And she feels a genuine obligation to her employer.

It's a relationship that works on give and take. When the company had needed Head to work a little extra, the odd weekend and night, she did so.

"My past record shows that I've been there for them and they've been there for me."

Imaginative companies prove there are ways to accommodate family leaves, advisers in the field note. They can bring back retired workers to fill in temporarily or give bonuses to employees who offer to do the additional work.

Head applauds her employer's progressive view. Richards bemoans that hers is still living in another age; not breaking the letter of the law, but certainly robbing it of any spirit.

—————————

Reprinted with permission—The Toronto Star Syndicate.

▼ ▼ ▼

1 **The benefits Cathy Head received are the results of union negotiation. Identify five other ways in which unions have benefitted workers.**

2 **Create a chart summarizing and comparing the two situations in the case study. Include each individual's feelings and the actions of the two companies. Compare your chart with a partner's.**

3 **What advice would you give to Ellen Richards?**

4 **Many fathers feel they too should have the right to stay home with their children, which is called paternity leave. What are the advantages and disadvantages of paternity leave? Do you support this initiative? Why or why not?**

Your View of Unions

Consider whether or not your views on unions have changed as a result of this study of unions. If your views have changed, explain in your journal how they have changed. If your views have not changed, explain why.

Make the Connection

UNIONS AND YOUR PLACEMENT

1 Divide your class into two groups, one group consisting of students whose placements do not involve a union and one group consisting of students whose placements do involve a union. The group whose placements have a union develops a questionnaire to explore the type of union, how the union was formed, the history of union negotiations and what was achieved, grievance procedures, who belongs to the union, and attitudes toward the union. The group whose placements do not include a union develops a questionnaire to gather information on attitudes toward unions at the placement and the history of the workplace structure.

2 At your placement, discuss with your supervisor whom you may approach with your questionnaire. Interview at least two people at your placement. Try to interview people with different viewpoints.

3 Write a report summarizing your findings and present it to the class.

WHAT HAVE YOU LEARNED?

1 What are the advantages and disadvantages of collective action?

2 Describe why unions first developed.

3 Explain the process of collective bargaining and what happens if it fails.

4 Why are grievance procedures important?

5 Outline the legislation that directly affects you in your placement.

Human rights

After completing this chapter, you should be able to:

▼ ▼ ▼

- Understand the importance of human rights legislation.
- Determine what constitutes discrimination and harassment.
- Describe how to make a formal complaint of discrimination.
- Recognize techniques for preventing discrimination.
- Understand the concepts of pay equity and employment equity.

▼ ▼ ▼

human rights
discrimination
Canadian Human
  Rights Act

Canadian Charter of
  Rights and Freedoms
harassment
sexual harassment

pay equity
employment
  equity
Employment
  Equity Act

Human Rights on the Job

M ost people accept that everyone is born free and equal, although this belief is not always reflected in daily life. Everyone does have basic **human rights,** including the right to be respected at all times. Canadians have the right not to be placed at a disadvantage based on factors such as race, place of origin, religion, age, gender, marital or family status, or disability. Everyone has the right to live and work in an environment that is free from such **discrimination**. The Canadian Human Rights Commission administers the **Canadian Human Rights Act,** which applies to industries under federal jurisdiction, such as air transport, radio and television broadcasting, banking, and telecommunications. Each province and territory also has similar human rights legislation to protect against discrimination for any person not covered under the federal legislation.

Basically, every person in Canada has the right to freedom from discrimination in the areas of:

All human beings are born free and equal in dignity and rights.
UNIVERSAL DECLARATION OF HUMAN RIGHTS

- Services, goods, and facilities
- Housing
- Contracts
- Membership in vocational associations and craft unions
- Employment

The chart on page 175 shows the prohibited grounds of discrimination in employment for each province and territory as well as for organizations under federal jurisdiction.

Exceptions to the human rights acts may apply in some situations. Generally, the discriminator must be able to show that there is a genuine and reasonable basis for imposing a discriminatory requirement. For example:

- An employer may impose hiring restrictions if the physical demands of a job prevent hiring an individual who is physically challenged.
- Certain special interest organizations, such as a senior citizens club, may restrict employment to the group that is the focus of its services.

The freedom of no one is safe unless the freedom of everyone is safe.
CANADIAN CIVIL LIBERTIES ASSOCIATION

Every individual has a responsibility to respect the rights of others. Every employer has a responsibility to stop or prevent discrimination in the workplace. Every employee has the right to lodge a complaint of discrimination, and the employer is expected to listen to and act on complaints. Human rights legislation incorporates many aspects of employment, including recruiting, hiring, training, transferring, promoting, apprenticeship terms, dismissals, and layoffs. Terms and conditions of employment—for example, rates of pay, overtime, hours of work, vacation time, shift work, discipline procedures, and performance evaluations—may also be included in this legislation.

The **Canadian Charter of Rights and Freedoms** also protects human rights within Canada. Its purpose is to state the rights of every citizen of Canada clearly so that these rights can be understood and protected by the legal system. The Charter is entrenched in the Canadian constitution, which helps to protect these rights from being abolished by federal or provincial

Prohibited grounds of discrimination in employment **

Jurisdiction	Federal	British Columbia	Alberta	Saskatchewan	Manitoba	Ontario	Quebec	New Brunswick	Prince Edward Island	Nova Scotia	Newfoundland	Northwest Territories	Yukon
Race	●	●	●	●	●	●	●	●	●	●	●	●	●
National or ethnic origin[1]	●				●	●	●	●	●	●	●		●*
Ancestry		●	●	●	●	●		●				●	●
Nationality[7]				●	●							●	
Based on association[8]										●			●
Place of origin		●	●	●		●		●			●		
Colour	●	●	●	●	●	●	●	●	●	●	●	●	●
Religion	●	●		●	●			●	●	●	●	●	●
Creed[2]			●	●	●	●				●	●	●	●
Age	●	● (45-65)	● (18+)	● (18-65)	●	● (18-65)	●	● (19+)	●	● (40+)	● (19-65)	●	●
Sex[6]	●	●	●	●	●*****	●	●	●	●	●	●	●	●
Pregnancy or childbirth[6]	●		●	●	●	●	●						●
Marital status[3]	●	●	●	●	●	●	●	●	●	●	●	●	●
Family status[3]	●				●	●	●		●			●	●
Pardoned offence	●					●	●				●		
Record of criminal conviction		●					●						●
Physical handicap or disability	●	●	●	●	●	●	●	●	●	●	●	●	●
Mental handicap or disability	●	●	●	●	●	●	●	●	●	●	●	●	●
Dependence on alcohol or drug[9]	●									●			
Place of residence												●	
Political belief		●			●		●			●	●		●***
Assignment, attachment or seizure of pay[4]											●		
Source of income					●								
Social condition[4]							●						
Language							●						
Social origin[4]											●		
Sexual orientation[5]					●	●	●						●
Harassment[5]	●					●****	●				●		●

1 New Brunswick includes only "national origin".
2 Creed usually means religious beliefs.
3 Quebec uses the term "civil status".
4 In Quebec's charter, "social condition" may include assignment, attachment or seizure of pay and social origin.
5 The federal, Ontario, Quebec and Yukon statutes ban harassment on all proscribed grounds. Ontario and Newfoundland also ban sexual solicitation.
6 Sex includes ground of pregnancy. Pregnancy or childbirth is included within ground of sex. Based on policy for B.C., N.B., P.E.I., Nova Scotia, Newfoundland, Northwest Territories. Supreme Court of Canada has held that sex includes sexual harassment.
7 Ontario's Code includes only "citizenship".
8 Association with individuals determined by prohibited grounds of discrimination.
9 Based on the policy for British Columbia, Saskatchewan, Manitoba and P.E.I.

* Includes linguistic background.
** Any limitation, exclusion, denial or preference may be permitted if a bona fide occupational requirement can be demonstrated.
*** Includes political activity or political association.
**** Does not include sexual orientation.
***** Includes gender determined characteristics.

legislation. Among the rights included in the Charter are the right to freedom of conscience and religion; freedom of thought, belief, opinion, and expression (including the media); freedom of peaceful assembly; and freedom of association. Discrimination based on race, national or ethnic origin, colour, religion, sex, age, or mental or physical disability is prohibited under the Charter.

ACTIVITY
Which Rights Do You Value Most?

1 You are a passenger in a hot-air balloon. Your precious cargo is your rights. Unfortunately, you have miscalculated the fuel required for your journey and your cargo—you must lighten your balloon or you will crash. Read the list of rights below and determine the order in which you value them. Which right will you toss out first? Which one will you try to hang onto the longest? Your right to:

- A clean environment
- Vote
- A safe community
- Demonstrate or protest
- An education

- Freedom from discrimination
- Live where you choose
- Food, water, and housing
- Freedom of speech

2 Compare lists with a partner. Present your arguments for your list ordering.

ACTIVITY
What Do You Know About Your Rights?

In small groups, write two examples of freedom from discrimination for each of the areas listed under human rights legislation, including: services, goods, and facilities; housing; contracts; membership in vocational associations and craft unions; and employment. For example, "All people have the right to eat in any restaurant they choose" is an example of freedom from discrimination in the area of services, goods, and facilities.

My disability is that I cannot use my legs. My handicap is your negative perception of that disability, and thus of me.
RICK HANSEN

Harassment

Harassment is a form of discrimination and is defined as any unwelcome physical, verbal, or visual conduct. Derogatory comments, threats, actions, or jokes against a person, and offensive posters are forms of harassment. Even an offensive attitude, leer, or other type of intimidating conduct may be considered harassment if the behaviour is known or ought to be known as unwelcome. Employers, people acting for employers, and co-workers are prohibited from harassing employees and prospective employees in some regions (see the chart on page 175). Ideally, employment decisions should be based on merit, and not on criteria that are unrelated to job performance.

Any unwelcome comment or action about colour, national or ethnic origin, or the adornments and rituals associated with cultural or religious beliefs is harassment. Teasing, taunting, or other actions against people who are older or younger as well as people with disabilities are also forms of harassment.

Unwelcome sexual advances made by a co-worker or a person in a position of authority or a reprisal because a sexual advance has been refused are forms of sexual harassment. One company defines **sexual harassment** as any conduct that includes unwelcome and repeated sexual advances, requests for sexual favours, and other sexually-related verbal or physical conduct or visual display that interferes with an individual's work or creates an intimidating or unpleasant work environment. There are three types of sexual harassment that are prohibited by human rights legislation:

1 An unwelcome comment or conduct.

2 A sexual advance made by a person who is in a position to grant or deny a benefit to another. It is considered a violation when the person making the solicitation or advance knows, or should know, that such behaviour is unwelcome.

3 A threat or reprisal against a person who rejects a sexual advance.

Examples of sexual harassment include:

- Displaying sexually offensive material.
- Insults or jokes of a sexual nature.
- Inappropriate remarks about a person's physical appearance.
- Sexually suggestive gestures.
- Comments about an individual's sex life.
- Unwelcome touching or leering.

It is important to note that sexual discrimination includes discriminating against women who are pregnant or have just given birth as well as paying women and men unequally for doing work of equal value.

I have a dream that my four little children will one day live in a nation where they will not be judged by the colour of their skin, but by the content of their character.

MARTIN LUTHER KING, JR.

ACTIVITY

Destroying Myths About Age

Discrimination based on age violates human rights. The myths and realities concerning older workers are outlined below. Read the list, and then in small groups list as many myths about young workers as you can.

Myth: Employees over the age of 50 are less productive than younger workers.
Reality: Workers between 17 and 44 call in sick an average of 3.7 days annually while those over 45 have a 3.1 average.

Myth: Older workers are more likely to leave their jobs.
Reality: Older workers are more stable. Women 50-plus change jobs 88 percent less than younger women.

Myth: Older bosses are not as decisive and do not evaluate information as well as younger bosses.

Reality: Studies prove that older managers, with more experience, do take longer to make decisions but evaluate information more capably and make fewer errors in judgement.

Myth: Older workers are set in their ways, unwilling to learn new methods.
Reality: Research has shown older people learn as well as younger people; teaching methods may have to be modified, but not content.

Myth: Older workers have more accidents.
Reality: The accident record of mature workers is better than that of younger workers.

Myth: Older workers are more expensive for a firm to employ.
Reality: Health-care premiums are lower for older workers because they usually have no dependent children and are sick less often.

Myth: Most older workers are interested in slowing down.
Reality: More 55- to 65-year-olds are entering the work force than ever before. Half the retirees in one research sample were interested in full- or part-time work.

. . . .

How to Make a Complaint of Discrimination

No one should have to dance backward all their lives.
JILL RUCKELSHAUS

Discrimination in any form should not be ignored. During the period of discrimination, the case should be documented by keeping a written record of the incidents, including times, places, and witnesses. Initially, a person who is being harassed or discriminated against can tell the discriminator that his or her behaviour is not welcome. If the harassment continues, the victim is not defenceless. He or she can tell the supervisor, and, if the situation is not resolved in a satisfactory manner, he or she can write to senior management. It is an employer's legal responsibility to prevent and stop discrimination. Many employers have procedures in place that outline the steps to be taken if an employee has a complaint of discrimination or harassment. They may also outline the levels of action to be taken against the harasser. Some unions also have complaint procedures for dealing with discrimination or harassment. Examples of actions taken against a discriminator include fines, reprimands, apologies to the victims, demotions, transfers, and terminations of employment.

Both federal and provincial human rights commissions provide frameworks to protect workers' rights and dignity. If a situation is unresolved by management, the complaint may be lodged with the appropriate human rights authority. An example of how a complaint would be handled by the Canadian Human Rights Commission follows.

What Happens to Your Complaint?

When a complaint is lodged with the Canadian Human Rights Commission, it follows the process described below. At each stage, an attempt is made to settle the complaint. If it is not resolved, it moves to the next stage in the process. The complaint may also be dismissed at any stage, and either party can appeal to a higher authority.

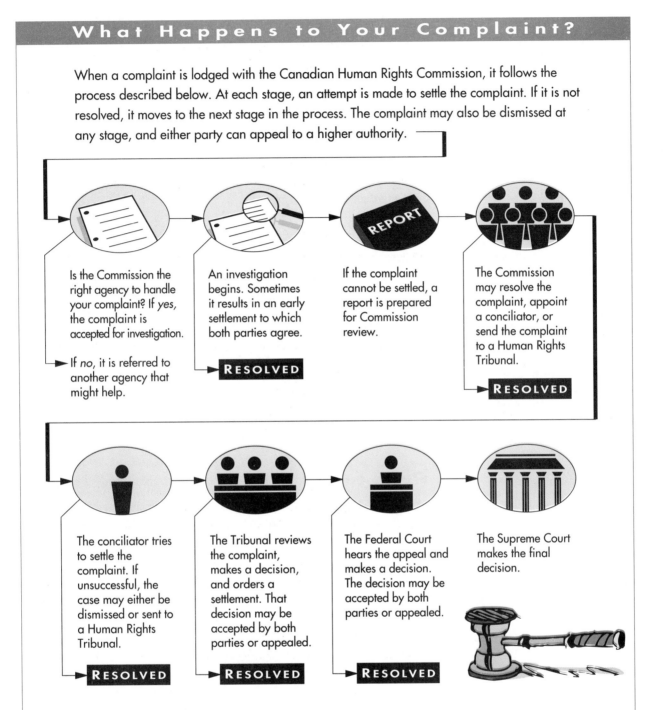

Is the Commission the right agency to handle your complaint? If *yes*, the complaint is accepted for investigation.

If *no*, it is referred to another agency that might help.

An investigation begins. Sometimes it results in an early settlement to which both parties agree.

RESOLVED

If the complaint cannot be settled, a report is prepared for Commission review.

The Commission may resolve the complaint, appoint a conciliator, or send the complaint to a Human Rights Tribunal.

RESOLVED

The conciliator tries to settle the complaint. If unsuccessful, the case may either be dismissed or sent to a Human Rights Tribunal.

RESOLVED

The Tribunal reviews the complaint, makes a decision, and orders a settlement. That decision may be accepted by both parties or appealed.

RESOLVED

The Federal Court hears the appeal and makes a decision. The decision may be accepted by both parties or appealed.

RESOLVED

The Supreme Court makes the final decision.

From "Equality: We All Have a Hand in It," courtesy Canadian Human Rights Commission.

A C T I V I T Y

Discrimination in the News

1 Find newspaper and magazine articles about discrimination in the workplace. Choose one case of discrimination and outline the events and the various points of view of the individuals involved.

2 In small groups, discuss your cases and how discrimination is presented in the press.

3 Write an essay about how cases of discrimination are presented in the press. Do you agree with how these cases were handled? How would you present a case of discrimination?.

Journal Entry

What Can You Do About Discrimination?

Consider what you think constitutes discrimination. In your journal, write a letter of advice to someone who has been discriminated against. The person could be fictitious or someone you know.

Preventing Discrimination

It can be difficult to lodge a complaint of discrimination because of the fear of losing a job or making matters worse. But it is essential that cases of discrimination be reported. Effective complaints procedures and reporting of incidents are important components of prevention—if these cases are not reported, then discrimination will likely continue.

The keys to preventing discrimination are education and training to heighten awareness of discrimination and harassment in the workplace. As well, educating discriminators is essential. Employers can act to prevent harassment by ensuring that:

- Derogatory or demeaning posters are removed from the workplace.
- Discriminatory comments or jokes are known to be unacceptable.
- Everyone understands what types of actions and comments are discriminatory.
- A policy against harassment is available and accessible, including the names of individuals who have been trained to handle complaints of discrimination.
- A complaint procedure is established.

Unions can help prevent discrimination by educating their members and other workers, providing guidelines for the complaint process, discussing discrimination at union meetings, and including discrimination prevention in training programs.

Native issues are almost never just Native issues. Native issues are human issues.
BUFFY SAINTE-MARIE

The heart never knows the colour of the skin.
CHIEF DAN GEORGE

Action Against Discrimination

AN INAPPROPRIATE PICTURE

A prospective employee was asked by the person interviewing her if she liked the poster of a nude woman hanging on his wall. She felt she had to reply. She did not express her true reaction, however, because she believed her answer would affect her chances of getting the position.

A settlement was reached during an investigation by the Canadian Human Rights Commission. The complainant received a letter of apology from the interviewer. A letter of reprimand was placed in his personnel file and he attended a training session on sexual harassment. The employer also destroyed the poster and revised its office policy on harassment to make it consistent with the provisions of the Act. The revised policy was circulated to ensure that all employees were aware of it.

EFFECTIVE ACTION BY THE EMPLOYER

A black employee of Canadian Pacific Rail, Phil F., filed a complaint with the Canadian Human Rights Commission alleging harassment because of his race and colour. Among the incidents he reported was one in which his locker and its contents were destroyed with black paint. When CP Rail became aware of the incident, Phil F.'s immediate supervisor was told to find out who was responsible. The supervisor was unable to determine responsibility, so he asked CP police to investigate. Although they were prepared to lay criminal charges, they were unable to discover the culprit. However, two employees, who were responsible for similar racially-motivated incidents that came to light during the investigation, were warned that such actions would not be tolerated in the future.

The Canadian Human Rights Tribunal that investigated the complaint held that the employer had met the requirements of the Act and could not be held liable for the incident:

CP Rail did not consent to or condone the incident. It "acknowledged throughout that it was reprehensible and unacceptable to the Company," which viewed the incident "as criminal activity."

CP Rail did everything proper to prevent discrimination. It "had a clear policy to prevent discrimination...[which was] communicated to its employees and [was] to be acknowledged in writing from time to time by supervisory personnel...."

The employer also did everything possible after the discrimination occurred to lessen its effect by undertaking a thorough investigation and reprimanding employees who participated in other incidents discovered during this investigation. The company also compensated Phil F. for damage to his property.

The employer's attempts to deal with the harassment apparently worked: "similar incidents have not occurred since."

JUST JOKING

A woman working in a word processing position in a federal department filed a complaint with the Canadian Human Rights Commission after she experienced what she said was harassment because of her Italian origin. Several co-workers allegedly directed derogatory remarks about Italians to the complainant and called her names. She complained to her supervisor, who told her that kind of thing went on in the office and she was over-emotional. He did not investigate her allegations. She then spoke to the department's harassment co-ordinator and requested a transfer, saying the situation was intolerable.

The complainant alleged that her work was

more carefully scrutinized after she met with the harassment co-ordinator, and believes the extra scrutiny was due to this meeting and her request for a transfer. She submitted an official complaint to the harassment co-ordinator and shortly afterwards was told that her position would be abolished. The complainant believed this action was in retaliation.

The Commission concluded that the complainant was harassed. A conciliator was appointed and a settlement reached. The department agreed to pay the complainant $1200 as compensation for hurt feelings. Her performance appraisal for the time in question was destroyed. A memorandum was circulated to all employees reminding them that discriminatory remarks about a person's ethnic origin are a form of harassment; even remarks apparently made "in fun" may be discriminatory and hurtful to others, and all such remarks should be avoided.

MAKING FUN

Dolph B. was a general employee of the National System of Baking. His foreman harassed him by calling him "stupid" and "dummy," unjustifiably criticizing his work in front of other employees, threatening to fire him, and forcing him to eat a pie that had been baked without sugar. Dolph B. eventually quit his job because the harassment upset him so much he became ill.

The Board members [of a provincial human rights council] accepted the evidence given by co-workers that Dolph B. was a good employee and that no serious problems existed with his work. The Board found that David W. engaged in the harassing conduct because Dolph B. has a mental illness. They also found that David W. was an agent of the employer and part of the

"directing mind" of the Corporation. Consequently, the employer was liable for the harassment. David W. and the National System of Baking were ordered to pay Dolph B. $3000 in general damages, $340 in compensation for lost wages, and $549 in interest on the award.

PERSISTENT PRESSURE

A settlement was reached in the complaint of a consumer loans officer who took medical leave from her bank for osteo-arthritis, a spinal condition. The loans officer maintained that on her return from leave she was treated differently from other employees. She said that, among other things, she was threatened with disciplinary action, pressured to resign, urged to transfer to another branch or accept a part-time job, and denied a loan. She received an unsatisfactory performance appraisal and was counselled on her work. She eventually resigned because of the stress she felt at being constantly criticized.

The Commission's investigation supported the loans officer's allegation that she was treated differently from other loans officers after she took medical leave. A conciliator helped the parties reach a settlement. The complainant received a letter of apology and $22 000 in compensation.

Harassment Casebook: Summaries of Selected Harassment Cases, Canadian Human Rights Commission. © Minister of Supply and Services Canada, 1991.

▼ ▼ ▼

1 Complete a chart like the one on the next page in your notebook.

2 In small groups, discuss the cases and compare your charts.

CASES	HUMAN RIGHT BEING VIOLATED	YOUR REACTION TO THE SITUATION	YOUR REACTION TO THE OUTCOME
An Inappropriate Picture Effective Action by the Employer Just Joking Making Fun Persistent Pressure			

Confronting Discrimination

In your journal, complete one, two, or all three of the statements below.

- I have been a victim of discrimination. Here is my story...
- I have been a victim of harassment. Here is my story...
- I will no longer behave in a discriminating manner. In the past, I have...

Pay Equity

Any two people performing the same job or substantially the same job should be paid the same wage without discrimination based on gender. In fact, legislation passed in the 1950s required equal pay for equal work. But just a few years ago, differences in pay for the same job were not unusual. For example, the legal minimum wage in some parts of Canada was lower for women until the early 1970s.

Jobs that are traditionally labelled "women's work" have always paid lower wages than those considered "men's work," even if the output from the different jobs is equally valuable to a company. This wage gap has narrowed very little since 1960. Today, women who work full-time make an average of only 66 cents for every dollar earned by men. Canadian economists have estimated that 20 to 30 percent of the wage gap is due to discriminatory attitudes toward women and the jobs they have traditionally held—attitudes that have, unfortunately, become part of the economic system. The underpayment of women workers has a direct effect on the financial well-being of many Canadian women and

In 1987, Hospital Services Groups of the Public Service of Canada was awarded a $30 000 settlement to ensure pay equity. Similarly, in 1990 a settlement of $317 000 000 in back pay plus $76 000 000 in ongoing annual salary adjustments was awarded to 70 000 federal public servants.

their families. For this reason, provincial and territorial governments have passed pay equity legislation.

Pay equity legislation regulates equal pay for work of equal value. Broadly speaking, pay equity means that women should be paid the same as men for jobs that are different but of similar value. In order to make payment practices less discriminatory, the value of a job is calculated in terms of skill required, level of responsibility, effort required, and working conditions. Pay equity acts require job evaluation plans, which are used to determine the value of each job in a company in a consistent, equitable manner. Each job is rated in a way that is fair, unbiased, and uniform. To do this, the content of each job is broken down into the four categories mentioned above—skill, responsibility, effort, and working conditions. Points are awarded to jobs according to a standard scoring system. In this way, jobs that are quite different may still receive the same final score. If there is a wage gap between jobs of equal value, the lower wage must be raised to the level of the higher wage. The higher wage is *not* reduced. Adjustments to salaries in female-dominated fields are the right of all employees who have not been paid fairly in the past.

Most jurisdictions in Canada have legislation that requires employers to pay female and male employees the same wages for work of equal value. Some provinces have pay equity acts, while others include pay equity under human rights legislation. The list that follows shows the relevant legislation by province and territory. The procedure for enforcing this legislation varies only slightly among jurisdictions. An employee who believes that she or he is not being paid fairly files a complaint with the appropriate commission, and then an officer of the commission investigates the complaint to determine its merit and a resolution. If necessary, the complaint may be referred to a tribunal for a hearing.

PAY EQUITY LEGISLATION

Alberta	Individual's Rights Protection Act
British Columbia	British Columbia Human Rights Act
Manitoba	Pay Equity Act
New Brunswick	Employment Standards Act
Newfoundland	Newfoundland Human Rights Code
Nova Scotia	Pay Equity Act
Ontario	Ontario Pay Equity Act
Prince Edward Island	Pay Equity Act
Quebec	Quebec Charter of Human Rights and Freedoms
Saskatchewan	Labour Standards Act
Yukon	Yukon Human Rights Act

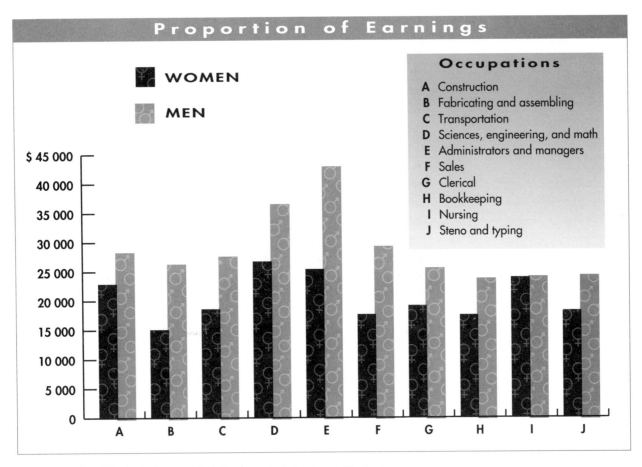

Proportion of Earnings

WOMEN

MEN

Occupations

A Construction
B Fabricating and assembling
C Transportation
D Sciences, engineering, and math
E Administrators and managers
F Sales
G Clerical
H Bookkeeping
I Nursing
J Steno and typing

Statistics Canada, 1986, obtained from *Infoflash*, Number 2, Ontario Women's Directorate.

Employment Equity

Women, aboriginal people, people who are physically or mentally challenged, and visible minorities have often been denied **employment equity,** or equal employment opportunity due to discriminatory practices. These groups should enjoy a representative share of employment opportunities in all occupations and at all levels. An example of discrimination that denies equal opportunity is the practice of allowing members of these four groups to advance within a company only to a certain level. The company may appear to be equitable by including members of these groups in management positions. However, the top executive positions are still out of reach for members of these groups not because these people are not qualified for the jobs, but because they are discriminated against. Legislation, including the federal **Employment Equity Act,** exists to ensure employment equity. Such legislation requires employers to report what proportion of their employees belong to these four groups. Employers must then prove that all groups are equally represented at all levels within their organizations.

By the year 2000, white males will likely account for only 15 percent of new workers— 85 percent of new workers will consist of women, aboriginal people, physically or mentally challenged people, and members of visible minorities.

Your Observations About Equity

In your journal, complete the statements below.

- At my placement, I have observed these examples of discrimination...
- At my placement, I have observed these examples of discrimination prevention...

EQUITY AT YOUR PLACEMENT

1 Human rights legislation varies depending on the area in which you live and the type of employer for which you work. Divide the class into five groups, with each group researching one of the following topics: human rights legislation, discrimination complaint procedures, prevention of discrimination, pay equity, and employment equity.

2 Once you have completed your research, think of questions you would like to ask at your placement that relate to your research topic. Try to word your questions in a sensitive and unbiased manner.

3 As a class, compile your questions into an interview questionnaire.

4 Schedule time with your placement supervisor for an equity interview using the class questionnaire. Ask for copies of company policies that relate to equity.

5 In small groups, compare your findings. For example, is one company more actively involved in discrimination prevention than another? How do company policies differ?

6 Prepare a report about equity at your placement. Be sure to include the legislation that affects you, how you can file a complaint of discrimination, and techniques for preventing discrimination in the workplace.

WHAT HAVE YOU LEARNED?

▼ ▼ ▼

1 What is the purpose of human rights legislation?

2 What are an employer's responsibilities when an incident of discrimination has occurred in the workplace?

3 What are an employer's responsibilities toward preventing discrimination in the workplace?

4 What actions can you take if you are harassed or discriminated against at your placement?

5 Do you treat others in the same way you wish to be treated? Explain why or why not.

CHAPTER 11

HEALTH

WHAT YOU WILL LEARN

After completing this chapter, you should be able to:

▼ ▼ ▼

- Understand current health issues in the workplace.
- Outline employee and employer responsibilities to ensure a safe workplace.
- Practise preventive measures to ensure a healthy workplace.
- Identify how health affects productivity in the workplace.
- Understand ergonomics and its purpose.

TERMS TO REMEMBER

▼ ▼ ▼

stress	noise	ventilation
monotony	vibration	humidity
job rotation	illumination	radiation
fatigue	airborne	productivity
repetition	contaminants	ergonomics

Occupational Health Issues

*O*ur working environment can affect our physical and mental health. Illness caused by a poor working environment can influence the performance of employees, organizations, and, thus, the economy. In other words, an unhealthy working environment is harmful to everyone. The conditions in any workplace should be adequate to maintain the health of all workers, prevent and control disease, and reduce lost working time.

Chronic or recurring illness is often the result of long-term exposure to inadequate working conditions. Excessive exposure to such factors as the following can cause work-related illness:

- Stress due to personal or job-related pressures
- Monotonous tasks
- Fatigue
- Repetition
- Prolonged standing or sitting
- Noise
- Vibration
- Poor illumination
- Poor air quality
- Radiation (from, for example, X-ray machines or computer monitors)
- Lack of cleanliness

Preventing and controlling working conditions is imperative for healthy workers and a healthy economy. Employees, employers, and designers of workplaces share the responsibility of maintaining health. Social awareness of health issues combined with government legislation helps to ensure healthy working conditions.

STRESS

Stress is physical, mental, or emotional pressure, and it can have a positive or negative influence on health. For example, one person may enjoy the challenge and excitement of giving a speech to a group of people, while another person may be filled with terror at such an event. The stress of intense competition can bring about peak performance in some actors, athletes, and salespeople, and many people feel that they work best under pressure. A person can have too little stress, such as an idle and bored retiree, or too much stress. Everyone needs some stress in order to be healthy and happy.

Negative stress due to personal or job-related pressures can affect a person's behaviour and health and the working atmosphere. Personal stresses, such as school exams or an illness in the family, can affect a person's job performance. Changes in work responsibilities, problems with a supervisor or fellow employee, a transfer to a new job or city, the possibility of layoffs, shift work, and more can cause job-related stress. Physical working conditions, such as excessive noise and vibration, extremes in temperature, poor illumination, and excessive humidity can also cause stress. Symptoms of negative stress include the following:

- Tense muscles and backache
- Pounding or racing of the heart
- Increased perspiration
- Forgetfulness and lack of concentration
- Loss of self-confidence
- Frequent anger and frustration
- Decreased productivity at work
- Avoidance of others
- Sleep disorders
- Depression and anxiety
- A tight or fluttery stomach
- Shortness of breath
- Cold hands or feet
- A desire to cry or run away
- Irritability or edginess
- Nail biting or teeth grinding
- Absenteeism from work
- Change in personal appearance

Stress-related illnesses account for 75 percent of all lost work time.

Ideally, people should manage their negative stress by ignoring what is uncontrollable and managing what can be controlled. Some uncontrollable factors can be reduced, though, such as talking to your supervisor when you are not given enough time to complete your work. Stress can be controlled by developing a sense of humour, practising proper nutrition and sleep habits, alternating between types of stresses, forming realistic goals, understanding stress, learning to relax, preparing for tasks thoroughly, maintaining financial security, and creating a stable home.

MONOTONY

Monotony of tasks, or wearisome sameness, can cause boredom, which in turn can lead to lack of concentration and poor job performance. In contrast, varied and interesting jobs challenge workers to make decisions and be responsive. Enlarging the demands of a job, matching the right person to a job, demonstrating the meaning and value of a job within an overall operation, and job rotation are all methods of reducing monotony and improving employee interest and satisfaction. **Job rotation** is a system in which employees change activities periodically. Its purpose is to reduce monotony by providing variety.

FATIGUE

Fatigue is physical or mental exhaustion, and it can impair work and increase susceptibility to disease. Fatigue on and off the job due to overexertion or lack of sleep can usually be fixed with sleep. Fatigue due to repetitive physical tasks, boredom, stress, mental strain, or other psychological reasons is not so easily remedied. Long-term exhaustion can lead to chronic fatigue syndrome, a condition of recurring fatigue and related symptoms, such as an inability to concentrate, irritability, and a weakened immune system.

REPETITION

Repetition—doing the same physical task over and over—can cause repetitive strain injury, which is the fastest-growing health problem in

Canada. Also called occupational overuse, repetitive strain injury is a general term used to describe a range of problems, including carpal tunnel syndrome (compression of nerves in the wrist due to repeated wrist action), tendonitis (chronic inflammation of the tendons), and bursitis (chronic inflammation of shoulder joints). Repetitive strain injury is caused by holding unnatural positions or repeating motions over long periods of time, and it results in painful wrists, elbows, shoulders, or fingers. Workers who use heavy equipment such as a jackhammer are susceptible as well as workers who do a lot of computer keyboarding. If these problems become chronic, the methods of treating them are limited. The strain must be alleviated through physiotherapy, supportive devices such as gloves and wrist splints, and, in severe cases, surgery. Preventive measures eliminate the need for therapy and surgery. Although repetitive strain injury has been affecting workers for decades, it is difficult to relate the symptoms to a specific job or task because they appear gradually over time. The true impact of chronic job-related illness is just beginning to be realized.

PROLONGED STANDING OR SITTING

Prolonged periods of standing or sitting can cause tension and discomfort. For example, a computer operator may develop tension in the neck, upper and lower back, shoulders, and even wrists and fingers. A restaurant server may have a chronically tense and achy lower back and legs. Taking breaks, stretching, and changing sitting position can reduce tension and loosen the affected muscles. Improving the design of office furniture and equipment can also reduce problems (further information on this topic appears later in this chapter).

NOISE

Noise, which is measured in decibels (dB), is unwanted or valueless sound vibrations. One decibel is the softest sound that can be heard by humans, and 120 decibels is the pain threshold. The harmfulness of noise depends on its level, frequency, duration, and a person's exposure to it over a lifetime. Noise can affect a person's hearing capacity as well as other functions. For example, hearing has an effect on balance, so hearing loss can cause poor balance. Excessive and prolonged exposure to noise can cause damage to the ear drums, hearing loss, speech problems, irritability, distraction, and fatigue. Some noisy industries include iron and steel making, automobile manufacturing, forestry, and textile manufacturing. Excessive noise can be controlled by directing the path of the noise, absorbing the noise with special materials and equipment, and providing employees with noise-muffling headphones or earplugs.

A substantial number of Canadians suffer from chronic disease, disability, or emotional stress and lack the community support to cope with these problems.
STATISTICS CANADA

White noise is the sound that is created when the whole range of audible sound frequencies are produced simultaneously at the same level. It is sometimes used in offices to help mask distracting noises.

When continually distracted by noise or other factors, a person's alertness fades significantly after only 30 minutes.

TYPICAL EXAMPLES OF SOUND PRESSURE LEVELS

Sound Pressure Levels, (dB)	Source	Subjective Response
0	No sound	Hearing threshold
10	Rustle of leaf	Faint
20	Buzzing insect	
30	Quiet whisper	
40	Quiet office	
50	Window conditioner	Moderate
60	Conversation	
70	Freight train	
80	Computer print room	
90	Heavy vehicle	Limit of exposure for 8 h
100	Subway station	
110	Rock drill	
120	Propeller plane	Pain threshold
130	Riveting hammer	Feeling threshold
140	Jet engine at 30 m	Danger

Courtesy Canadian Standards Association, CAN/CSA Z412-M89: *A Guideline on Office Ergonomics.*

VIBRATION

Vibration, or a rapid back and forth motion, from machinery or power tools can cause tingling, numbness, pain, loss of dexterity, less sensitivity, and whiteness in the fingers. The result of long-term exposure to vibration can be vibration syndrome, which often affects the fingers. Vibration of the whole body may also create health problems. For example, driving a transport truck can contribute to lower-back pain and degeneration of the spine.

ILLUMINATION

In a 1989 survey, 44 percent of Canadian office workers identified eye strain as a major problem in their jobs.

Illumination refers to the quality and quantity of light. Factors that affect illumination include artificial light, sunlight from windows, colours and textures of surfaces, and the placement of partitions and furniture. Under proper lighting conditions, workers should be able to easily distinguish visual details. Poor lighting can cause headaches, eye strain, nausea, fatigue, stress, and irritability. Fluorescent lights, which are energy-efficient, are used in many offices, although natural lighting and full-spectrum lighting (which artificially recreates natural light) are gentler on people's eyes and show colours more accurately. Task lighting, such as a desk lamp, provides light for specific purposes. Ceilings, floors, walls, partitions, and furniture should help to reflect some light without glare. Ceilings are usually a light colour to reflect light, and floors are usually darker in colour. Textured surfaces tend to prevent glare; smooth surfaces tend to create glare.

INDOOR AIR QUALITY

The quality of indoor air depends on the following factors: **airborne contaminants** (pollutants), **ventilation** (air movement), temperature, **humidity** (moisture in the air), and carbon dioxide levels. Airborne contaminants can be generated inside a building by smoking and by emissions from building materials and furnishings. Since poor ventilation can cause contaminants to be recirculated, fresh and clean air should be continually pumped into a building. Dust particles can enter humans through inhalation or absorption through the skin. Inhaled particles pass into the lungs and may be absorbed into other parts of the body or ingested in small amounts. Extremes in temperature and high humidity can create physical stress. For example, high temperatures have been linked to tension and high blood pressure. Poor indoor air quality can also cause a disorder called sick building syndrome, which includes such symptoms as burning and watery eyes, headaches, dizziness, nausea, numbness of limbs, sore throat, breathing problems, and dry skin.

Plants such as the spider plant, peace lily, Chinese evergreen, banana plant, and philodendron absorb and thrive on airborne contaminants and can therefore reduce the level of these contaminants.

IDEAL INDOOR AIR QUALITY

Airborne contaminants	None
Air movement	3–5 m/min
Temperature	20–23°C in winter and 23–27°C in summer
Humidity	30–50%
Carbon dioxide level	600–800 parts/billion

RADIATION

Radiation refers to the act of atoms emitting light, heat, or other energy that travels in waves. Human beings are constantly exposed to radiation, but this exposure is not necessarily harmful. The sun emits radiation, as do common electrical devices such as irons, toasters, televisions, fluorescent lights, and computers. The effects of computer radiation are still being studied, but some legislation already gives pregnant employees who work regularly at computers the right to do alternative work during pregnancy. Special aprons have also been designed for pregnant workers who sit in front of computers. These measures are a result of concern over the possible harmful effects of radiation on unborn babies. X-ray machines, nuclear power, nuclear testing equipment, and other technology produce radiation that can be harmful if not used safely. For example, a concentrated type of radiation is used medically to assist healing and repair tissue in a specific part of the body, yet exposing the entire body to the same amount of radiation can be fatal. The positive or negative effects of radiation depend on the length and intensity of a person's exposure to it.

Lack of Cleanliness

A dirty workplace can foster mould, bacteria, corrosion, odours, and insects, all of which can affect people's health. Personal hygiene is also essential since germs can be transmitted from worker to worker.

Activity

Classify Your Stress

1 Create a chart like the one below to list the causes of positive and negative stress in your life for each category. Beside each entry, indicate whether it is positive (+) or negative (–). Place a check mark beside the negative stresses that you can control.

2 On a separate sheet of paper, write down ways in which you can reduce negative stress by changing a behaviour, situation, or other factor.

3 Share your chart and list with a close friend who can help you assess your situation and also assist with possible solutions.

FAMILY	SCHOOL	PLACEMENT	PART-TIME JOB	FRIENDS

Journal Entry

Managing Your Stress

In your journal, complete the statements below.

- I handle negative stress in my life by…
- Stress I enjoy occurs when…

▼▼▼▼▼▼▼▼▼▼▼▼▼▼▼▼▼▼▼▼▼▼▼▼▼▼▼▼▼▼▼▼▼▼▼

MONOTONY AND FATIGUE

1 Carefully analyze your tasks and activities at your placement. Are there any that you feel are monotonous? Does your placement provide a variety of activities? List any concerns and possible solutions you may have.

2 Do you generally feel tired or energetic? Analyze the amount of sleep you are getting and your eating habits. Are they adequate for keeping up your energy level? If you think your work conditions are causing fatigue, list the specific causes and possible solutions.

3 With a partner, discuss your observations of your tasks at your placement and how they affect you. How are your concerns and solutions similar or different? What can you conclude?

Make the Connection

Who Is Responsible for Prevention?

Preventing unhealthy working conditions, as well as promoting measures that maintain good health, is essential to healthy workers and a healthy economy. Employers as well as employees share these responsibilities. Individual and collective awareness of health issues combined with government legislation helps to ensure healthy working conditions.

Ideally, employers should provide opportunities and conditions for job satisfaction and employee well-being. They should establish health policies and support management and supervisory staff in enforcing these policies. They should also attempt to encourage and support awareness of health among employees.

Health policies may include ongoing campaigns to promote employee awareness of the issues, good work habits, physical and mental well-being, and stress control. A health support system, required under federal or provincial health legislation, that consists of a first-aid kit and sometimes trained personnel or on-staff doctors or nurses may be organized. Employers and employees may form a health committee whose purpose is to recognize health concerns, evaluate problems in order to effect solutions, and minimize harmful working conditions. Sometimes unhealthy or harmful working conditions can be eliminated or avoided by improving or modifying facilities and work procedures. In some cases, longer breaks, retraining, or job rotation may be necessary. Some legislation requires employers to isolate a process that can cause illness (such as excessive noise) and make the required physical changes to the workplace to resolve the problem.

Management may tend to focus on short-term health issues, which are usually more easily identified and solved, but overlook long-term issues. The costs involved in solving some problems may be a factor in making these decisions. If necessary, employees can work collectively to improve conditions through their unions or company health committees. The federal Canada Labour Code regulates workplace standards and procedures, which are enforced by government inspectors. This code gives employees the right to a healthy workplace, to know about foreseeable hazards, to participate in a health committee, and to refuse work that can endanger themselves or other employees. Provincial governments also have legislation to protect employees, to ensure healthy working conditions, and to compensate employees for work-related illnesses and accidents. Other organizations that are concerned with occupational health include federations of labour, occupational health committees, and public-interest research groups. (For more information on legislation that affects occupational health, see Chapter 12.)

Employees also have responsibilities toward promoting health in the workplace. For example, when you are on the job, report any conditions that you believe are unhealthy or dangerous, know how to use equipment properly, and maintain sensible working habits. Your personal lifestyle can also produce illness that can affect your job performance. Make sure you have regular physical examinations by your doctor, eye doctor, and dentist. In order to help reduce stress and fatigue and to maintain and improve your physical condition, try to fit exercise into your schedule at least three times a week. To maximize the benefits of exercise, keep your heart rate in the target zone for your age for 15 minutes. The lower end of the zone is 170 beats per minute minus your age; the upper end of the zone is 200 beats per minute minus your age. Proper nutrition will also help prevent illness. What you put into your body on and off the job affects your judgement, behaviour, and reaction times. To maintain your health, follow these nutritional guidelines:

- Eat a variety of foods.
- Emphasize cereals, breads, other grain products, vegetables, and fruit in your diet.
- Choose low-fat dairy products, lean meats, and foods prepared with little or no fat.
- Achieve and maintain a healthy body mass with regular exercise and a healthy diet.
- Drink eight glasses of water a day.
- Limit salt and caffeine in your diet.

A century ago, most of the population got enough exercise from work to stay in shape. Now, less than 1 percent of all energy expended in North American workplaces comes from human muscle.

1 In small groups, select six health issues from those listed on pages 189–194 to study further. Brainstorm jobs and work situations in which each issue would be important, and list possible solutions for each situation. For example, excessive noise is an important health issue for stage crews during rock concerts. The solutions might include wearing special headphones or earplugs. Include solutions that are the responsibility of the employer as well as the employee.

2 On your own, create a poster or a brochure to encourage prevention of one health issue that you discussed in your group. Your poster or brochure should be directed to a particular job or occupation and to either employers or employees.

Journal Entry

Maintaining Your Health

In your journal, complete the statement below.

- To ensure a healthy lifestyle I will...

CASE STUDY

Shared Solutions for Health Problems

SABRINA

Sabrina works in an office as a computer operator. She constantly complains about lower-back, neck, and shoulder pain, headaches, and eye strain. As a result, she has constant discomfort, her daily productivity is not what it used to be, and she is often absent from work.

SAM

Sam has read in a health and safety magazine that people working at computer terminals should switch to other tasks for 15 minutes out of every hour. He presents the information to his union, which includes it in contract negotiations. The union is unsuccessful in having this clause included in its collective agreement.

JEREMY

A few months ago, Jeremy's company moved into a new office building. Jeremy has noticed that about an hour and a half after he arrives at work he starts getting a headache and itchy eyes. Toward the end of the week, he often feels nauseous and tired. Shortly after leaving work, he begins to feel better. He has recently learned that other employees in the building are experiencing similar problems. Jeremy thinks he is suffering from sick building syndrome.

CAROL

Carol is a fit and healthy 15-year-old who works as a cashier in a plant nursery. She stands on a concrete floor for long periods and often has to peer over the counter to see customer merchandise on low, flat carts. Sometimes she lifts heavy items to find the price tags. At the end of a shift, she complains that her back, legs, and feet hurt. When talking with other cashiers, Carol learns that they, too, are feeling the same aches and pains.

▼ ▼ ▼

Complete a chart like the one below to list for each case the solutions that are the responsibility of management and the solutions that are the responsibility of employees. Rank your solutions using the following scale: 1—ideal, 2—good, and 3—acceptable.

MANAGEMENT SOLUTIONS	RANK	EMPLOYEE SOLUTIONS	RANK

Effects of Health on Productivity

*I*n business, **productivity** refers to the capacity of an employee to create or produce during a given period of time. The more a person produces, the greater his or her level of productivity. For employers, high productivity is desirable for higher profits. Recurring health problems affect productivity in that much energy can be misspent—that is, not directly used for production. For example, poor health can cause workers to slow down, thus reducing productivity. Employee illness can also cause increased absenteeism, more mistakes, loss of skilled employees, and poor morale. When morale is low, employees tend to disregard employer concerns and will arrive late, leave early, and work slowly. Employees may also be able to concentrate on their work for only short periods of time, make frequent trips to the washroom, or leave their desks or work stations frequently. For employees, poor health conditions cause physical or mental strain, resulting in pain, unhappiness, and lost working time. A healthy work environment increases efficiency, improves employee performance, stimulates morale, improves public and labour relations, and minimizes financial losses.

In any given week, about 6 percent of the work force in Canada is off sick for one or more days.

For every day's work lost in Canada due to strikes and lock-outs, six working days are lost through workplace accidents and disease.

ROGER I. SIMON, DON DIPPO,
ARLEEN SCHENKE
LEARNING WORK

"I know a healthy employee is an efficient employee, Brewer. But you're getting sweat all over accounts payable."

By Jef Mallett. Reprinted by permission.

Massage Therapist Takes the Pain Out of Work

by Allan Thompson

Massage therapist Adrian Symonds is building a profitable small business treating the aches and pains of Ontario workers.

The 45-year-old founder and owner of Creative Health Services does on-site physical therapy for workers at such companies as Canadian Tire, Levi Strauss, and Kimberly-Clarke. His simple pitch is that he can save companies thousands in Worker's Compensation Board claims by treating workers on the job before their aches and pains lead to costly injuries.

"It's a very difficult business to get into, because often companies will say, 'This is a very good idea,' but can't be convinced to spend the money on it," Symonds said. "But I save them money."

One of his best clients is Canadian Tire Corp. Symonds says it took him four years to persuade the company to hire him; now it has nothing but praise.

"It became really clear to me and I could see a lot of benefits from having him around," said Mary Jane Nodwell, health services co-ordinator with Canadian Tire.

"Having a professional health care person on-site can very often be effective in preventing people from going off work," Nodwell said. "People trust him and believe in the things he advises."

"And it's not just a passive treatment like traditional health care—this idea that somebody else will make you better."

Companies hire Symonds to be available in the workplace for two to five hours a week.

Workers can either request appointments through the supervisor or health nurse, or simply walk in the door and complain about a sore neck.

While most of his work involves strain injuries and lower back problems, Symonds has become much more pro-active in his work, encouraging workers to start exercise programs. He uses tai-chi workout techniques, conducts back education programs, and lately, has begun extensive job demand assessments.

"I've been around some factories so long I begin to stick my nose in as many places as I can that will affect health care. My role just keeps expanding."

Lately, he has been taking a photography course at Humber College so he can photograph people's work stations for better assessments of proper ways to do the job. He has also begun recording work practices on video for the same reason.

And he's very aggressively encouraging his clients to become more active. "The problem with life in a factory is that people confuse work and exercise, which is really too bad," Symonds said.

Even people doing hard physical work may not be getting proper exercise, since their tasks might focus only on certain parts of the body and totally neglect others.

But psychologically they feel they're working hard and don't need exercise, he said.

Symonds got into massage relatively late in his career. Before 1985, when he completed the course work required to be a registered massage therapist, he had already worked on the docks in Halifax, planted trees in British Columbia, and taught martial arts classes.

He started by doing some workshops for occupational health nurses and writing articles in a couple of industry journals. He began the company in 1985 and has built it through word of mouth.

Reprinted with permission—The Toronto Star Syndicate.

1 How can treating employee aches and pains save a company money?

2 How else can treatment of aches and pains benefit a company?

3 What forms of illness prevention does Symonds encourage?

Ergonomics

Employers began to understand the importance of productivity in the early 1900s. In order to improve employee efficiency, workplace designers tried to create more efficient work spaces and stations. For example, the Ford Motor Company introduced the assembly line in 1914, giving each employee the responsibility for a single repetitive action. Before that time, the assembly process included teams of employees working on all the steps of production. As a result of the new process, assembly time was cut drastically. But employees complained about the new technology; Ford responded by increasing wages in order to combat increased employee turnover.

Early workplace designers assumed that improving worker efficiency would always result in greater productivity, but they did not consider the physical and mental impact on workers and that these factors also influence productivity. In other words, the most efficient way to work may not be the most productive. High productivity occurs through the efforts of healthy, happy, and safe employees.

Ergonomics is the study of the physical and mental relationship between a person and his or her work tools, furniture, equipment, and work space. Its goals are to maximize productivity and efficiency and minimize human suffering. Knowledge from sciences such as physiology and psychology about the limitations and capabilities of human beings is integrated with knowledge from studies in such areas as engineering and management.

Ergonomic studies are done in offices, stores, factories, and other workplaces to evaluate working conditions and make recommendations for correcting problems. For example, office employees commonly use telephones, photocopiers, computers, calculators, filing cabinets, and chairs on wheels. All of this interaction should be evaluated in an ergonomic study of an office environment. Major areas of study in ergonomics include:

Henry Ford, founder of the automobile manufacturing company, once said that if you save ten steps a day for 12 000 employees, you save much wasted motion and misspent energy.

- Instrumentation, controls, and displays on equipment and machinery.
- Effects of work station design on attention, memory, and quality.
- Effects of noise, temperature, lighting, and other environmental factors on employee performance.
- Effects of fatigue due to shift length, night shifts, and other factors.
- Anatomy, body posture, strength, and workplace layout.
- Age, height, mass, ability, and gender differences.

The following checklist outlines other ergonomic concerns of workplace designers.

A CHECKLIST OF ERGONOMIC PRINCIPLES

1 Be aware of the structure and operation of the human body so that your design suits the needs of the user, rather than the other way around.

2 Allow for the variations between individual users of your design, such as their height, sex, age, weight [mass], strengths, and disabilities.

3 Leave enough space in and around what you are designing to permit safe and convenient use, ease of maintenance and repair, and space for moving doors, drawers, or other moving parts.

4 Avoid dangerous projections, sharp corners, and knife-like edges which cause cuts, bruises, torn clothing, and uncomfortable pressure points, especially on undersurfaces where they cannot be seen.

5 Reduce the need for unnecessary reaching, stooping, twisting, and walking, so that the design can be used more efficiently without causing excessive fatigue.

6 Design products which must be grasped or operated by the hand so that the hand is not forced into an uncomfortable, tiring, or weakened position.

7 Where use of the design involves the carrying out of a number of tasks, arrange things so that these tasks can be carried out in a logical, orderly sequence.

8 Design to take advantage of well-established patterns of human behaviour, such as in the perception of visual information, hand and eye movement, and in pedestrian traffic flow.

9 Avoid boring the user of your design or straining the vision by providing adequate lighting and visibility, clear legibility, and a sufficiently stimulating, colourful, and well-organized visual environment.

10 Design so that in the event of failure or emergency conditions the product cannot become unusually dangerous or injurious.

11 In all aspects of designing use common sense, remembering that the user, like the designer, is not always at peak performance and is capable of errors of judgement.

James Warren, "Simple Methods for Ergonomic Design," *Design Engineering*, Maclean-Hunter, Toronto, 1982. Reprinted with permission.

Your Occupation and Health

In your journal, complete the statements below.

- The occupation I have chosen has working conditions that, if not handled correctly, could lead to work-related illness. I need to ensure that both myself and my employer take preventive measures. The working conditions that could lead to illness are...

- The preventive measures that could be taken are...

CASE STUDY

Colour Goes to Work

THE WAY COLOUR AFFECTS US ON THE JOB

Colour is nothing more than the way we perceive light and its reflection. But colour in turn changes our perceptions, alters our mood, even raises our blood pressure. Such an important design element can't be left to chance or fashion in the workplace, where it has a direct impact on productivity. Instead, a well-designed colour scheme can become another effective tool in an office that's responsive to its occupants' needs. The ability to apply colour in imaginative ways is part skill, part gift, and it's an area that requires extensive design training. But all of us share certain thoughts and attitudes about colour—and that common ground is where design thinking starts.

IT'S PERSONAL

Colour, then, is really an individual preference. And certain personality types react differently to the same colour palette. An outgoing, active person will respond well to an intense or highly saturated colour. A more introverted person will work better in an office with a less saturated, less intense colour scheme. Colour can't change the behaviour of a person, but the right colour scheme can reinforce certain working patterns and behaviours. And for certain types of work—physical labour or reflective thinking—the use of colour can help reduce fatigue. A designer planning the colours for an office can take into account the personalities of the people who work there, in order to reinforce everyone's productivity.

SHEDDING LIGHT ON COLOUR

Lighting in an office has an impact on the colour scheme all its own. Light actually alters colour; and since different types of light will introduce new elements to colour, both must be designed in consideration of each other. A professional designer will be able to balance these two important aspects of design in order to create the best effect for both.

CHARTING COLOUR'S SUCCESS

Just to point out the effect that colour can have in the workplace, here are some results from a study conducted by the National Industrial Conference Board. In interviewing 350 companies that had changed or used colour in their offices, the research team found that 27.5 percent felt their productivity had increased because of the new colour scheme. A total of 64.7 percent said that the colour had improved lighting. In addition, 19.1

percent said fatigue had been reduced, and 14.7 percent said absenteeism had gone down. Overall, 75 percent of the companies interviewed had positive results to report, simply because of new applications of colour.

HOW DOES COLOUR FEEL?

Certain colours evoke almost universal feelings and responses. For example:

Red This colour overstimulates and raises blood pressure, but also creates a feeling of physical warmth.

Black and Brown These colours, except as accents, create feelings of fatigue and decrease the perception of light.

White It increases the feeling of light and space, but it's hard on people who work at computer screens.

Blue It decreases blood pressure and is relaxing to the point that its overuse makes people "feel blue" or depressed.

Yellow This colour can cause eyestrain in certain applications, but it stimulates and raises spirits.

Green A quiet and refreshing colour. Green is often perceived by people as their favourite colour, and has a calming effect.

_____

Design-Lines Colour Schemes, Volume 1, Issue 1, First Quarter, 1989, published by Schendel, the office people.

▼ ▼ ▼

1 Visit three different buildings, such as stores, restaurants, schools, or offices. Record the uses of colour in each place by taking notes, photos, or videos. You might want to study the colour scheme at your placement as well. In writing, comment on your reaction to each colour scheme.

2 Imagine that you are starting a small business with a few employees in an industry that interests you. How would you want your workplace designed? In writing, outline your workplace design, including diagrams where appropriate.

▼ ▼

ERGONOMICS ASSESSMENT

1 The ergonomics checklist that follows can be used to assess your work station and workplace. A copy of the checklist will be provided by your teacher; modify it as necessary for your placement.

2 At your placement, complete the checklist. With your supervisor's permission, gather any brochures or training materials your company may have that address health issues. Has an ergonomics assessment been completed for this workplace in the past? If so, ask your supervisor for information about this assessment.

3 Discuss with your supervisor the preventive measures that are taken at your placement to ensure healthy working conditions. Are training seminars given, do posters promote good practices, and is there a health committee? Are the employer's and employees' responsibilities clearly outlined?

4 In a report to your teacher, outline the results of your ergonomic assessment. List the ways in which you would modify your current work area and explain why you would make each change.

ERGONOMICS CHECKLIST

Company name: _____
Job title: _____
Brief job description: _____
_____
_____

Work Station	**Yes**	**No**
• Is there sufficient space for completing tasks and for the required equipment?	___	___
• Are frequently used items and equipment within easy reach for your body size?	___	___
• Is your body supported sufficiently most of the time?	___	___
• Can you stand or sit to complete tasks?	___	___
• Is the floor stable and not slippery?	___	___
• Is the height of the work surface adjustable for users of different sizes?	___	___
• Do you have a footrest?	___	___
• Is your movement around the work station impaired by any objects?	___	___
• Can you maintain a comfortable posture most of the time?	___	___
• Are you standing or sitting uncomfortably for long periods of time?	___	___
• Is the work station designed so that people assigned to the job are not restricted by their age, gender, or body mass?	___	___
• Was your work station modified in any way for ergonomic reasons? If so, how was it modified?	___	___

Seating		
• Is your chair stable and rotatable?	___	___
• In a normal working posture, is your back fully supported?	___	___
• Can the chair be adjusted easily from a sitting position? (The backrest and height should adjust.)	___	___
• Is the chair fabric breathable?	___	___

	Yes	No

- Is the seat contoured for the human body? ____ ____
- Are armrests suitable and detachable? ____ ____
- Can the chair be moved close to the work surface without difficulty? ____ ____
- Is entry and exit from the chair easy? ____ ____

Environment

- Is the air temperature within normal levels? ____ ____
- Does the air temperature fluctuate extremely? ____ ____
- Is there a continuous supply of fresh air? ____ ____
- Are humidity levels acceptable? ____ ____
- Can normal conversation be heard without difficulty? ____ ____
- Is noise kept to a minimum? ____ ____
- Do the workplace colours evoke a positive response from you? ____ ____
- Is there sufficient contrast for seeing? ____ ____
- Are the surfaces resistant to glare? ____ ____
- Is lighting and visibility adequate for all tasks? ____ ____
- Is there sufficient task lighting? ____ ____
- Are extremes in well-lit and dark areas avoided? ____ ____
- Are waste materials disposed of appropriately? ____ ____

Computer Use

- With your head and body in a comfortable position, is the image size on the monitor and its quality acceptable? ____ ____
- Is there a nonreflective surface on the monitor? ____ ____
- Are contrast and brightness controls within easy reach? ____ ____
- Can the keyboard be placed in a comfortable position for typing? ____ ____
- Do the keys respond well to a gentle touch? ____ ____

Controls/Displays

- Are displays legible? ____ ____
- Can information be obtained quickly? ____ ____
- Are unnecessary displays eliminated? ____ ____
- Are controls within easy reach? ____ ____
- Are dials located near their corresponding displays? ____ ____
- Do the controls respond to a minimal amount of force? ____ ____
- Is the control layout logical? ____ ____

	Yes	No
▪ Are controls easily identified and clearly labelled?	____	____
▪ Are controls colour-coded in a sensible way?	____	____

Machinery/Tools

	Yes	No
▪ Does the equipment operate smoothly?	____	____
▪ Does the equipment have sufficient safety guards?	____	____
▪ Does the equipment operate within reasonable noise limits?	____	____
▪ Are the controls easy to use and within easy reach?	____	____
▪ Do you use tools that have a quality handgrip?	____	____
▪ Can you avoid working with a bent wrist?	____	____
▪ Can you avoid vibration in your hands, arms, or body while you work?	____	____
▪ Can you avoid applying a lot of pressure or force with your hands or wrists while working?	____	____
▪ Can you avoid using a twisting motion of the wrist?	____	____

Posture/Movement

	Yes	No
▪ Can you change your position often?	____	____
▪ Do tasks involve focussing on items at a variety of distances?	____	____
▪ Do your arms and elbows hang loosely at the sides of your body?	____	____
▪ Are your wrists straight?	____	____
▪ Is your neck straight or at less than a 15-degree angle?	____	____
▪ Is your spine straight and well-supported?	____	____
▪ Is your posture correct and relaxed?	____	____
▪ Can you avoid leaning over excessively?	____	____
▪ Can you avoid working with your arms raised above your shoulders?	____	____
▪ Can you avoid working with your elbows out and away from your body?	____	____
▪ Can you avoid a lot of repetitive elbow and shoulder movement?	____	____
▪ Can you avoid repeatedly reaching above your head or behind your shoulder?	____	____
▪ Can you avoid lifting, loading, or unloading heavy materials (more than about 15 kg) from high or low spots?	____	____
▪ Can you avoid twisting or stretching your body in an uncomfortable manner?	____	____
▪ Can you avoid pushing or pulling on loads?	____	____

	Yes	No
▪ Do your muscles rarely get tired, weak, or sore while doing your job?	___	___
▪ Are there ways to change your job to reduce demands on your back?	___	___

Summary
- Is employee absenteeism within normal levels?   ___ ___
- Is productivity and efficiency high?   ___ ___
- Do employees rarely complain about working conditions or make mistakes?   ___ ___

- Can you think of ways to accomplish your job with less effort or stress?

_____

_____

_____

- What changes would you like to see in the tasks or equipment given to you to do your job?

_____

_____

_____

WHAT HAVE YOU LEARNED?

▼ ▼ ▼

1 What major health issues affect workers?

2 a How can workers influence occupational health policies?
b Why might workers ignore health concerns?

3 a How can employers influence occupational health policies?
b Why might employers not improve conditions to ensure a healthy workplace?

4 Describe how health affects productivity in the workplace.

5 How can the relationship among people, equipment, and work environment be improved?

6 List five basic principles of ergonomics that you think are the most important.

CHAPTER 12

SAFETY

After completing this chapter, you should be able to:

▼ ▼ ▼

- Describe the causes and types of common injuries in the workplace.
- Recognize employee and employer responsibilities for safe working conditions.
- Understand legislation that regulates safety in the workplace.
- Know how to report unsafe working conditions and work-related injuries.
- Recognize the benefits of workers' compensation.

▼ ▼ ▼

injury

Workplace Hazardous
    Materials Information
    System (WHMIS)

first aid

hazard

workers' compensation

Causes of Injuries

Feeling angry and frustrated at work can cause injuries. Take time to calm down before you continue to work.

Safety in the workplace should ensure good health among employees as well as freedom from **injury.** Most injuries on the job are caused by a combination of unsafe actions and conditions. Some literature on workplace safety discusses accidents, meaning undesired events that result in physical harm, but many safety officials favour the word "injury" in place of "accident." The word injury suggests that events are controllable. Safety officials believe that all injuries are preventable and, therefore, controllable. Below are some major causes and types of work-related injuries.

MAJOR CAUSES OF INJURIES	TYPES OF INJURIES
• Slips, trips, and falls	• Back problems, cuts, abrasions, concussion, breaks, and strains
• Improper use of equipment and poorly maintained or faulty equipment	• Injury to or loss of hands, fingers, eyes, other limbs, and hearing
• Improper lifting techniques	• Back problems, muscle strain, and torn ligaments
• Not turning off the power when repairing machinery	• Electrocution, burns, scalds, and drowning
• Entry into unsafe confined spaces	• Gas poisoning and suffocation
• Improper use or storage of chemicals and other hazardous materials	• Poisoning and severe burns

SLIPS, TRIPS, AND FALLS

If you fall, reduce your chances of injury by relaxing your muscles, absorbing the impact of the fall with your legs and arms, and rolling in the direction of the fall.

Most injuries both on and off the job are caused by slips, trips, and falls. Slips usually occur as a result of hidden steps, slippery surfaces (such as waxed, wet, or greasy floors), and loose flooring or carpeting. Trips are caused by clutter and obstacles in hallways or on stairs, improperly placed or secured electrical cords, dropped objects that are not picked up (such as a pencil or machine part), and poorly placed furniture. Falls are caused by improper use of ladders, makeshift ladders (such as a stack of boxes) or stools, improper use of safety equipment, and unstable platforms. All of these injuries can be foreseen and prevented. The employer should ensure that all repairs are completed, antislip materials are used, spills are cleaned up, and warning signs are used for wet floors or hidden steps. The employee should keep alert to potential hazards. To avoid slips, trips, and falls, wear shoes that are in good repair and that have low heels and rubber (not plastic) soles.

IMPROPERLY USED, MAINTAINED, OR FAULTY EQUIPMENT

Employers are responsible for ensuring that routine safety checks of equipment are conducted. Employees should use safety guards if required, wear protective gear designed to shield against injury, and follow all procedures as outlined in the operator's manual.

Before you use equipment, make sure you know exactly how it operates, its safety features, and how to use it properly.

Safety Equipment

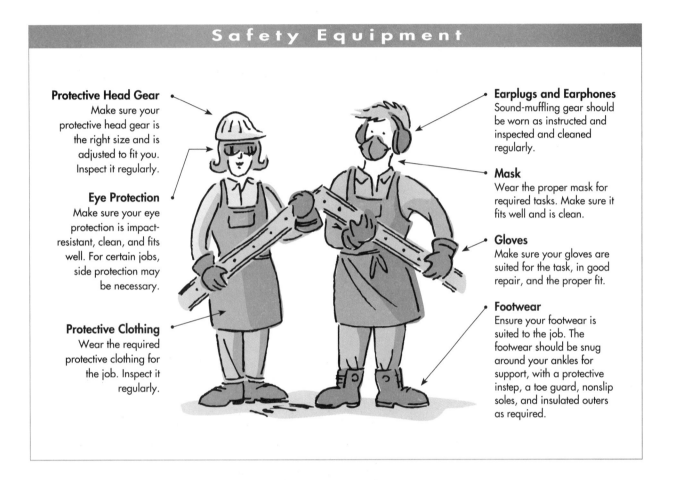

Protective Head Gear
Make sure your protective head gear is the right size and is adjusted to fit you. Inspect it regularly.

Eye Protection
Make sure your eye protection is impact-resistant, clean, and fits well. For certain jobs, side protection may be necessary.

Protective Clothing
Wear the required protective clothing for the job. Inspect it regularly.

Earplugs and Earphones
Sound-muffling gear should be worn as instructed and inspected and cleaned regularly.

Mask
Wear the proper mask for required tasks. Make sure it fits well and is clean.

Gloves
Make sure your gloves are suited for the task, in good repair, and the proper fit.

Footwear
Ensure your footwear is suited to the job. The footwear should be snug around your ankles for support, with a protective instep, a toe guard, nonslip soles, and insulated outers as required.

IMPROPER LIFTING TECHNIQUES

Before lifting or moving an object, assess its weight. Use good judgement and proper lifting techniques: bend your knees, keep your back straight, and lift with your legs, not with your arms or shoulders. Employers should have the necessary mechanical aids required to lift heavy objects, such as carts, dollies, and forklift trucks.

REPAIRING MACHINERY WITHOUT TURNING OFF THE POWER

Fatalities and serious injuries occur too often when maintenance work is being done and the power is inadvertently turned on or valves and pipes are opened before the work is complete. The power needs to be turned off and locked to prevent the machine from being turned on too soon. Workers should be provided with appropriate locks for this purpose, and they must also be trained in the proper safety procedures.

To be safe on the job, complete your tasks step by step—avoid shortcuts.

Entry into Unsafe Confined Spaces

Confined spaces include walk-in freezers, storerooms, sewers, culverts, vats, and silos. When working in a confined space, consider the following: Can someone outside open a line that lets in liquid, gas, or any other material by accident? Is there sufficient oxygen inside? Could there be poisonous gas? Could a machine accidently start up and cause an injury? Can you get out safely?

Improper Use or Storage of Hazardous Materials

Chemicals and other hazardous materials must be used and stored correctly. Not all hazards are visible—some toxic substances cannot be seen or smelled. In Canada, the **Workplace Hazardous Materials Information System (WHMIS)** is designed to protect Canadians and provide workers and employers with vital information about hazardous materials used in the workplace to promote safe working practices. Information is conveyed through labels, material safety data sheets, and worker training programs. The WHMIS symbols are shown below, along with a sample label, which would appear on a container of the hazardous material.

Class A—Compressed gas

Class B—Flammable and combustible material, including the following divisions:

1 Flammable gas   4 Flammable solid
2 Flammable liquid   5 Flammable aerosol
3 Combustible liquid   6 Reactive flammable material

Class C—Oxidizing material

Class D—Poisonous and infectious material, including:

1 Materials causing immediate and serious toxic effects
   Subdivision A: A very toxic material
   Subdivision B: Toxic material

2 Materials causing other toxic effects
Subdivision A: A very toxic material
Subdivision B: Toxic material

3 Biohazardous infections material

CLASS E—Corrosive material

CLASS F—Dangerously reactive material

Courtesy Industrial Accident Prevention Association

METHANOL

–Flammable liquid
–Vapour harmful
–May cause blindness

–Keep away from sources of ignition
–In case of fire, use alcohol foam
–Avoid prolonged or repeated breathing of vapour and contact with skin

IF INHALED: Move victim to fresh air. If breathing has stopped, give artificial respiration or oxygen.

IF SWALLOWED: If the victim is conscious, give one glass of warm water containing one tablespoon [15 mL] of salt in order to induce vomiting. Keep victim warm and cover eyes to exclude light. Contact a physician immediately.

IF SPLASHED ON SKIN OR EYES: Flush affected areas with water for 15–20 minutes.

SEE MATERIAL SAFETY DATA SHEET

NAME AND ADDRESS OF SUPPLIER:

Courtesy Industrial Accident Prevention Association

A C T I V I T Y

Are You Safe?

1 Use the safety questionnaire below to evaluate how safe you are at work. In your notebook, write the number of each statement and respond with Never, Occasionally, Almost Always, or Always.

SAFETY QUESTIONNAIRE

1 I take time to calm down before acting when I am emotional. _____

2 I seek information about safe practices and procedures. _____

3 I focus on my tasks without distraction. _____

4 I remind others of safe practices. _____

5 I use equipment for its intended purpose only. _____

6 I do not cover up other people's unsafe practices. _____

7 I use the appropriate safety equipment. _____

8 I inspect my work area for safety hazards. _____

9 I lift items properly in order to prevent back injuries. _____

10 I turn off all equipment before repairing or adjusting it. _____

11 I put items in their proper places after using them. _____

2 In small groups, compare your answers. Discuss how you can change your Never and Occasionally responses into Almost Always or Always responses.

Journal Entry

Improving Your Safety Habits

In your journal, complete the statement below.

- I can improve my safety habits and practices by...

Injury Prevention

*P*reventing injury is the most important aspect of safety in the workplace. Injuries can be prevented in three ways: with proper safety education and training, with responsible behaviour by both employees and employers, and by reporting unsafe conditions.

During safety education and training:

- Employees participate in a thorough workplace orientation conducted by the employer.
- All staff reads the appropriate operation manuals carefully and learns the proper procedures.
- Supervisors carefully monitor employees when they are learning how to operate new machinery.
- Employees attend seminars and workshops on safety conducted or organized by the employer.
- All staff takes courses in general safety for the workplace. Some or all employees may receive training in **first aid** (emergency medical care or treatment).
- Employees learn emergency action plans developed by their employer; for example, what to do in case of a fire, chemical hazard, or robbery.

Responsible employee behaviour is important, since injuries are often caused by individuals who conduct themselves improperly, take short-cuts, or are physically unfit. An employee who practises safe work habits will gain respect from his or her co-workers and the community. Co-workers prefer to work with a responsible person because he or she helps to reduce the risk of injury. Employers also seek responsible employees because they help prevent injuries, absenteeism, and reduced productivity, and they encourage other workers to stay in the company because of safe working practices.

Employers must also act responsibly by providing a complete safety program that includes training, safety equipment, a safe environment (for example, providing fire extinguishers, fire alarms, sprinkler systems, emergency exits, and first-aid kits), and properly maintained and serviced equipment. Every employer's safety program should include a procedure for reporting unsafe conditions. Many workplaces have established joint health and safety committees that include members of management as well as employees. These committees conduct inspections, identify **hazards** (potentially harmful equipment or conditions), listen to or read reports from employees, make recommendations to management, and monitor clean-up operations to ensure that hazards are eliminated. Unions often play a key role in forming and maintaining health and safety committees.

Statistics show that young people who are new to the work force are the employees most likely to be injured. People who have recently been transferred to a new job are the next group most likely to be injured. The

Over one million Canadians are injured every year in work-related accidents. In one year, approximately 60 percent of these injuries were sufficiently severe or disabling that employees needed time away from work for recuperation, rehabilitation, or hospitalization.
STATISTICS CANADA

About 10 000 Canadian workers are killed on the job every year.

graphs that follow show percentages of specific reported injuries in relation to age of injured workers. Notice how younger workers reported more finger injuries and amputations while older workers reported more back injuries. Good safety practices can prevent injuries and can even save your life. In fact, it is the legal responsibility of every worker to practise safe work habits.

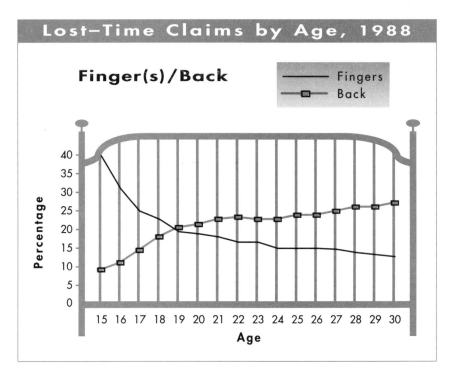

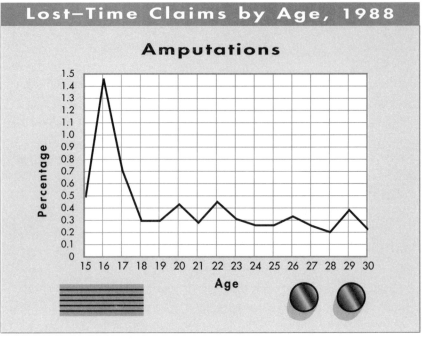

Courtesy Industrial Accident Prevention Association

In small groups, discuss the following questions:

1 Why do you think finger injuries and amputations are high among 15- to 18-year-olds?

2 What jobs would have a high risk potential for injury to fingers and limbs?

3 a What stories can you share regarding injuries from unsafe practices on and off the job?

b How could these injuries have been prevented?

Taking Unnecessary Risks

In your journal, respond to the questions below.

- What unnecessary risks do I take in my daily life?
- How can I change this behaviour?

CASE STUDY

He Should Have Stayed in Bed

Sam Ng is late for work and in a hurry to make up for lost time. The traffic is all snarled and Sam's patience is wearing thin. Once in the parking lot, he has a difficult time finding a parking space. There is a space at the back of the lot, which causes Sam to feel even more rushed. Dashing up the sidewalk, Sam slips on the ice. After he picks up all his belongings, he continues to rush, but this time with a slight limp. Rounding a corner in the hall, Sam bumps into Nicole and causes her to bang her hip on the corner of the photocopier. She, too, now limps to her desk. Sam is relieved to finally be at his desk. He swivels in his chair to answer the telephone and the chair tips over, causing Sam to bump his head on the wall. While trying to take the telephone message, he searches through a drawer for a pencil or pen. In the search, he cuts his finger on a sharp object and stabs himself with a thumbtack. Angrily, he slams the desk drawer shut—on his fingers. Thinking a cup of coffee would be a welcome relief, he walks toward the coffee maker and trips over a box of pamphlets that has just been delivered. Anxious to rid his office of this safety hazard, he stoops over to pick up the box and wrenches his back. Once he recovers, he decides the pamphlets should be filed. He opens the top drawer of the file cabinet and loads it with pamphlets. Luckily, Nicole, no longer limping, is able to quickly assist Sam before the whole cabinet topples. A very shaken Sam pours a steaming mug of coffee. Fortunately, his suit jacket absorbs the coffee he spills before it burns his skin.

▼ ▼ ▼

1 Complete a copy of the chart below in your notebook. List each hazard outlined in the case study and its cause, as well as prevention methods for both employees and management.

2 Compare charts with a partner, and discuss the similarities and differences between them.

HAZARD	CAUSE OF THE HAZARD		PREVENTION METHODS	
	EMPLOYEES	MANAGEMENT	EMPLOYEES	MANAGEMENT

Regulating Health and Safety in the Workplace

*T*he occupational health and safety section of the Canada Labour Code outlines safety regulations for industries that are under federal authority. Similar provincial legislation exists for other industries. This legislation was the first to deal exclusively with health and safety in Canada. Under this code, employees have the right to a safe and healthy workplace. The three basic rights outlined in this code are the right to know, the right to participate, and the right to refuse dangerous work.

The right to know means that employers must inform employees of foreseeable hazards in the workplace as well as prevention measures. Employers are also responsible for displaying the Canada Labour Code in the workplace, details of the company safety program, and other health and safety information. The right to participate means that employees may assist in identifying health and safety issues and in resolving these issues through a health and safety committee. The right to refuse dangerous work means that if an employee has reason to believe that a situation presents a danger to herself or himself, she or he can refuse to work without disciplinary action from the employer providing that proper reporting procedures are followed.

The provinces and territories have legislation that clearly outlines workplace health and safety regulations for industries that are not under federal authority. The requirements of these health and safety acts are similar to the requirements of the Canada Labour Code. The following excerpt from the Ontario Occupational Health and Safety Act defines the responsibilities of employers, supervisors, and workers.

Legislation gives Canadian workers the right to know about forseeable health and safety problems, participate in a health and safety committee, and refuse work when their health and safety could be endangered.

14—(1) An employer shall ensure that,

(a) the equipment, materials, and protective devices as prescribed are provided;

(b) the equipment, materials, and protective devices provided by him are maintained in good condition;

(c) the measures and procedures prescribed are carried out in the workplace;

(d) the equipment, materials, and protective devices provided by him are used as prescribed; and

(e) a floor, roof, wall, pillar, support, or other part of a workplace is capable of supporting all loads to which it may be subjected without causing the materials therein to be stressed beyond the allowable unit stresses established under the *Building Code Act*.

(2) Without limiting the strict duty imposed by subsection (1), an employer shall,

(a) provide information, instruction, and supervision to a worker to protect the health or safety of the worker;

(aa) in a medical emergency for the purpose of diagnosis or treatment, provide, upon request, information in the possession of the employer, including confidential business information, to a legally qualified medical practitioner and to such other persons as may be prescribed;

(b) when appointing a supervisor, appoint a competent person;

(c) acquaint a worker or a person in authority over a worker with any hazard in the work and in the handling, storage, use, disposal, and transport of any article, device, equipment, or a biological, chemical, or physical agent;

(d) afford assistance and co-operation to a committee and a health and safety representative in the carrying out by the committee and the health and safety representative of any of their functions;

(e) only employ in or about a workplace a person over such age as may be prescribed;

(f) not knowingly permit a person who is under such age as may be prescribed to be in or about a workplace;

(g) take every precaution reasonable in the circumstances for the protection of a worker;

(h) post, in the workplace, a copy of this Act and any explanatory material prepared by the Ministry, both in English and the majority language of the workplace, outlining the rights, responsibilities, and duties or workers;

(i) prepare and review at least annually a written occupational health and safety policy and develop and maintain a program to implement that policy;

(j) post in a conspicuous location in the workplace a copy of the occupational health and safety policy;...

16—(1) A supervisor shall ensure that a worker,

(a) works in the manner and with the protective devices, measures, and procedures required by this Act and the regulations; and

(b) uses or wears the equipment, protective devices, or clothing that his employer requires to be used or worn.

(2) Without limiting the duty imposed by subsection (1), a supervisor shall,

(a) advise a worker of the existence of any potential or actual danger to the health or safety of the worker of which the supervisor is aware;

(b) where so prescribed, provide a worker with written instructions as to the measures and procedures to be taken for protection of the worker; and

(c) take every precaution reasonable in the circumstances for the protection of a worker.

17—(1) A worker shall,

(a) work in compliance with the provisions of this Act and the regulations;

(b) use or wear the equipment, protective devices, or clothing that his employer requires to be used or worn;

(c) report to his employer or supervisor the absence of or defect in any equipment or protective device of which he is aware and which may endanger himself or another worker; and

(d) report to his employer or supervisor any contravention of this Act or the regulations or the existence of any hazard of which he knows.

(2) No worker shall,

(a) remove or make ineffective any protective device required by the regulations or by his employer, without providing an adequate temporary protective device and when the need for removing or making ineffective the protective device has ceased, the protective device shall be replaced immediately;

(b) use or operate any equipment, machine, device, or thing or work in a manner that may endanger himself or any other worker; or

(c) engage in any prank, contest, feat of strength, unnecessary running, or rough and boisterous conduct.

Occupational Health and Safety Act. © Reproduced with permission from the Queen's Printer for Ontario.

Who Is Responsible?

BATA INDUSTRIES

Investigators for the Ontario Ministry of the Environment discovered large quantities of toxic waste and solvents improperly stored at a Bata Industries plant site. Many of the 285 barrels and drums, as well as a large storage tank, were found to be decaying and leaking chemicals into the ground. Charges of environmental pollution were laid against the chairman and two other Bata executives as well as against the company.

▼ ▼ ▼

1 What are the implications of individuals being held responsible for unsafe company practices?

2 Do you think fines are an effective means of preventing similar situations? Explain why or why not.

MEAGHAN

Meaghan works in a pizzeria. Her job is to chop the onions, peppers, and pepperoni. The owner has instructed Meaghan on the necessity for high standards of personal hygiene. Special soap is provided in the washroom, and Meaghan thoroughly scrubs before she starts work. During her chopping, something irritates her contact lens. She rushes to the washroom, where she removes her lens with her hand. The soap irritates her eye and Meaghan screams! After rinsing her eye with the eyewash in the first-aid kit with the help of her supervisor, she goes home. It is discovered that Meaghan has suffered an allergic reaction to the soap. It is several days before her eye is back to normal.

▼ ▼ ▼

1 Is Meaghan responsible for what happened to her? Explain why or why not.

2 Why might high standards of personal hygiene be important in some jobs?

Reporting Unsafe Working Conditions

Every worker must report unsafe working conditions, and the employer must respond by making the workplace safe. A worker may legally refuse to work if she or he believes that equipment, a physical condition, or another condition of the workplace presents a potential danger. Although legislated procedures for reporting unsafe conditions vary from province to province, the following procedure is typical. The employee must immediately report the reason for refusing to work to the employer or supervisor, who investigates the report, usually with a health and safety committee member and the employee. The employee has the right to remain in a safe place until the investigation is complete. Once the dangerous conditions have been corrected to the employer's satisfaction, the employee may once again refuse to work if she or he still feels that the conditions are unsafe. The employer is then required to notify a government health and safety inspector, who analyzes and reports on the situation and then responds to both the employer and the employee. The employee once again has the right to remain in a safe place during the investigation. The employer may assign the employee to alternative work during this period, but the employee must still receive full pay. No other employee can be assigned to work in the area being investigated unless this person is informed of the refusal to work and the reasons for it. Once the investigation is complete and the safety issue is resolved, the employee must return to work.

CASE STUDY

The Right to Refuse Work

ERIN

Erin is working in a restaurant and is assigned to wash windows during slow periods. She must stand on the top step of a ladder to reach the top of the window. Erin tells her supervisor that the ladder is not safe and that she is afraid of heights. Her supervisor claims that the job is safe and that the only reason for Erin's objection is her fear of heights. The supervisor insists that Erin continue.

AHMED

Ahmed, a graphic artist, is told to clean silk screens in the basement of his employer's stu-dio. The label on the cleaning solvent says to use it only in a well-ventilated area. The employer tells Ahmed to open the basement window.

▼ ▼ ▼

1 Explain why you do or do not think these situations entitle the employee to refuse to work.

2 What other steps could be taken to ensure safer working conditions?

3 Write a letter to either Erin or Ahmed to give advice about what to do in the situation.

A C T I V I T Y
*Role-Playing
Refusing to Work*

1 In groups of five, think of a situation in which a refusal to work may be in order.

2 Role-play the situation, including an employee, an employer, a co-worker, a supervisor, and a government inspector. In your role-play, find a solution for the situation and consider these questions: Was the supervisor told about the danger? How did the employer respond to the situation? Was the co-worker knowingly working in unsafe conditions? Was the co-worker concerned or did he or she choose to ignore the situation? Did the co-worker and employee work together to improve the situation?

3 After each group performs for the class, discuss the effectiveness of the solutions presented.

Ensuring Your Safety

In your journal, complete the statement below.

- If I thought a work area was unsafe, I would...

Workers' Compensation

When a work-related injury or illness occurs, provincial **workers' compensation** legislation assists the employee and employer. Benefits from workers' compensation cover the injured employee's medical costs, hospitalization, rehabilitation, and disability pension, and compensates her or him for lost income. Workers' compensation protects employers from long, expensive court cases since compensation benefits replace a worker's right to sue an employer for damages. Employers pay premiums to support the program based on the number of their employees; employees do not pay at all.

In the event of an injury or illness, the employer must follow the regulations of the Workers' Compensation Board. The employer must make sure first aid is given immediately and must provide emergency transportation to the doctor, hospital, or home of the injured worker if required. The employee's full wages are usually paid by the employer for the day of the injury or illness. The employer must notify the Workers' Compensation Board of the injury or illness within a specific

In one year, Workers' Compensation Boards paid about $3.9 billion for nearly 1.1 million claims.
STATISTICS CANADA

period of time using a special form. Employers may be fined if they file a late report. Under certain conditions, they must offer to re-employ a seriously injured worker. In some cases, workers return to an alternative job because the damage from their injury prevents them from doing their original job. When necessary, the work or the workplace must be modified to accommodate the needs of an injured worker. Workers are often unable to return to any job with the employer. Compensation then includes education and retraining for them so that they can do other work.

ACTIVITY
Reporting Accidents

Read the accident report form on page 225, and then describe what you think happened on the job. Outline both the employee's and the employer's responsibilities in this case. What could have prevented this accident?

ACTIVITY
Researching Health and Safety Information

1 As a class, organize a duty roster to gather and display information on health and safety policies in your area. List all possible sources of information (government departments, safety associations, Workers' Compensation Board, training programs, etc.). Beside each, identify who will contact that source to request information. Identify who will create the display on a bulletin board or other display area in your school.

2 Once the information has been gathered, assign someone to invite a speaker to conduct a health and safety seminar for your class.

WCB
WORKERS COMPENSATION BOARD
BOX 2415. EDMONTON. ALBERTA
T5J 2S5

WORKER'S REPORT OF ACCIDENT

COMPLETE AND RETURN FORM AT ONCE

PLEASE PRINT YOUR FULL NAME. ADDRESS. SOCIAL INSURANCE NUMBER. EMPLOYER S NAME AND ADDRESS IN AREA BELOW IF NOT SHOWN CORRECTLY AT RIGHT ➡

FILE NO.	CLASS	CLAIM NO.	ACCIDENT DATE	LBP CODE

EMPLOYER'S NAME AND ADDRESS

MAILING ADDRESS WORKER'S NAME AND ADDRESS

SOCIAL INSURANCE NO.

LAST NAME
S a h a r i

PREVIOUS LAST NAME (IF APPLICABLE)

FIRST NAME(S)
K a t h l e e n

MAILING ADDRESS
903-43 Street S E
Edmonton, Alberta
T2A 1H2
POSTAL CODE

HEALTH CARE INSURANCE NUMBER   PROVINCE

SOCIAL INSURANCE NUMBER	PHONE	MARITAL STATUS	DATE OF BIRTH	OCCUPATION
123 456 789	555 - 4321	Single	17/01/70	nurse

EMPLOYER S NAME	EMPLOYER'S MAILING ADDRESS	EMPLOYER'S PHONE NO
Central Hospital	3111-112 Ave. NW, Edmonton, AB T5W 0M1	555-1234

1 A. DATE AND HOUR OF ACCIDENT   THE 30th DAY OF May   19— AT 9 O'CLOCK A.M.

B. WHEN DID YOU REPORT THE ACCIDENT TO YOUR EMPLOYER? May 30, 19— at 9:10 a.m.

C. WHO DID YOU REPORT TO? NAME Dr. Rachlis   TITLE Head of Emergency

D. IF NOT REPORTED IMMEDIATELY. GIVE REASON. _____

E. IN WHAT CITY. TOWN OR PLACE DID THE ACCIDENT HAPPEN? Edmonton, AB Central Hospital

F. DID IT HAPPEN ON THE EMPLOYER'S PREMISES? STATE EXACTLY WHERE The Emergency Department exit door.

2 WAS THE WORK YOU WERE DOING FOR THE PURPOSE OF YOUR EMPLOYER'S BUSINESS? YES ☒ NO ☐

WAS IT PART OF YOUR REGULAR WORK? YES ☒ NO ☐

3 HOW DID THE ACCIDENT HAPPEN AND WHAT INJURY DID YOU RECEIVE? DESCRIBE FULLY. (STATE RIGHT OR LEFT. IF APPLICABLE)

A co-worker was entering through the door as I was exiting the door. The index finger of my right hand jammed between the door and door jam.
My finger was broken.

MARK PART INJURED

Right   Left

IMPORTANT PLEASE LIST ANY WITNESSES Sergio Altitia

NAME	ADDRESS
Kathleen Sahari	903-43 Street S E, Edmonton, Alberta T2A 1H2

Courtesy The Alberta Worker's Compensation Board

Make the Connection

▼▼▼▼▼▼▼▼▼▼▼▼▼▼▼▼▼▼▼▼▼▼▼▼▼▼▼

SAFETY ASSESSMENT

1 Use a copy of the survey below provided by your teacher to assess safety at your placement. Then interview the person or committee that is responsible for safety at your placement. With your supervisor's permission, gather any brochures or other training materials your company may have that address safety issues. If your workplace has a health and safety committee or gives any safety seminars, ask if you can attend a meeting or seminar.

2 Using the information you gathered from your assessment, prepare a presentation on safety procedures at your placement. Highlight any protective equipment, machinery, tools, chemicals, or hygiene standards that assist you in completing tasks. Outline the safety program at your workplace and list ways in which it could be improved.

3 Create a list of safety procedures for the student who will follow you at your placement.

SAFETY SURVEY

1 What type of business is it?

Office _____ Manufacturing _____ Retail _____

Construction _____ Other _____

If manufacturing, what do they manufacture? _____

_____

What area do you work in?

Office _____ Other _____

2 How many full-time employees work in the business in total? _____

Do they have a joint Health and Safety Committee? _____

Identify the members who represent the workers. _____

_____

_____

3 Do they have a written and signed copy of the workplace health and safety policy? _____

Do they have an emergency procedure? _____

Is the emergency procedure written down? _____

Did anyone explain the emergency procedure to you before you asked about it? _____

How often do they have emergency drills? _____

4 Are you required to wear any personal protective equipment? _____

What type? _____

Do you work in any confined spaces? _____

Do you work at heights? _____

5 Did you receive any health and safety training the first day on the job? _____

Who did the training and what is his or her title? _____

_____

Do you do any lifting as part of your job? _____

Did anyone train you in how to lift something properly? _____

Did you receive some health and safety training before doing every new job? _____

If not, what jobs did you do for which you did not receive any health and safety training? _____

_____

6 List all the equipment/machinery you will work with. (Indicate which ones have a written work procedure.) _____

_____

_____

7 What are the major hazards identified for you so far? _____

_____

_____

8 What chemicals do you work with? _____

_____

_____

Were any health hazards identified for you? _____

Briefly describe the health hazards. _____

_____

_____

9 What were you told to do if you see a hazard in the workplace?

_____

_____

10 What health and safety information is posted in the workplace?

_____

11 Whom do you tell if you get hurt and what is his or her responsibility in the workplace? _____

_____

12 Where are the first-aid supplies kept? _____

13 Do you have first-aid training? _____

If you have first-aid training, did you let your boss know that you do? _____

Courtesy Industrial Accident Prevention Association

WHAT HAVE YOU LEARNED?

▼ ▼ ▼

1 Why are safe working habits so important?

2 What factors contribute to a safe working environment?

3 Outline how legislation in your province or territory affects health and safety in the workplace.

4 Describe what an employer must do in the event of a work-related injury or illness.

5 Describe what an employee must do in the event of unsafe working conditions.

6 How does workers' compensation help injured workers?

PART 4

EXPLORING THE WORKPLACE

Experience is not what happens to you; it is what you do with what happens to you.

ALDOUS HUXLEY

SUCCEEDING ON THE JOB

After completing this chapter, you should be able to:

▼ ▼ ▼

- Adjust to new workplace situations.
- Recognize the necessary attitudes, knowledge, and skills to succeed on the job.
- Analyze problems and find solutions.
- Understand the importance of managing your time effectively.
- Understand how to keep and advance in a job.

TERMS TO REMEMBER

▼ ▼ ▼

attitude	decision making
working knowledge	time management
problem solving	mentor

Adjusting to the Workplace

Once you find a job, you must be able to adjust to the job and the workplace. As well, as a new employee you will likely want to work toward keeping and advancing in your job. In order to do this, you need to develop the necessary attitudes, knowledge, and skills. Problem-solving and time-management skills are two other essential aspects of employee success.

Any person who is starting a new job will feel some excitement and anxiety. New employees may wonder whether their co-workers will like them and whether they will like their co-workers. Before starting a job, a new employee often speculates about it: Will the supervisor be patient? Will the supervisor expect me to know everything? What will I learn first? The supervisor will likely be speculating about the employee, too. He or she may be considering how to help the employee feel comfortable, fit in, and become a good worker.

Anyone in a new situation is never completely comfortable at the beginning, and people react differently to change. There are steps you can take, however, to make the first few weeks at a new job as comfortable as possible. As a new employee, you will be reacted to and studied by others, since any change in a work environment attracts attention. Therefore, the first impression you make is important. A positive attitude, a willingness to learn, friendliness, the ability to remember names, and good grooming are essential aspects of making a good first impression. They will also help you to keep your job.

I feel anxious because I really want to get the first day over with and get rid of the first-day jitters. I really hope my experience gives me the career direction I want.

STUDENT

BENT OFFERINGS, by Don Addis. By permission of Don Addis and Creators Syndicate.

ATTITUDE

Attitude is the beliefs and feelings that cause a person to behave in a certain way. By displaying a positive attitude toward yourself and your new workplace, people will respond positively to you. The moment your new supervisor and co-workers sense that you have a sincere desire to be with them and a willingness to learn and contribute, you will be on your way to full acceptance.

I am anxious to make a good impression. Besides the expected jitters, I feel a surge of energy because I want to do the best job I possibly can.
STUDENT

WILLINGNESS TO LEARN

A willingness to learn involves accepting responsibility and performing duties with enthusiasm. In your workplace, you learn by doing the tasks of your job as well as by observing. Be open to new ideas and tasks, even if they are not what you expected.

FRIENDLINESS

To communicate friendliness, try to avoid extreme shyness or aloofness, as well as excessive enthusiasm and nonstop chatter. Use these guidelines when you first meet someone:

- Shake hands firmly.
- Look the person in the eye.
- Smile.
- Say something polite, such as "Pleased to meet you" or simply "Hello."
- Try to remember the person's name and use it in conversation.

REMEMBERING NAMES

When you start a new job, you will meet many new people in a short period of time. When you make an effort to remember people's names, you demonstrate courtesy and friendliness. Use these guidelines to help you remember names:

- Be interested in every person you meet.
- Listen carefully and concentrate on what the person is saying.
- Repeat the person's name to yourself several times.
- When you get a chance, write down the names of the people you have met.
- Associate a picture, phrase, or character with the name of each person.
- Look around you and say the names of the people to yourself as they come into view.

GROOMING

Good grooming, or physical appearance, communicates a positive image to others. Pay attention to your appearance, but do not confuse good grooming with wearing the latest fashions—good grooming is just as important for people who wear a uniform to work. You need to dress appropriately for your work and be clean and neat. Observe how most of your co-workers dress for work. Select a positive role model among your co-workers, and use that person as your guide.

Starting Up

In your journal, respond to the questions below.

- When was the last time I started something new (for example, a new school, class, part-time job, or team)?
- How did I feel when I first started? How did I feel after a few weeks or months?

ACTIVITY

Role-Playing Meeting People

1 With a partner, role-play meeting people and introducing yourself. One of you plays the part of a new employee, while the other plays someone who already works for the employer. Once the introductions are over, try to continue the conversation for a few more minutes. In the first role-play, concentrate on shaking hands, and use your own name.

2 In a second role-play, use a fictitious name. See if your partner is able to remember the name you use.

3 Role-play several more introductions, making sure that each of you plays both roles.

ACTIVITY

Rating Your Grooming Habits

Use the questionnaire that follows to evaluate your grooming habits. In your notebook, write the number of each statement and respond with Always, Usually, Sometimes, Seldom, or Never. Develop strategies to improve your rate of Always responses.

GROOMING QUESTIONNAIRE	Rate
1 Hair is neat and clean.	____
2 Skin is clean and free from odour.	____
3 Clothing is clean, pressed, mended, and fits well.	____
4 Footwear is clean, safe, and in good repair.	____
5 Clothing is not too casual and is appropriate for work.	____
6 Fingernails are clean and trimmed.	____
7 Teeth are brushed and breath is fresh.	____
8 Face is clean and fresh.	____
9 Posture is straight.	____

Your First Day on the Job

In your journal, complete the statements below.

- As I look forward to my first day at my placement,
  I feel...

- I feel confident starting my new job because...

Attributes for Success

*I*n order to succeed on the job, a person needs to determine the attitudes, knowledge, and skills that employers want. A study to identify and rank those attributes that make an individual ready for entry-level employment was conducted by the Alberta government. The study identified 42 important attributes, and employers and career specialists were surveyed in order to rank them in order of importance. The results, which are listed below in order of priority, demonstrate that acquiring skills is not sufficient preparation for an entry-level job—in general, attributes that relate to values and attitudes are considered more important.

PERSONAL ATTRIBUTES FOR ENTRY-LEVEL EMPLOYMENT

1	Attitude to work	**17**	Free from addictions
2	Dependability	**18**	Quality oriented
3	Ability to motivate self	**19**	Job-specific skills
4	Personal initiative	**20**	Promoting personal strengths
5	Self-esteem	**21**	Understanding of the world of work
6	Basic skills (e.g., numeracy, reading)	**22**	Time-management skills
7	Work with others	**23**	Realistic career goals
8	Interpersonal communication skills	**24**	Writing skills
9	Integrity	**25**	Willingness to start at the bottom
10	Decision-making skills	**26**	Making use of training opportunities
11	Ability to adjust to change	**27**	Job interview skills
12	Problem-solving skills	**28**	Identifying potential job opportunities
13	Commitment to employer		
14	Understanding of own capabilities	**29**	Independence
15	Appearance, dress, and hygiene		
16	Interest in self-improvement		

30 Assertiveness skills

31 Skills for dealing with negative attitudes

32 Perseverance regarding career goals

33 Job search documentation (résumé, application)

34 Employment/volunteer experience

35 Having job-search strategies

36 Work and lifestyle balance

37 Stress-management skills

38 Optimism about future

39 Establishing personal support systems

40 Follow-up on job application

41 Money-management skills

42 Performance on hiring tests

From *A Study to Identify and Rank Those Factors Which Make an Individual Job Ready for Entry Level Employment*, Alberta Career Development and Employment, 1992.

My first day was basically an orientation. I found that I was exposed to much exciting new information.
STUDENT

Every job requires certain knowledge and skills in order to complete tasks and be a competent worker. This **working knowledge** is unique for each job, and a new employee will not know everything right from the start. By observing others, listening to instructions, and asking questions, you will acquire this working knowledge. The sooner you do, the more quickly you will feel part of your new surroundings.

During the first work days, you will receive instructions and learn new tasks. In order to ensure that you complete tasks correctly, you must listen carefully to all instructions and make notes, if necessary. Remember that a supervisor would rather spend time explaining a task than redoing it. At your placement, if you are unclear about something or do not have enough information, ask questions. Sometimes people forget to provide all the necessary information because they are so familiar with it. For example, a supervisor may forget to tell you about coffee and lunch breaks, what to do in an emergency, or how your job fits into the flow of work. Make a list of questions to ask your supervisor at a time that is convenient for the supervisor. As well, you may want to ask for any reading material that relates to your job, such as employee manuals or product information.

In order to be an effective worker in any job, you need to determine what working knowledge is needed. Some aspects of working knowledge are described below.[1]

WORKPLACE MATERIALS

These are materials and objects that are basic to a workplace, such as tools, equipment, decor, supplies, raw materials, finished products, and protective clothing. A new employee may need to learn how to operate equipment, identify products, or order supplies, for instance.

---

[1] From Roger I. Simon, Don Dippo, and Arleen Schenke, *Learning Work*, p. 28. © The Ontario Institute for Studies in Education, 1991. Published by OISE Press, an imprint of Greenwood Publishing Group, Inc., Westport, CT. Reprinted by permission.

WORKPLACE LANGUAGE

This refers to the specialized words and phrases, technical jargon, abbreviations, codes, and forms as well as names, nicknames, slang, clichés, tones of voice, gestures, and modes of conversation. A new employee may hear unfamiliar language and should not hesitate to ask what the terms mean.

WORKPLACE "FACTS"

The workplace "facts" are the information and beliefs taken as objectively true and accurate by at least some people in a workplace. These facts include not only task-related information but also employee reputations and workplace customs, rituals, and traditions. As a newcomer, some of these facts may not make any sense initially. Observe and ask questions until they become clear.

SKILLS AND TECHNIQUES

These are the capacities and competencies necessary to perform certain procedures and complete certain tasks required by the work. As a co-operative education, or work experience, student your school subjects will form the basis of your skills and techniques, and your training plan will outline them for you.

I read many books and training manuals before I started my job. There was a lot of information to absorb.
STUDENT

THE FRAME OF REFERENCE FOR EVALUATING WORKPLACE EVENTS

This refers to the principles used by workers to determine the good or bad qualities of things, people, events, and ideas. For example, certain criteria may be used by people to determine a "fair day's work," a "job well done," or a "good supervisor."

RULES AND MEANINGS

These refer to both written and unwritten rules, understandings, and expectations that regulate interactions among people in various situations. Rules and meanings include power structures, lines and areas of authority, questions of responsibility, status, prestige, and influence.

. . . .

1 In your notebook, rate yourself from 1 to 5 for each attribute on the chart on pages 235–236. Use the following scale: 5—excellent, 4—good, 3—average, 2—adequate, and 1—limited.

2 Create a copy of the chart that follows to categorize your results and outline ways in which to improve. A strength is an attribute with a rating of 4 or 5, while a weakness is an attribute with a rating of 1 to 2.

. . . .

A C T I V I T Y
Determining Your Job Attributes

STRENGTHS	WEAKNESSES	WAYS TO IMPROVE WEAKNESSES

Make the Connection

▼▼▼▼▼▼▼▼▼▼▼▼▼▼▼▼▼▼▼▼▼▼▼▼▼▼▼▼▼▼▼▼▼▼

ACQUIRING WORKING KNOWLEDGE

1 In small groups, discuss aspects of working knowledge. List five examples of working knowledge from your placements under each of these categories: workplace materials, workplace language, workplace "facts," skills and techniques, frame of reference for evaluating workplace events, and rules and meanings.

2 On your own, make a list of information you would like to know about your placement.

3 Return to your group and plan strategies for acquiring the information. Consider how your supervisor and co-workers might assist you.

Journal Entry

Learning the Ropes

Everyone makes mistakes, especially in a new situation. In your journal, describe a mistake you made as a result of not being familiar with the workplace rules, customs, equipment, and so on. Then respond to the questions below.

- What did I learn from my mistake?
- What could I have done to prevent this mistake?
- What could my supervisor or co-workers have done?

How to Solve Problems

Any new job involves unexpected challenges. For example, consider the situations in the chart that follows. In order to meet the challenges, a person needs to be able to define the problem and find a suitable solution. A second important aspect of meeting challenges is being able to make decisions that are carefully considered and appropriate for the situation. Effective **problem solving** and **decision making** are essential for success in the workplace.

Ideal Situations	Challenges
▪ Your supervisor has confidence in you.	▪ Your supervisor is very demanding.
▪ Your co-workers are friendly and helpful.	▪ You do not receive the help you need.
▪ You have a variety of tasks.	▪ Your work is very repetitive.
▪ Your supervisor and co-workers understand that you are still learning.	▪ There is some pressure from others to learn faster.
▪ You are made to feel welcome.	▪ Not everyone welcomes you.
▪ You have been given a good orientation.	▪ You are tired and flustered at the end of the first day.

Try to make the most of each day and learn whatever you can from every situation. When a problem occurs, consider it a challenge and work to find a solution. The problem-solving model that is described below may help you.

Do not face trouble; outface it.
Robin Skelton

Step 1: Identify the problem. Examine the situation carefully. Often the real problem is hidden behind other, more obvious problems.

Step 2: Brainstorm possible solutions. Make as long a list as you can, even if you think some of your ideas are far-fetched or impossible. One of these alternatives may be a great solution.

Step 3: Analyze the alternatives to make a final decision. There are several ways to analyze your alternatives and practise effective decision making:

1 Consider each alternative in turn, and list all the reasons why that alternative would be the best.

2 Create a chart that lists your alternatives down the side and factors involved in making the decision along the top.

Example: You need to find the best way to travel to work.
You may also want to create a chart that lists your alternatives and the advantages and disadvantages of each.

	COST	FINANCES AVAILABLE	TRAVELLING TIME	CONVENIENCE
Bus				
Taxi				
Walk				
Car pool				
Drive car				
Fly				
Ride bicycle				
Drive motorcycle				

3 Ask yourself "What if..." questions about each alternative. Continue asking these questions until you have isolated the real reason for considering the alternative and the values behind it.

Example: You have been offered an excellent job in another city. Should you take it?
Questions: What if the job is not as attractive as it seems? What if I cannot find a place to live? What if I do not make any friends? What if I come home once a month? What if this is an ideal opportunity?

4 Create a general description of the ideal solution. Compare your alternatives to the ideal solution, and choose the alternative that is closest to the ideal.

5 Sometimes it is difficult to analyze the best alternative, but you must still make a decision. At this point, choose an alternative and do your best to make it work.

We are continually faced with great opportunities brilliantly disguised as insoluble problems.
ANONYMOUS

Step 4: Try what appears to be the best solution. Act on your decision.

Step 5: Evaluate the effectiveness of the solution. After a period of time, evaluate the effectiveness of the solution. Has the problem been solved? Did you make the best decision?

Example: You decide to take the job that is out of town. After three months, you assess your situation by examining your comfort level on the job, whether the job is what you expected it to be, whether you like the city in which you are living, whether you have made friends, and so on.

Step 6: If the solution is ineffective, repeat steps 3 to 6.

Decisions are not usually irreversible—try something else if your first decision does not work.

To demonstrate the problem-solving model, consider this problem: You have been doing the same tasks for days at your placement, and you feel you are ready to learn something new.

Step 1: The obvious problem is repetitive work. The real problem is how to obtain more challenging work.

Step 2: Alternatives include quitting, complaining to co-workers, talking to your supervisor, talking to your teacher, waiting to see if the situation improves, and checking your training plan.

Step 3: The chart below shows the advantages and disadvantages of each alternative.

ALTERNATIVES	ADVANTAGES	DISADVANTAGES
▪ Quit.	▪ The solution is immediate.	▪ The people are nice. ▪ You will be giving up instead of facing the situation.
▪ Complain to co-workers.	▪ You will be heard.	▪ You will be seen as a grumbler.
▪ Talk to your supervisor.	▪ You may learn that there is a good reason for doing the same tasks. ▪ You will be acting in a mature way.	▪ You will be nervous. ▪ The supervisor might not listen. ▪ The supervisor might get angry.
▪ Talk to your teacher.	▪ You can get advice.	▪ The teacher may not understand.
▪ Wait to see if the situation improves.	▪ You will not have to approach your supervisor.	▪ The situation may not change.
▪ Check your training plan.	▪ The tasks you will complete are clearly outlined.	▪ You may still have to approach your supervisor.

Step 4: You feel the best solution is to talk to your supervisor. Plan what to say in advance, and ask your teacher ahead of time for advice on what to say and how to say it.

Step 5: You talked with your supervisor, who said it is essential that you fully understand certain tasks before learning new ones since the tasks are progressive. You will learn a new task next week. You are satisfied with this solution.

Problem Solving

JOSÉ

José really likes his supervisor and his placement, and he is getting along just fine on the job. He enjoys listening to his co-workers during coffee break. They are older than he is, and they talk about everything—movies, cars, sports, and dates. He enjoys their company and feels good about being included in the group. Then they start talking about the supervisor. They ask José how he likes working with "the old crab." They tell José that the supervisor is really tough on students and that only by being a real "goody-goody" can anyone get along with him. Later in the day, José's supervisor starts telling him about what a terrible job the last student did. The supervisor says the student spent too much time socializing and gossiping with the other workers, who too often demonstrate a negative attitude toward their work.

JONI

Joni is a very bright, industrious worker. She completes her tasks quickly and accurately. She is also constantly late for work and frequently leaves early. Joni rationalizes that this is acceptable because she always completes her work on time. She is surprised when her supervisor tells her that if she is late or leaves early one more time, she will be put on probation. One more violation after that and she will be fired. Joni wants to keep her job.

▼ ▼ ▼

Use the problem-solving model to identify the problem in each case study and find a solution.

Your Problem-Solving Ability

In your journal, describe a job-related problem you have had. Then respond to the questions below.

- How did I solve the problem?
- How did I feel about the outcome?
- Would I solve it differently now? If so, how?

Time Management

Managing your time wisely enables you to get the most out of your work and your leisure time. Good **time management** means organizing and planning tasks and events for greater efficiency, productivity, and reduction of stress. These skills demonstrate a positive attitude toward your work. Good time management also means that your co-workers can rely on you to be on time and to complete tasks on time. Poor time management can result not only in lost productivity but a great deal of stress. In order to manage your time effectively, use these guidelines:

- Use an engagement calendar or desk diary to log your professional and personal commitments.
- Create a daily list of things to do. Beside each entry, indicate the priority of the task: *A* means must do, *B* means hope to do, and *C* means would be good to do if there is time. Review your list at the end of the day and cross off the tasks you completed. Unfinished tasks become part of tomorrow's list.
- Use a calendar to outline major projects or events. You may need to look at activities in blocks of time—weekly, monthly, three months at a time, or yearly. Plan your other activities around these dates to prevent you from double-booking your time. Pocket-sized computerized calendars are also available to help you keep track of your time.

These hints can help you complete tasks more efficiently on the job:

- Visualize each task. Mentally see yourself performing the task before you actually do it.
- Always leave complete messages when telephoning people. If possible, tell people when you are available to receive calls. If you have to wait on the phone, complete small tasks while you wait. When you return a call, throw away the message.
- Have all business-related phone numbers ready for quick access beside your phone.
- Keep the notes you made when receiving instructions and the instruction manuals for the equipment you use in an accessible place.
- Make sure your work area is arranged so that you can move easily from one task to another. Organize your tools and equipment and keep your work area neat.
- Complete less important tasks during slack times. Demonstrate initiative and willingness to learn by seeking out new tasks.

To choose time is to save time.
FRANCIS BACON

Procrastination is the thief of time.
EDWARD YOUNG

Reprinted by permission of Tribune Media Services.

A C T I V I T Y

How Do You Spend Your Day?

Draw a circle in your notebook to represent a 24-hour day. Divide the circle into parts to show the time you spent on each activity (such as school, home-work, time with friends, sleep, chores, and so on) before you began your placement. Draw a second circle to show how you spend your time now that you are at your placement. Then answer the following questions:

1 What conclusions can you draw about the changes in how you spend your time?

2 How did your time management change when you started your place-ment?

1 Use the questionnaire that follows to determine how well you manage your time. In your notebook, write the number of each statement and respond with Sometimes, Always, or Never.

TIME-MANAGEMENT QUESTIONNAIRE

		Rate
1	I am self-disciplined.	_____
2	I can focus on a task without being distracted.	_____
3	I do not procrastinate.	_____
4	I complete all tasks.	_____
5	I prioritize my tasks.	_____
6	My work area is neat and organized.	_____
7	I do not waste time on unimportant tasks.	_____
8	I do one task at a time.	_____
9	I have received the necessary instructions to do each task.	_____
10	I ignore unnecessary details.	_____

2 List the steps you could take to change your Never responses to Sometimes or Always responses. What difference would it make to your life if more of the responses were in the Always column?

MANAGING TIME AT YOUR PLACEMENT

Make the Connection

1 For one week at your placement, keep a log of everything you do and how long each activity takes. List tasks, phone calls, interruptions, breaks, and so on. Start by writing down your arrival time.

2 After a week, review your log. Is there a pattern that tells you how you manage your time and what demands are made on you? For example, does a co-worker constantly interrupt you for purposes other than the task at hand? Are you late returning from your breaks?

3 Make a list of the types of time-management tools and methods that are used at your placement. Can you identify one person who is much better at time management than anyone else at your placement? Why is this person a good manager of time?

4 Create a poster about the importance of time management as it relates to your placement.

Your Time Management Ability

In your journal, complete the statements below.

- I manage my time well when...
- I can improve my time management by...

Job Advancement

Once a person has developed the attributes needed to keep a job, she or he often wants to advance in the job. A person seeking advancement must understand the typical levels of jobs in a company or an occupation and the criteria required for promotion into these levels. She or he needs to form goals and plans for advancement and work to achieve these goals. Through words and actions, employees can let others—such as supervisors, managers, or employers—know that they are planning to move ahead.

Finding a **mentor,** or an adviser, in your occupation can also help. Mentoring describes a relationship in which a young person is supported, promoted, and nurtured by an older person who serves as a role model, teacher, and strategist. The mentor may offer opportunities for an employee to gain the experience needed to be promoted or may introduce the employee to other people who can help. In order to find and connect with a potential mentor, use these guidelines:

- Actively seek and plan ways to meet a mentor. Do not wait to be found.
- Develop a high profile at work in order to demonstrate your attributes. Show independence, competence, and a willingness to learn. Most people meet as they work together and develop common interests and goals.
- Join groups connected with your occupation and attend social functions related to your job. Many people meet their mentors in an informal setting.
- Watch for clues that a mentor may be interested in you. Respond to these clues appropriately.
- If you do not find a mentor immediately, continue to use your network as your support system.

TYPICAL ROUTE FOR JOB ADVANCEMENT

Entry-Level Job

This job is usually not well-paid and may involve little prestige and authority. It is an opportunity to demonstrate a positive attitude, develop knowledge and skills, create a network, and seek a mentor. There are often several different types of entry-level jobs within a company or an organization.

Intermediate Job

After an entry-level job, a person may progress through one or more intermediate jobs that demonstrate increasing skill, knowledge, and responsibility. A pay increase usually accompanies each change in level. Sometimes it is a good idea to take a job that is on the same level as your current one in order to gain new skills and to broaden your experience, even if it does not involve a pay increase.

Supervisory Job

At the supervisory level, a person is responsible for his or her own work as well as that of others. Effective management skills are necessary and working knowledge must be broader.

Management Job

A manager is responsible for an area of work or a department that includes supervisors and intermediate workers and entry-level workers. A manager is responsible for dealing with groups of people, equipment, budgets, production, and so on. Depending on the company or organization, there may be several levels of management.

Employer/Entrepreneur

An employer is responsible for the entire company or organization and everyone who works there. Whether the company is a new venture or an international organization, the same attitudes, knowledge, and skills are essential.

Making Career Moves

Vladimir worked on the public relations team of a large company. It was an exciting position and he did very well. After a year on the job, he realized that the greatest opportunities for advancement were in sales, not public relations. He asked for an interview with the sales manager and inquired about becoming a salesperson. Salespeople had to have either diverse experience in various departments of the company or extensive sales experience with other companies. Some of the positions he would have to move through did not appeal to Vladimir. These positions would not be promotions, but lateral moves—different jobs but at the same level and the same pay.

▼ ▼ ▼

1 In small groups, brainstorm a list of alternatives for Vladimir.

2 Outline what you think Vladimir should do, and why.

Make the Connection

JOB LEVELS AT YOUR PLACEMENT

1 Ask your supervisor about the different levels of jobs at your placement and the qualifications required for each level. For example, upward moves may require additional experience or education.

2 Create a chart showing the various levels and required qualifications.

3 In small groups, compare your charts. What conclusions can you form?

WHAT HAVE YOU LEARNED?

▼ ▼ ▼

1 What can a person do to adjust to a new job and workplace?

2 What attitudes, knowledge, and skills do you think are necessary for your job at your placement?

3 Describe how a person can obtain the necessary job attitudes, knowledge, and skills to keep and advance in a job.

4 Explain the steps involved in solving a problem.

5 List six reasons why time management is important.

6 a Describe a typical route for job advancement.

   b Why is it important to know the job levels and requirements?

CHAPTER 14

Ethics

WHAT YOU WILL LEARN

After completing this chapter, you should be able to:

▼ ▼ ▼

- Understand employee, company, and societal ethics.
- Recognize the importance of ethics in the workplace.
- Identify the responsibilities of an ethical employee.
- Understand how company policies and practices are based on ethical standards.
- Appreciate the impact of environmental ethics on the workplace.

TERMS TO REMEMBER

▼ ▼ ▼

ethics	integrity	environmental
honesty	confidentiality	awareness

What Are Ethics?

Always do the right thing. This will surprise some people and astonish the rest.

MARK TWAIN

*E*thics are the rules of right or wrong that form a system of behaviour. They can apply to an individual, a company, or a society. Ethics form the basis for the kind of person you are as well as the organization you represent and the society you are a part of. Fundamental values are at the centre of any code of ethics. Recall from Chapter 2 that values are the moral principles you use to make decisions. A person decides what is important in his or her life and acts based on those values. An employer determines its code of ethics based on personal values. A society has a code of ethics based on generally accepted values.

Ethics are learned through experience, education, and interaction with other people. There are three levels of ethics that may guide a person. First, there is the most difficult category to define—the moral stance an individual takes when making decisions that are not covered by written rules. Second, ethical policies exist in some form in most large companies and organizations. The guidelines and policy handbooks published by some companies give them an opportunity to explain what is important to the company, what the company can offer, and the beliefs on which company operations are based. Organizations within some professions, such as the medical profession, also publish guidelines for their members. Third, there is the law, which is how society formalizes its code of ethics. The connections among personal, organizational, and societal values are shown in the following chart:

PERSONAL VALUES	ORGANIZATIONAL VALUES	SOCIETAL VALUES
▪ Caring for family	▪ Caring for the organization (employees and management)	▪ Caring for other members of that society
▪ Caring for friends and relatives	▪ Caring for the public (customers, creditors, and suppliers)	▪ Caring for the global society
▪ Obeying family rules and the law	▪ Obeying company rules and the law	▪ Obeying societal rules and the law
▪ Being a responsible citizen (community)	▪ Being a responsible citizen (community, province, country, and the world)	▪ Being a responsible member of society
▪ Protecting and caring for the home and community	▪ Protecting and caring for the human and physical environment	▪ Protecting and caring for the human and physical environment

1 Answer the questions below in your notebook. There are no right or wrong answers. For each answer, explain how your family influenced your response and, if possible, which family member was the greatest influence.

2 Compile the class responses and create a chart to summarize them. What conclusions can you form?

---

1 Which is most important in a friendship?
____ Loyalty.
____ Generosity.
____ Honesty.

2 If you had a powerful government position responsible for housing, to whom would you give the highest priority?
____ Unemployed people.
____ Physically challenged people.
____ Homeless people.

3 Which government initiative do you think should receive funding first?
____ Job creation programs.
____ Stay-in-school initiatives.
____ Day-care centre development.

4 You are an animal rights activist. You find out that your best friend helps fund lobbying for increased hunting in your area. You:
____ Discontinue the friendship.
____ Overlook the difference in views.
____ Try to change your friend's viewpoint.

5 Which freedom is most important to you?
____ Economic freedom.
____ Religious freedom.
____ Political freedom.

What Do You Value?

Every day, you face life situations that call for thought, decision making, and action. Everything you do, every decision you make, is based on your values. Throughout your life, you decide what it is that you value—what is important to you. You break away from, but are often still guided by, the beliefs of your family. In your journal, respond to the statements below.

- Describe something you have done recently that you are proud of because it will make a difference for others.
- Describe a controversial issue on which you have openly expressed your views recently.
- Describe a situation in which you observed someone not being treated fairly. How did you feel?

Being a Responsible Citizen

CASE STUDY

In Nassir's family, caring for people in the community is just as important as caring for oneself and one's family. Every time there is a food drive for the local food bank, Nassir's family cuts down on meals so that they can donate more food. Nassir and his two younger sisters often buy small gifts with their own money to include in the food packages. At 17 years of age, Nassir is very aware of his social responsibilities. He also feels that his family is closer because of this commitment to others.

Nassir's close friend Antonio does not understand Nassir's belief in social responsibilities. Antonio's family also helps other people, but they feel that family and friends always come first. Antonio's family is having a party over the holidays, and Antonio invites Nassir.

Unfortunately, Nassir is planning to help prepare a holiday dinner at a shelter for the homeless. Nassir cannot convince Antonio that he values their friendship but needs to honour this commitment as well.

▼ ▼ ▼

1 **Outline Nassir and Antonio's values.**

2 **a What is the basis of their difference of opinion?**
  b What compromise could they come to?

3 **Continue to tell the story. Explain what happens on the day of the party.**

4 **In small groups, describe incidents in which you clashed with a friend because of differing values initiated by your family.**

Ethics in the Workplace

*I*t is important for everyone to be aware of the ethical issues that concern companies and organizations. The Conference Board of Canada asked executives in 300 companies worldwide how important certain ethical issues are in the workplace. Listed below are the top 13 issues and the percentage of positive responses to each issue. Some of these issues concern the interests of the employee (such as employee privacy), others concern the consumer (such as product safety standards), and others concern the organization (such as employee conflicts of interest).

ETHICAL ISSUES	PERCENT
Employee conflicts of interest	91
(Involvement in a project that is in competition with the employee's company or in a project that gives an employee a competitive advantage due to his or her position.)	
Inappropriate gifts to corporate personnel	91
(Gifts given by suppliers or other people who have been granted or hope to be granted contracts and other money-making favours.)	
Sexual harassment	91
(Unwelcome sexual advances made by a co-worker or a person in a position of authority.)	
Unauthorized payments	85
(Payments made to suppliers or others to reward or ensure favours.)	
Affirmative action	84
(Employment and pay equity programs.)	
Employee privacy	84
(Privacy of employees' personal lives as long as it does not affect their workplace behaviour.)	
Environmental issues	82
(Such as pollution, proper storage of hazardous materials, packaging, and waste disposal.)	
Employee health screening	79
(Such as testing employees for viruses or use of alcohol or illegal substances.)	
Conflicts between company ethics and foreign business practices	77
(Such as a difference in the environmental stance of a company and the environmental laws of the country it is located in.)	

For our discussion is on no trifling matter, but on the right way to conduct our lives.
PLATO

Security of company records   76
   (Confidentiality of company financial records as well as
   business plans and production processes.)

Workplace safety   76
   (The responsibility of employers and employees to ensure
   safe work practices.)

Advertising content   74
   (Promotional material that honestly reflects a product or
   service and does not demonstrate prejudice or bias.)

Product safety standards   74
   (Such as sample testing, written product standards,
   and required labelling on products.)

Ron Berenbeim, "Ethical Issues?" *Business & Society Review,* (Fall 1987), pp. 22–25.

A C T I V I T Y

Debating Ethical Issues

In groups of six, organize a debate on one of the statements below. Three members of your group prepare the points that support the statement, while the other three prepare the arguments against the statement. Both groups may need to research information about the topic. The two groups should work out of hearing distance of each other. Select a spokesperson from each side to present the initial argument. Once the initial arguments are presented, the other group members may participate in the debate.

- Employee health screening is acceptable when it affects employees' job performance.
- Responsible advertising does not promote any stereotypes of people.
- An employee may discuss company issues with a spouse or close friend.
- Corporate executives are responsible for ensuring safe environmental practices.
- Gifts or payments to a supervisor from an employee are acceptable.

Employee Ethics

Individual employees have certain ethical responsibilities toward their employer, customers, and community. A commitment to the employer and other employees and promoting an atmosphere of mutual respect, integrity, and open and honest professional relationships encourages the success of the company and its employees.

A successful company is more likely to offer its employees more opportunities and valuable work experience. Therefore, it is advantageous for an employee to understand and adopt the company's policies and objectives, act in a professional manner, and give their best effort.

They should act responsibly to avoid conflicts of interest and other situations that are potentially harmful to the company. Of course, if a company's practices are unethical or illegal, an employee has a responsibility to improve or report the situation to the appropriate authorities. If a company's practices conflict with an employee's values, the employee will need to evaluate the situation to determine his or her options, such as finding a job elsewhere or discussing the problem with his or her supervisor or employer.

In most companies, employees are expected to act with honesty and integrity. **Honesty** is the quality of being honourable and fair in character and actions—in other words, refusing to steal, cheat, lie, or misrepresent something. **Integrity** means having high ethical standards and refusing to compromise those standards. An important aspect of honesty and integrity is respecting company time. Since employees' time is money spent by companies, poor working habits can cost companies billions of dollars a year. Employees may mismanage company time by making personal telephone calls, leaving work early or coming in late, taking care of personal matters on company time, and slowing down their work during company time. In essence, misusing company time can be compared to stealing from a company.

Respecting **confidentiality,** or privacy of information, is another important ethical issue for employees. Not only should employers respect employees' right to privacy, but employees should respect the right to privacy of the company and its customers and suppliers. This means not discussing or publicizing certain information. For example, discussing a company's future plans may lead to these plans becoming known to a competing company and being used to gain an advantage. It is never appropriate to discuss confidential information, such as a doctor's file on a patient, with anyone. As well, employee records may contain information that is no one else's business. Remember, though, that employers have a limited right to know about aspects of an employee's personal life that affect work performance and safety.

Reprinted by permission of Tribune Media Services.

In small groups, discuss confidentiality, considering the following:

1 a List the types of information about employees that you think should be kept confidential.

b List the types of information about companies that you think should be kept confidential.

2 Why might people be interested in confidential information?

Use the questionnaire that follows to evaluate your honesty. In your notebook, respond to each statement with Always, Usually, Sometimes, Seldom, or Never. Circle the questions you answer with Sometimes, Seldom, or Never. For each one, indicate what you could do to improve and why it is important to you to improve.

HONESTY QUESTIONNAIRE

	Rate
1 Do you tell the truth all the time?	_____
2 Do you admit your mistakes?	_____
3 Do you avoid making excuses?	_____
4 Do you avoid talking behind people's backs?	_____
5 Do you handle money transactions carefully at work?	_____
6 Do you work hard even when your supervisor is not there?	_____
7 Do you get back to work quickly after breaks?	_____
8 Do you give customers a good product or good service?	_____
9 Do you pay for things you take from work (food, clothing, equipment, and office supplies)?	_____
10 Do you handle company products and equipment carefully to avoid waste and damage?	_____

Employer Ethics

Any company or organization has a moral responsibility to employees, customers, shareholders, and the community. To promote productivity among employees and, thus, achieve its own goals, a company should create an environment that promotes professional growth, encourages each person to achieve her or his highest potential, and promotes individual creativity and responsibility. It should also provide for open and honest communication and clearly defined expectations, and reward employee contributions to company objectives. In terms of quality of work life, employers are required by law to ensure a healthy and safe environment, equal employment opportunities, and equal pay for work of equal value. Every employee should be respected, and employers should ensure that employees have a sense of security in their jobs. Employees should feel free to make suggestions and file complaints. Management should be competent, and their actions should be fair and ethical.

In order to create a successful business, a company should provide quality products and services that fill customer requirements at appropriate prices. Customer orders and concerns should be addressed promptly and accurately. Companies should also continue to research and develop new products and services and purchase new technology to improve customer service. Without satisfied customers, a company cannot maintain and advance its business.

In order to maintain and increase the number of its shareholders, a company should strive to provide consistent growth of profits and a good rate of return on investment. It should try to maintain a good market position and reputation, protect shareholder investments, and provide relevant information. Achievement of these goals is dependent upon the successful development of the company's commitment to employees, customers, and the community.

A company is also responsible to the communities in which it operates and to the global community. The stability and health of a community and its members ultimately affect the success of a company. It should constantly strive to improve the quality of community life through charitable and community work, payment of taxes, promotion of employee participation in community projects, and health and education programs. A company should maintain its property in good order and protect the environment and natural resources.

In the past, companies were considered to act responsibly toward the community if they merely produced and distributed goods and services. They could use natural resources as long as they complied with the few rules imposed by governments. By making profits, organizations were considered to contribute to a community. In recent times, this concept of community responsibility has changed. Employers are now responsible for examining the impact of their actions on the well-being of the community. Legislation has required companies to practise pay and employment

Conduct is three-fourths of our life and its largest concern.
MATTHEW ARNOLD

We can't live for more than a few minutes without air, a few days without water, a few weeks without food. Yet we continue to destroy the very things that keep us alive and in the process rob our children of a future.
ANITA GORDON AND DAVID SUZUKI

Genetic diversity, in both human and nonhuman species, is a precious planetary resource, and it is in our best interests to monitor and preserve that diversity.

DAVID SUZUKI

There are indications that preserving and cleaning up the environment will become a big money-making industry. Experts have predicted a growth rate of as high as 20 to 30 percent for this industry.

equity. More and more, companies are expected to share in the responsibility of providing education. As well, there is a growing public **environmental awareness** or realization of the need to improve, maintain, and protect the conditions and influences that affect the development of living things. Environmental issues are gaining importance, and companies are increasingly encouraged or required to ensure the following:

- Conservation of natural resources.
- Protection of the environment.
- Clean-up of the environment.
- Reduction, reuse, and recycling of materials and energy.
- Limited use of packaging.
- No product testing on animals.

In the workplace, an environmental economic philosophy is developing as employers consider such questions as:

- What is the company's environmental policy?
- How can we reduce product packaging?
- How can we safely dispose of wastes and hazardous materials?
- How can we recycle supplies and materials?
- How can we build products that last?
- Do we use nonhazardous substances when possible?
- How can we educate our employees about environmental hazards?
- How can we try to conserve energy?
- Do we encourage employees to submit proposals on how to reduce waste?
- How can we ensure that our operations do not have a negative impact on the communities in which we operate?

There are many cases of conflicts between the interests of a company and the interests of society. Consumers, public interest groups, and governments are aware of environmental issues and pressure companies to accept their responsibilities. In fact, businesses that do not consider these issues in their day-to-day operations are beginning to be seen as unethical.

Many companies have a written code of ethics. These codes formalize the concerns of the company for employees, customers, and members of the public. The following is the ethical code of McDonnell Douglas, an aircraft manufacturer.

McDonnell Douglas Code of Ethics

Integrity and ethics exist in the individual or they do not exist at all. They must be upheld by individuals or they are not upheld at all. In order for integrity and ethics to be characteristics of McDonnell Douglas, we who make up the Corporation must strive to be:

- Honest and trustworthy in all our relationships;
- Reliable in carrying out assignments and responsibilities;
- Truthful and accurate in what we say and write;
- Co-operative and constructive in all work undertaken;
- Fair and considerate in our treatment of fellow employees, customers, and all other persons;
- Law-abiding in all our activities;
- Committed to accomplishing all tasks in a superior way;
- Economical in utilizing company resources; and
- Dedicated in service to our company and to improvement of the quality of life in the world in which we live.

Integrity and high standards of ethics require hard work, courage, and difficult choices. Consultation among employees, top management, and the Board of Directors will sometimes be necessary to determine a proper course of action. Integrity and ethics may sometimes require us to forego business opportunities. In the long run, however, we will be better served by doing what is right rather than what is expedient.

Courtesy of McDonnell Douglas.

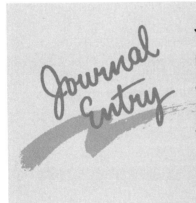

Your Ideal Company

In your journal, list what you think are the most important ethical concerns of an ideal company. Assume you are hired at your ideal company. Write a letter to a friend telling him or her about the new company that you are working for. Outline why the company is a good place in which to work.

The Body Shop

The Body Shop was founded by Anita Roddick in Brighton, England, in 1976 on the concept of offering cosmetics that were based on natural ingredients such as aloe vera, cocoa butter, jojoba oil, almond oil, and rhassoul mud from the Moroccan mountains. Today, The Body Shop operates more than 741 stores in 41 countries including Japan, Finland, the United Arab Emirates, and Australia.

The Body Shop is a unique retailer that is highly respected for its distinctive approach to retailing and its commitment to profits with principles. This commitment is expressed in all aspects of the company's business such as using minimal packaging, not testing on animals, raising awareness and funds for environmental groups and social issues, paying staff for their volunteer work in communities across the country, supporting developing nations through its Trade Not Aid projects, and initiating an innovative refill system to reduce packaging waste.

Right from the beginning, The Body Shop pledged to be *"the most honest cosmetics company in the world."* It intentionally avoids the traditional path taken by other cosmetics companies. "We do not promise the fountain of youth in a jar," says Margot Franssen, president of The Body Shop Canada. "We are always honest and straightforward in explaining what our products can do for people's skin and hair."

A basic principle of The Body Shop's philosophy is its opposition to the animal testing of cosmetics. "Not only do we not test our products on animals, but we also require our suppliers to guarantee in writing that they are not

testing on animals on our behalf and that they have not tested our ingredients on animals for at least five years," explains Margot. Instead, The Body Shop uses reliable and safe alternative tests. The Body Shop has also been an innovator in developing substitutes for animal-based products.

In addition to developing and selling its products in an environmentally and socially responsible manner, The Body Shop initiates and participates in a continual program of environmental and social campaigns. Store windows and Body Shop delivery trucks are used as high-profile billboards, and customers and staff are encouraged to donate money, sign petitions, and, generally, get involved in worthy causes. For example, The Body Shop joined an international campaign to raise awareness of the burning of the Amazon rain forests.

The Body Shop Canada participates in international programs organized through The Body Shop International's *Trade Not Aid* projects. The company establishes trading initiatives that use traditional skills and materials, pay fair market prices, trade in replenishable natural resources, create successful and sustainable trade links, and respect all environments, cultures, and religions. For example, The Body Shop purchases handmade paper from traditional papermakers in Nepal. It pays a fair price plus a premium, which goes into a fund for training and education.

In Canada, The Body Shop has its own corporate commitment to the environment and the community. Each Canadian Body Shop donates 16 hours of paid employee time every month to local charitable activities. The Body Shop Canada recycles paper and cardboard, prints its letterhead on post-consumer recycled stock, reuses warehouse and shipping materials, and uses environmentally safe cleaning products. It operates its own unique recycling program for its plastic bottles and contributes money to social services in different regions across Canada through The Body Shop Canada Foundation.

The Body Shop Canada

1 With a partner, make a list of the ways in which The Body Shop acts in a socially responsible manner.

2 Do you think the ethical practices of The Body Shop help to attract customers? Explain why or why not.

3 Why should companies be responsible for more than just making a profit?

Societal Ethics

M any of the ethical concerns of employees and employers relate to societal concerns such as honest dealings with consumers, human rights, and environmental awareness. The values that govern a society shape the ethics of its work force and its businesses and institutions.

In some countries, caring for people who are disadvantaged or who cannot care for themselves is another societal concern. This has led to the creation of social welfare programs such as Unemployment Insurance, the development of organizations that represent certain groups of people (such as organizations for the blind), and foreign aid to less developed countries that need help to meet the basic needs of their citizens.

Environmental awareness has become a major societal concern in the past decade as resources have been or are in danger of becoming depleted, more species have become endangered or extinct, and pollution has threatened the health of humans and wildlife. While some governments try to enact legislation to counteract these problems, everyone should make an effort to act reponsibly toward the environment to ensure a healthy future for all.

These social issues and many others reflect our values as citizens. Values are also embodied in a society's laws and system of government. The aims of law and government are to ensure safety, fair treatment, and equal opportunity for all citizens. These laws have a great impact on the workplace, including the manner in which employees are treated and the expectations placed on employers. For example, there are laws to ensure the rights of workers to form a union and to bargain collectively

The true measure of civilization rests upon how it cares for its vulnerable members.
Reva Gerstein

with an employer to improve working conditions. There are laws to ensure that workplaces are healthy, safe, and equitable for employees. Sometimes it seems that certain citizens enjoy more advantages while others are penalized. Public pressure can help to create the changes that are necessary to ensure that all members of society are treated equally and fairly.

ACTIVITY
Exploring Local Social Issues

1 Consider how you can become involved in helping Canada to improve and promote a social value such as protection of the environment or caring for homeless people. Contact a lobby group that is involved in a social issue that interests you. What is this group doing to address the issue? Do research to determine the impact of this issue in your community and how it is being addressed by government and industry.

2 Write a letter to your Member of Parliament asking how her or his local office is addressing these issues.

ACTIVITY
Start in Your Own School

1 As a class, co-ordinate a study of your school's environmental practices. Consider the use of paper, disposable cups, glass, cans, water, and energy.

2 Compile your information and brainstorm improvements that could be made. Prepare a written report outlining your suggestions and present it to your principal.

3 Design posters to promote environmental awareness in your school.

Overcoming Resistance to Change

Imagine that you are an environmental expert who has been hired by a local company that makes, packages, and sells greeting cards. The company president has hired you to advise the company on how to reduce waste in its manufacturing process.

Your university environmental degree did not prepare you for employee resistance to change. Several employees say, "We've always done it this way." At the end of the first day of your study, you go home and gather your thoughts. In your journal, outline your day and its frustrations. Include some positive resolutions for tomorrow that will help the employees see the ethical importance of following your recommendations.

ETHICS AT YOUR PLACEMENT

1 Choose one issue from the list on pages 253–254. Investigate how this issue is addressed at your placement. You may need to research your topic at the library. In your investigation, determine what the company policy is, how this policy is presented to the employees, and how customers are made aware of policies.

2 Write a newspaper article or present a television broadcast about the ethical issue you investigated at your placement. If you have access to video equipment, tape your television broadcast. If not, role-play it for the class.

Make the Connection

WHAT HAVE YOU LEARNED?

▼ ▼ ▼

1 Explain how personal values, company policies, and laws are affected by ethics.

2 What major concerns do companies have about employee behaviour? Why?

3 What impact do company ethics have on customers, shareholders, and a community?

4 What do you think are the major societal issues facing companies today?

INTERPERSONAL RELATIONS

Interpersonal Relations in the Workplace

*I*nterpersonal relations refers to the pattern of associations and communications among people. The ways in which people relate at work are affected by workplace factors, such as the division of labour and lines of responsibility and influence, as well as by personal factors, such as personalities, values, and attitudes. In many ways, interpersonal relations influence the self-esteem of employees and the success of the employer. Good interpersonal relations involve understanding the qualities of a valued employee and supervisor or employer as well as the dynamics of relationships between people in the workplace. Although ideally everyone works to avoid personal problems at work, problems do occur. Interpersonal skills involve knowing how to resolve problems, deal with emotions such as anger, and accept and give constructive criticism.

CHARACTERISTICS OF VALUED EMPLOYEES

Statistics Canada surveyed workers to determine what characteristics they felt were important to maintaining their jobs. The results of the survey are as follows:

1 Be dependable.

2 Follow instructions.

3 Know what an employer expects.

4 Manage time and materials efficiently.

5 Get along with a variety of people.

6 Maintain good health.

7 Be punctual.

8 Adapt to varying work situations.

9 Work without close supervision.

10 Be loyal to employer.

11 Work as a team member.

12 Work under tension or pressure.

13 Use initiative and imagination.

14 Make decisions on your own.

15 Be neat and clean in appearance.

16 Follow safety regulations.

17 Use information, materials, and equipment.

18 Have basic speaking skills.

19 Have basic arithmetic skills.

20 Have basic writing skills.

21 Organize work activities of others.

A dependable employee is valued by fellow workers and by employers. A good rule is to give as much as you can all the time. Other qualities that are valuable to have as an employee are a positive attitude and the ability to take initiative. People who take initiative are usually enterprising, show interest in their work, and make decisions about how to proceed with their work without supervision. This behaviour presents a positive image to an employer.

My employer believes in me.
STUDENT

CHARACTERISTICS OF VALUED SUPERVISORS AND EMPLOYERS

In order to attract and keep good employees, supervisors and employers must have certain characteristics. The valued supervisor and employer:

- Speaks with each employee on a regular basis.
- Has realistic expectations about the amount of work employees can complete in a specific period of time.
- Is aware of individual employees' goals and supports people in these goals where possible.
- Encourages employees to work as part of a team.
- Gives positive feedback frequently.
- Gives negative feedback in a way that is not upsetting and that incorporates suggestions for improvement.
- Listens to what employees have to say and acts on these suggestions or complaints, if necessary.

Junior Workers Must Show They're Willing, Reliable

by Janis Foord Kirk

Several years ago I tried to help a young woman find work. Let's call her Mary Setter.

After spending two years in university working toward a B.Sc., Setter had decided she was on the wrong career path. She was hoping to get a start in the business world.

I knew of a junior clerical position in a major firm. The money wasn't great but the company was. It had a policy of promoting from within so it was a good opportunity for Setter. She got the job.

She'd only been working for the firm for about a month when she called me to complain about her duties—filing, photocopying, and basic accounting. The work was too menial for her. She was overqualified, she said.

In fact, she wasn't. Although bright, Setter had minimal experience and no accounting training.

We went over the same ground we had covered a month earlier: Lots of young people had started in junior jobs with this firm and moved into better positions. Once she had proven herself, she could do the same. But she had to be patient.

Concerned, I called her employer. "There are a few problems," he acknowledged. "But I'm hoping we can work them out."

Three months later, he called me. Setter had been fired.

It turned out that in the four months she'd worked with them, she had missed ten days of work, most of them Mondays or Fridays. At least twice a week she was late. Numerous times, rush jobs had been found on her desk days after they'd been given to her. On two occasions, her supervisor had talked to her about these problems, to no avail.

The final crunch came when it was discovered that she had photocopied several copies of her brother's thesis on the company's photocopier and on company time.

With all her abilities and intelligence, Setter had a terrible attitude. She was spoiled. She claimed to desperately want a career. But she wasn't willing to be patient and work hard for it.

Good junior workers are a rare breed, employers tell me. Far too often, young people feel it's their right to step into a perfect job. If the job they land isn't ideal, they, like Setter, don't give their full effort.

Positive careers are built by those who are willing to pay their dues. Proving yourself and your abilities on the lower levels of the business world is essential if you want to make it to the upper echelons.

When they hire or promote, employers are looking for a particular type of individual. Experience, skills, and training play a key role, of course. But the less-definable attributes like work ethic or attitude are equally important.

Employers use words like initiative, honesty, reliability, loyalty, and capacity for hard work when describing the kind of attitude that impresses them. Consider what these words mean.

Employees with initiative are self-starters. They take their responsibilities seriously. Once trained, they don't need to be told time and again what to do.

Honest employees don't take advantage of their employers. They give "a full day's work for a full day's pay," as one employer put it. They don't use the products or services of their employer for their personal use.

Valued employees are reliable. Unless they are truly ill, they're at work and on time.

Hard-working people put their full effort into their job. They do their best to see that the objectives of the company are met.

Loyal employees don't "move across the street for an extra 25 cents an hour," another employer suggested. They hang in through frustrating or difficult times. If they have criticisms, they make them behind closed doors to management.

Good employees have a professional attitude.

© Janis Foord Kirk. Reprinted by permission.

▼ ▼ ▼

1 How do you think other workers react to a worker like Mary Setter? Why?

2 What do you think was Mary's biggest problem as a worker?

3 How could the employer have helped Mary?

4 If you were the employer and you had one piece of advice to give Mary as she was fired, what would it be?

1 Below is a list of work-related personal characteristics that are important to success and advancement at work. Read the list and consider which characteristics you possess.

- Attitude: Approaches tasks positively and willingly.
- Appearance: Reports for work suitably dressed and groomed.
- Dependability: Meets job responsibilities with minimum supervision.
- Punctuality: Arrives for work on time. Returns from breaks and lunch on time.
- Interest: Displays interest in tasks.
- Initiative: Observes a job that needs to be done and does it without being asked.
- Co-operation: Is tolerant of and helpful to others.
- Courtesy: Shows appreciation for and politely addresses others.
- Judgement: Shows common sense and thinks before acting.

2 Write a letter to Mary Setter's ex-employer (from the previous case study) outlining your strengths as a worker to replace Mary.

Journal Entry

Relations on the Job

In your journal, complete the statements below.

- When I consider the characteristics of a valued employee, I realize…
- When I consider the characteristics of a valued employer, I realize…
- An employer can help an employee succeed by…
- My employer expects…
- I expect…

Make the Connection

▼ ▼

WHO WAS YOUR BEST BOSS?

1 The letter that follows was written in response to the question: Who was your best boss ever? Read the letter and list the characteristics that Margaret appreciates in a boss.

Dear Nadia,

Who was my best boss ever? What a question! It is so difficult to answer. I would rather tell you about the characteristics that I appreciate in someone—anyone—for whom I work.

I like to work for someone who is tough. This person demands of himself or herself, and everyone who works for him or her, maximum output and excellence. This person believes in his or her employees and is willing to stand up for them. This person works hard, plays fair, remembers to say thank you, and knows when it is time to give workers responsibility and independence. This person is not afraid of being in charge.

I have worked for this person. I was happy because I was forced to produce more and better work than I thought possible. I thrived because someone believed in me.

Yours sincerely,

Margaret

2 In small groups, prepare a list of questions to use to interview a person at your placement about her or his best boss ever. You might ask questions such as:

- When you work for someone, what personal characteristics do you like her or him to have?

- What methods of giving direction, or orders, do you prefer?

- Outline three characteristics of a good boss.

3 After the interview, share your results with your group. As a class, compile a list of characteristics of a good boss.

Getting Along With Others

*T*he ability to get along with others involves being able to deal with emotions effectively, resolve conflicts, give and receive criticism, and act assertively.

Handling Emotions

Sometimes emotions are so overwhelming that people cannot function effectively. Specifically, **anger**—the feeling of frustration resulting from a situation that is seen to be wrong or unfair—can be hard to handle at the workplace. Anger and other emotions can be dealt with by expressing or repressing them. **Repression** is a defence mechanism people use to put unacceptable or painful emotions or memories out of their minds. Repressed feelings can actually lead to poor health and can cause displays of uncontrolled anger, which may cause hurt feelings and damaged relationships. When a person becomes angry, he or she may express other repressed feelings. Common symptoms of repressed negative emotions include putting other people down, transferring anger from work to friends and family, and muscle tension.

People can control and use their anger in constructive ways by understanding themselves and the situations that make them angry. Negative emotions signal a problem or challenge to be overcome, so careful analysis of a situation can lead to a solution. (See the problem-solving model on pages 239–240 of Chapter 13.) If you become angry, use these guidelines to control your anger:

- Try to calm down. Remove yourself from the situation by going outside. If you cannot go out, picture yourself on a beach or another place you enjoy. Concentrate for a few minutes on the scene and the peace it inspires. Emotion has a physical effect on your body, so you need to relax your tense muscles, slow your breathing, and return your body to normal. Afterward, you will be more relaxed and better able to tackle your work and the problem.
- Avoid getting co-workers involved in a situation by talking about the problem unnecessarily. Gossiping will only cause additional problems. Talking over a problem with a friend or family member may help you to feel better, but you should resolve the situation with the person you are angry with.
- Identify the source of your anger. Consider the situation in order to determine what you want to accomplish, how you can accomplish it, and whether or not you are trying to dominate a situation.
- Acknowledge responsibility for your emotions. No matter what another person has done to make you feel angry, you are responsible for your actions and feelings. Other people are not responsible for your reactions.
- Express your feelings calmly and coherently. Avoid blaming or lecturing a person. Respond to an angry person with statements such as: "I

People are more likely to become angry when they are hungry, tired, or upset for another reason.

am also upset over this situation. Let's talk about the problem." Then you can help to defuse the situation. Open and direct communication is the key to solving any situation. Try to offer suggestions to resolve the problem.

Dealing With Emotions

In your journal, identify occasions during which you became emotional or tense, and explain why. Describe how you released this emotion.

Keep a record for a week of times when you experience extreme emotion or tension at your placement. Describe the physical signs. What time of day was it? What were you doing and with whom? What feelings and thoughts did you have at the time? How did you respond?

RESOLVING CONFLICTS

A **conflict** is a clash of opposing ideas, interests, or activities. Conflicts can occur at work or at home—anywhere where people interact. When a conflict occurs, finding a resolution can involve much co-operation and compromise on the part of the people involved.

The best way to prevent and resolve conflicts is to have open and direct communication with others. The ability to deal with emotions in a constructive way helps to resolve some conflicts. If a resolution is not attempted, more difficulty can result later. Here are some guidelines for resolving conflicts:

- If you are emotional, take time to calm down. It is more difficult to resolve a situation when you are emotional, and it may even make the situation worse.
- Consider why the conflict occurred and some possible solutions. (See the problem-solving model on pages 239–240 of Chapter 13.)
- Be prepared to apologize for an inappropriate action. An **apology** is an acknowledgement to another person of a mistake or failure one is responsible for. In an apology, you should admit your mistake and ask for forgiveness. Although apologizing can be difficult, most people feel better after admitting and acknowledging their actions. On the other hand, avoid apologizing too much. You may be apologizing

for situations that are not your fault, or you may need to improve behaviours for which you are often apologizing.

- Consider the other person's point of view. Listen to the other person with an open mind and without preconceived notions. Different perspectives are not necessarily wrong, and everyone has a right to her or his own feelings and beliefs.

- Offer possible solutions calmly and coherently. With the other person, decide on the best possible solution. Everyone who is involved must be willing to try the solution. After a period of time, reevaluate the solution to determine whether it was effective. Discuss the success or failure of the solution. If it was not effective, propose another solution.

If there is one secret of success, it lies in the ability to get the other person's point of view and see things from that person's angle as well as your own.
HENRY FORD

Dealing With Conflict

In your journal, respond to the questions below.

- How do I react when:

  Someone takes a seat that I feel is mine?

  I am criticized for not doing a task properly?

  Someone is late meeting me?

  A friend breaks an appointment with me?

  I am asked to complete a task just before going to lunch?

- How can I prevent these minor problems from becoming major issues?

- How can I react positively to a person I am in conflict with?

1 Think of three conflicts you have had recently, and complete a chart similar to the one below. Record who you were in conflict with, what the conflict was about, how you managed the situation, and how you and others felt about the results.

ACTIVITY
Analyzing Your Conflicts

CONFLICT	HOW I MANAGED THE SITUATION	RESULTS

2 For each conflict, list five strategies you could have used to prevent or lessen the conflict.

Giving and Receiving Criticism

Everyone has ways in which they can improve, times when they do not perform to the best of their abilities, and moments when they make mistakes. Although criticism may not always be given in a constructive way, everyone can learn to accept and profit from it. **Criticism** is the act of making judgements about another person's behaviour or actions, and it may involve positive or negative comments. Knowing how to give and receive criticism is a valuable skill and can help to prevent conflict. Constructive criticism from someone such as your supervisor can help you to better perform your job and understand your supervisor's needs. Follow these guidelines when receiving criticism:

No one can please everyone all of the time.

- Try to stay calm and consider the validity of the criticism—even if it is presented in a negative manner. Perhaps your behaviour could be improved.
- Try not to think of the criticism as a personal attack. It may be difficult for the person to express the criticism.
- Listen to the person carefully and try to interpret nonverbal communication.
- Examine the qualifications of the critic to determine whether or not he or she knows the subject and has valid reasons for the criticism. Perhaps something can be learned from the experience.

Follow these guidelines when giving criticism:

- Consider the person you are criticizing and the situation in order to direct your comments. Be aware of the other person's reaction to your criticism by observing her or his nonverbal communication.
- Consider why the person you are criticizing may have behaved inappropriately. Does the person fully understand what is expected? Perhaps he or she has a valid explanation.
- Do not pass judgement or interpret actions. Explain why you are suggesting a change and give examples of how the person might change. Give the person the motivation to change by explaining the reasons behind your criticism.
- Remain positive throughout the conversation. Mention the positive aspects of the person's performance and accomplishments. Try to present a balanced perspective of the person's behaviour.
- Comment on improvements to the person's behaviour when you see improvement.

Handling Criticism

Hamid had been working at his job as a shipping clerk in a lumberyard for two weeks when his employer called him into his office. He told Hamid that he had been doing a great job and that the other employees really enjoyed working with him. The employer pointed out that Hamid had been making quite a few errors in filling the orders, however, and asked him to be more careful. Hamid was furious. He stormed out of the office thinking, "I don't have to take this abuse. Who does he think he is?"

▾ ▾ ▾

1 What should be Hamid's next step if he wants to keep his job?

2 If you were the employer, what would you do next?

3 Write an ending to this case study.

ACTIVITY

Role-Playing Criticism

1 Below are some nonconstructive criticisms that an employer might make. With a partner, role-play the employer and the employee. The employee should try to respond to the criticism in a positive manner.

- You work too slowly. You are holding up the others.
- You do not seem to be fitting in here.
- You take too long on your coffee break.
- Do you know how much each mistake you make costs me?

2 Now repeat the role-plays with the employer expressing the same problems in a more positive manner.

3 As a class, discuss how you felt about giving and receiving the negative and positive criticisms.

ASSERTIVE BEHAVIOUR

Behaviour that is **assertive** expresses a person's feelings, preferences, needs, or opinions while still respecting others. Assertive people tend to be confident in their opinions. They can honestly express feelings in a positive manner and encourage others to do the same.

Aggressive behaviour is intended to achieve one's own goals at the expense of others, or to impose opinions on others. Many aggressive people express themselves without demonstrating respect and sensitivity for other people.

Passive behaviour—not expressing oneself and protecting one's rights—allows a person to be victimized. Passive people tend to have a poor self-concept and often think that everyone else is always right. They put themselves down, allow others to make choices and solve problems for them, and do not express their true feelings because they are afraid others will not agree with or like them if they do. Passive people are often taken advantage of by aggressive people, or passive people may tend to encourage others to take on their decisions and work.

The chart below shows examples of assertive, aggressive, and passive statements.

ASSERTIVE	AGGRESSIVE	PASSIVE
■ I would prefer the day shift next week. ■ Thank you, I enjoy the work.	■ I am taking the day shift next week. ■ I know. I am the best worker you have.	■ Whatever you think is best. ■ Oh, I'm not really that good.

In the workplace, you will need to maintain a good working relationship with all kinds of people. When dealing with aggressive people, remain firm in your opinions without becoming aggressive. Rather than responding to hostility, calm the aggressive person by focussing on relevant information. For example, if a co-worker is complaining loudly about a mix-up, ask what exactly is the problem. As the aggressive person goes into detail, hopefully she or he will vent the anger. Then you can more easily discuss the problem rationally. If an aggressive person demonstrates insensitivity, respectfully explain that you do not agree with this behaviour. When dealing with passive people, ask several questions to determine whether the person understands the situation and her or his true feelings. Give support to a passive person without taking on her or his tasks or problems. Be aware of how you respond to a passive person—be respectful and considerate.

"Good morning, students. I am going to be your teacher for this Assertiveness Training course . . . that is . . . I mean . . . if you don't mind."

Douglas Blackwell, Blackwell Cartoon Service.

1 In groups of three, role-play a workplace situation that involves an assertive, an aggressive, and a passive person. You may want to use one of the following situations:

- You have broken a piece of equipment and your employer is angry.
- A co-worker is busy with personal telephone calls, while you are so busy that you have people on hold on the telephone.
- You are lining up to buy lunch and the person ahead of you lets three friends join her in front of you.

2 Reflect on how you felt playing each role. Which role felt most like you? Why?

Common Relationships in the Workplace

*G*ood relationships with other people at work are critical to the happiness and well-being of most people. Three common work relationships are employee–employer, employee–employee, and employee–customer.

EMPLOYEE–EMPLOYER RELATIONSHIP

An employee's success on the job often depends on the employer's assessment. If you do not get along with the boss for whatever reason, you may find it difficult to enjoy work no matter how satisfactory other aspects of the job are. Whether you work for an understanding, considerate employer or a difficult, demanding one, these guidelines can help you to have a successful relationship:

- Respect your employer's authority.
- Listen to and follow your employer's instructions.
- Ask questions if you do not understand.
- Exhibit a positive attitude.

Our chief want in life is somebody who will make us do what we can.

RALPH WALDO EMERSON

"What I like about him is he never tells you to stay in line, he asks you to stay in line."

Drawing by Ross; © 1981 The New Yorker Magazine, Inc.

EMPLOYEE–EMPLOYEE RELATIONSHIP

Establishing good interpersonal relations with co-workers makes good sense. Liking people and being liked in return will make the time you spend at work more pleasant. When employees like one another, morale tends to be higher, absenteeism tends to be lower, and mutual respect and consideration are more common. Most work requires being part of a team to achieve the company's goals. When employee relations are good, individuals realize that they will inconvenience their co-workers if they do not complete their own tasks. These guidelines will help you to have good employee relations:

- Be friendly, supportive, and co-operative.
- Be a responsible member of the team.
- Show respect for other feelings, levels of ability, and opinions.
- Avoid discussing anything personal that you would not want repeated to others.
- Make the best of any situation.
- Seek assistance when needed.
- Compliment others when they deserve it.
- Communicate in a relaxed, patient, and pleasant manner.
- Give listeners and speakers your complete attention.

EMPLOYEE–CUSTOMER RELATIONSHIP

Whether the company has three employees or three thousand, whether the product is rubber washers or gold jewellery, and whether the interaction is by fax or in person, quality service is the basic requirement of successful employee–customer relations. A business that provides good **customer service,** or conduct that is helpful to and considerate of customers, creates a healthier personal work environment and will likely have repeat customers.

The basic rules of customer service are courtesy and common sense. Treat people as you would like to be treated. Employees do not just do a job—they also add a personal element to it. Some employers publish guidelines to help their staff learn how to respond well to customers and they hold customer service and product knowledge seminars for new employees. Staff meetings also give employees up-to-date information and an opportunity to share experiences.

Reflections on Customer Service

In your journal, complete the statements below.

- When I go into a store, I prefer a salesperson who...
- When I am a customer in the presence of other customers who are rude and inconsiderate toward an employee, I usually...
- I dislike returning items or complaining about a flaw in an item because...
- If I were in charge, I would tell my employees to always...

ACTIVITY

Role-Playing Relationships at Work

1 Write each of the following scenarios (or some of your own) on a piece of paper and put them all in a hat. With a partner, choose a scenario to role-play for the class.

- An employee does not understand how to complete a task. The employer is on a long telephone call.
- A difficult-to-please customer is in a sporting goods store buying a track suit for a friend. The salesperson is trying to be helpful.
- An employee with a personal problem discusses it with a co-worker. The co-worker then tells a few more people at the workplace.
- A customer is calling the customer service department of a credit card company because he or she was wrongfully charged for something.
- An employee is having trouble understanding a new computer program. A co-worker has just been to a seminar on the computer program.
- An employer is giving instructions to an employee on how to complete a task.
- A regular customer is calling a wholesale lumber dealer because three tractor-trailer loads of lumber for a building site seem to have disappeared in transit.
- An upset driver arrives at the counter of a muffler shop with a tail pipe in hand and a plea for help. The driver is on the way to the airport and is late.
- An employee is late for the third time in one week. The employer is standing at the door watching the employee arrive.

- A customer breaks a small ornament in a gift shop and refuses to pay for it.
- An employee accidently breaks a part on a piece of equipment. Another employee says, "Just put it back. No one will notice."
- The head engineer of a large mining company is getting ready for the annual shareholders' meeting. One of the major shareholders calls to say that she or he has arrived a day early by mistake.
- Two employees are unloading a truck just before quitting time. The unloaded boxes are supposed to be placed on the shelves where they belong for safety reasons. One employee turns to the other and says, "Let's just unload the boxes and get out of here. We can put them away tomorrow."
- A gas meter reader is delayed by a tearful person who has just received news that his or her spouse has had a heart attack at work.

2 Choose one of the situations you did not role-play and write a script outlining how you think the scene would unfold.

Resolving Interpersonal Problems

CASE STUDY

HIROKO

Hiroko works as a data clerk in the local hospital on the day shift. The night data clerk cannot leave until she arrives, and Hiroko's supervisor must cover for her on her coffee and lunch breaks. Hiroko has worked at the hospital for two years. She is popular with her co-workers because of her outgoing personality and generous nature. Her one fault is that she is often late—as much as 30 minutes. She never calls to let anyone know that she will be late. One day, she is not only late, but she falls asleep during her break and is late returning to her desk.

▼ ▼ ▼

1 If you were Hiroko's supervisor, what would you do?

2 What, if anything, should her co-workers do?

3 Write an ending for this case study.

ROB

Rob is a valued employee at the Always Open Gas Bar. The customers compliment him and mention his excellent service to his supervisor. Rob is able to handle three customers at once and make them all feel that they are important, and he also gets along well with his co-workers. But Rob will never stay late when there is extra work. No matter how busy or short-staffed the gas bar is, Rob leaves the moment his shift ends. Rob's supervisor is frustrated. He wants to keep Rob as an employee but cannot accept this behaviour.

▼ ▼ ▼

1 What can Rob's boss do about the situation?

2 How could Rob justify his actions?

3 If you were working with Rob, how would you react to his behaviour?

▼ ▼

RESOLVING SITUATIONS AT YOUR PLACEMENT

1 Write a case study similar to the ones on page 280 about a person at your placement who is, in your opinion, creating problems for the supervisor and co-workers. Write questions for your case study.

2 Exchange case studies with a partner and discuss your answers.

Make the Connection

WHAT HAVE YOU LEARNED?

▼ ▼ ▼

1 List ten important employee characteristics and explain why each is important.

2 List ten important employer characteristics and explain why each is important.

3 Outline strategies for dealing with the following situations:

   a An angry co-worker.

   b A conflict between two employees.

   c Negative criticism from an employer.

   d An aggressive person.

   e A passive person.

4 Describe the three common relationships in the workplace.

5 How can you make sure you get along with your employer, co-workers, and customers?

6 Why is the employee–customer relationship important?

CHAPTER 16

EVALUATING YOUR WORK EXPERIENCE

WHAT YOU WILL LEARN

After completing this chapter, you should be able to:

- Evaluate your performance in the workplace.
- Respond to feedback from your teacher and supervisor.
- Understand formal and informal employee evaluation in the workplace.
- Evaluate your placement.
- Reevaluate your personal career goals and plans.

TERMS TO REMEMBER

self-evaluation
performance review
probationary period
letter of recommendation

Reflecting on Your Progress

Throughout your work experience, **self-evaluation** of your placement, your career plans, your performance, and feedback from others is important. An individual is often the best judge of his or her progress and can more easily identify obvious and subtle personal changes. Changes in attitude or ways of thinking are not easily measured and sometimes are not easy to talk about. Learning to judge yourself fairly and determining ways to improve are valuable skills. Reflecting on and evaluating your experiences will help you to:

- Determine whether the objectives of your training plan are met.
- Summarize the information and concepts you learn.
- Determine the changes in your attitude.
- Determine how well you apply your knowledge, skills, and attitudes to real-life workplace circumstances.
- Determine your strengths and weaknesses.
- Summarize your responses to your experiences.
- Reconsider the direction of future studies and your career plans.

Only action can testify to the validity of thoughts and emotions: action alone verifies the personality. It is the only authentic form of self-expression. "I act. Therefore I know who I am."

STEPHEN VIZINCZEY

Reflecting on Self-Evaluation

In your journal, respond to the questions below.

- Why do people hesitate when asked to talk about themselves?

- How do I feel when I am asked to talk about myself?

- "There is no value-judgement more important to humans than the estimate we pass on ourselves." Why do I agree or disagree with this statement?

- What are the advantages of being able to express my strengths and weaknesses?

▼ ▼

EVALUATING YOURSELF AT YOUR PLACEMENT

1 In your notebook, respond to the questions that follow to evaluate yourself in the workplace.

- Are you happy in your job?
- Are you reporting to work appropriately dressed?

- Are you practising the safety code of the workplace?
- Are your job skills improving?
- Are you a useful member of the staff?
- Do you communicate well with your co-workers?
- Do you display confidence when fulfilling your duties?
- Have you developed and maintained a positive work attitude?
- Is the quality of your work high?
- Do you have open communication with your supervisor?
- Are you meeting the responsibilities of your job with minimum supervision?
- Are you receiving and giving positive feedback?
- Do you speak well of the business, your supervisor, and the other employees?
- Do you fit in with your co-workers?

2 Ask five employees at your placement what they consider to be the three characteristics that students need most to be successful at their placements.

3 Write a report about your participation at your placement based on this information, and share it with your class.

What Are You Learning?

Each week for several weeks respond to the questions below in your journal.

- What new knowledge did I gain this week that I did not have before?
- How did this new knowledge make me feel?
- What do I expect this new knowledge to add to my life?

Responding to Feedback

Your teacher and supervisor will provide you with feedback to help you evaluate your performance and monitor your progress. When meeting with the team, listen to their suggestions and think of ways to act on their feedback. Listening in a courteous and attentive manner conveys a positive image and gives other people the confidence to speak frankly.

You should ask questions about or comment on some of their observations. This meeting is an opportunity for you to offer your opinions as part of the team and to indicate your desire to make improvements. You may want to ask questions such as: Is my progress satisfactory? Am I following instructions quickly? Does my quality of work meet the company standards? Do I use my time well? In what specific ways would you like me to improve? What suggestions do you have for me? The discussion may include the following topics:

- Punctuality and attendance
- Dependability
- Strengths and weaknesses
- Listening skills
- Ability to follow instructions
- Initiative
- Duties performed
- Quality of work
- Attitude toward work
- Use of time
- Specific job skills and tasks
- Other components of your training plan

Nothing ever becomes real until it is experienced—even a proverb is no proverb to you till your life has illustrated it.
JOHN KEATS

Reflecting on Feedback

After meeting with your teacher and supervisor, jot down their suggestions. Then, in your journal, complete the statements below.

- When I met with my teacher and supervisor, I felt...
- I wish that I could have...
- Next time we meet, I will be sure to...

Formal Employee Evaluation

In many workplaces, an employee is regularly evaluated in a **performance review,** which is an exchange between a supervisor and an employee to discuss the employee's work. Performance reviews may be conducted once a year or every six months. Their purpose is to give the employee an assessment of his or her work and to allow the employee to discuss the job from his or her perspective. The meeting is not meant to be one-sided. In fact, it is the perfect forum for an employee to raise any concerns about the job and tasks as well as the future prospects of the organization. Most companies give new employees a three-month **probationary period,** or trial period. During this time, the supervisor assesses the new employee's skills, attitudes, and performance. At the end of the three months there is a performance review. At this point, a new employee who is performing well becomes a permanent employee. Then performance reviews are conducted regularly, according to company policy.

CASE STUDY

Performance Review Policies

NATIONAL SPORTS CENTRES
Your first three months of employment are your orientation period. Upon successful completion of this term your manager will review your performance. You can expect a performance review at least once more during your first year of employment. If your job performance continues to be satisfactory, you may receive another increase. After one year all employees will usually be reviewed once a year. Performance reviews are intended to help you and your manager reach an understanding of your job responsibilities and the performance standards by which you are measured. Your manager will discuss your strengths and weaknesses with you and provide you with the opportunity to plan improvement and career development. You will be asked to sign a copy of the review to indicate your participation. We will stress the importance of your participation in the review by offering you the opportunity to respond in writing and to request further discussion if you wish. Discussions of your job performance are not limited to formal reviews. Your supervisors are available throughout the year for a full and frank discussion of your work performance. This communication should be a continuous process to ensure an open, harmonious working relationship between you and National Sports Centres.

Courtesy of National Sports Centres

BEAVER LUMBER
The first three months of your employment is actually a period of getting to know one another for you and the company.

We want to observe your performance on the job and we expect you to look the company over and come to some conclusions about the suitability of your job and about our company as your employer.

Your performance will be reviewed with you just prior to the completion of three months' service. It is at this point that employees hired as full- or part-time are confirmed as permanent, assuming, of course, that their performance has been satisfactory and they have completed the required training programs. You will be reviewed again after the completion of 12 months' service.

Thereafter, your supervisor will be expected to keep you regularly appraised of your performance on the job. In order to eliminate any possibility of this being neglected, every manager is required to hold a performance appraisal interview with each member of his or her staff once a year on a formal basis. Your supervisor will use the results of these interviews to make recommendations for your future development. Performance appraisals are not intended to be a frightening or intimidating experience for anyone. You should see them as an opportunity to meet with your supervisor in an uninterrupted meeting to discuss your job.

From Beaver Lumber Training Plan, "Very Important Points for the New Employee." Beaver Lumber Company Limited.

Your concerns, questions, and input are important to us, as we want you to feel good about your job and experience success!

▼ ▼ ▼

1 Why do you think businesses outline their probationary period and performance review policies so carefully?

2 Why do you think a probationary period is necessary?

3 a How does a performance review help the employee?

b How does a performance review help the employer?

4 List five topics that you consider to be important to discuss in a performance review. Explain what should be discussed for each topic and why each point is important.

5 If you were a new employee for one of these companies, what would you want to know about the three-month probationary period and the performance review that is not outlined in these policies?

Informal Employee Evaluation

Although many companies and organizations have formal evaluation procedures, employee evaluation may also be informal. This is often called feedback. You will often receive feedback when people in the workplace say or do something to indicate their feelings. Here are some examples of informal feedback:

- Raj responded with a smile when the receptionist passed on thanks from a customer he had helped.

- As the supervisor walked around the building, she stopped to compliment Lesia's paint job.
- Martin's most valuable feedback at the day-care centre came from the children's fondness for him.
- The supervisor scowled as he passed Dave and Mary laughing and talking at the water cooler.
- The supervisor thanked Sergio for staying a few minutes late to complete the job.
- The accountant slammed the door as she left his office.

Informal feedback may be positive or negative. When responding to positive feedback, a smile, a "Thank you," or a statement such as "I'm happy that you are satisfied" is sufficient. Negative feedback, however, is more difficult to respond to. Consider the message and the mode of delivery. For example, the supervisor who scowled at Dave and Mary at the water cooler probably wanted them to return to work. He could have stopped and spoken to them about his concern in a friendly, but firm, manner. The message is to return to work, but the mode of delivery is negative. Sometimes the recipient of negative feedback can approach the sender later to ask how the situation could have been improved or to state an intention to improve.

Experience is never limited, and it is never complete; it is an immense sensibility, a kind of huge spider-web of the finest silken threads suspended in the chamber of consciousness, and catching every airborne particle in its tissue.

HENRY JAMES

CASE STUDY

Interpreting Informal Evaluation

Jackie had been working at Bosley Plastics for one week when her teacher, Mr. Garmes, came to visit her at her placement. First he met with her supervisor for 20 minutes. Then Jackie and Mr. Garmes had a visit over coffee in the lunchroom. While they were sitting there, passing employees smiled and spoke to Jackie. She told Mr. Garmes that she felt she was getting along with her co-workers. Mr. Garmes told Jackie that her supervisor was impressed with the quality of her work and the initiative she had shown. But Jackie wondered why her supervisor had not given any of this praise to her. Then, as Jackie thought about the past week, she remembered that her supervisor had used a sample of Jackie's work to instruct another employee. And on another day, her supervisor had commented that the quality of placement students was excellent. As well, the supervisor had trusted Jackie to organize her own time and had assigned her several tasks at the same time.

▼ ▼ ▼

1 What was the supervisor's informal evaluation of Jackie?

2 How can Jackie respond to this informal evaluation?

Responding to Praise

Imagine that you are at your placement and have put in several days of hard work on a particular task. You submit it to your supervisor, who praises you in front of your co-workers. In your journal, explain how you would feel and how you would react. Then respond to the questions below.

- When was I last praised at work, at home, or somewhere else? What was my reaction? What was I thinking?

ACTIVITY
*Role-Playing
Responses to Feedback*

1 With a partner, role-play this situation to show positive feedback: You and your supervisor are in the elevator at the end of your first week at the placement. The opening line might be, "How did the first week go?" Either person can ask this question.

2 Role-play another situation to show negative feedback: An extremely nervous new employee spills his or her coffee in the company cafeteria. The employee's supervisor sees this and says something negative about him or her to a co-worker, which is heard by the new employee.

3 After the role-plays, discuss how it felt to give and receive positive and negative informal feedback.

Leaving Your Placement

As you leave your placement, your reflections on your experience can be very useful to your teacher in assisting her or him to successfully place students in the future. In the evaluation of your placement, you and your teacher will:

- Determine whether the placement had a supportive atmosphere.
- Determine whether the placement was organized to make learning possible.
- Determine whether the objectives of your training plan were met.
- Decide whether this placement should be used in the future.
- Decide whether any improvements to the workplace experience could be made in the future.

Before you leave your placement, you may want to ask a co-worker, your supervisor, or your teacher for a **letter of recommendation**, which

The experience of work gives you a chance to do things you did not know you were able to do.

TEACHER

What lies behind us and what lies before us are tiny matters compared to what lies within us.

OLIVER WENDALL HOLMES

ACTIVITY

Writing About Your Placement

outlines your progress at your placement. Although these letters should be dated, they do not need to be addressed to anyone in particular. Ask the writer to outline the length of your placement, the duties of your position, the quality of your work, and the employable skills you demonstrated. You can use a letter of recommendation as a reference when applying for a job in the future.

Write a letter to the student who will follow you in your placement. Describe a typical day and outline the features of the position as you experienced them. Make suggestions that will help the next student to get the most out of her or his experience.

Make the Connection

EVALUATING YOUR PLACEMENT

The following form describes some possible features of a work experience. On a copy provided by your teacher, describe *your* particular experience by filling in the appropriate number from 1 to 5. Use the following rating scale: 1=Practically Never, 2=Once in a Great While, 3=Sometimes, 4=Fairly Often, 5=Very Often.

PLACEMENT EVALUATION

	Rank
1 I have enough work to keep me busy.	_____
2 What I do is interesting.	_____
3 I find my tasks challenging.	_____
4 I am given enough training to do my tasks.	_____
5 I do things myself instead of just observing.	_____
6 I have adult responsibilities.	_____
7 I am learning things that will help me in my future employment or education.	_____
8 I am given clear directions.	_____
9 I have a variety of tasks to do at the site.	_____
10 Adults at the site take a personal interest in me.	_____

11 I have freedom to develop and use my own ideas.   _____

12 I feel I am helping people or improving my community. _____

13 My job is just busy work.   _____

14 I think the site is a safe place to work.   _____

15 I am appreciated when I do a good job.   _____

16 I get help when I need it.   _____

17 I discuss my experience with my supervisor
or co-workers.   _____

18 I feel I am doing a good job at this site.   _____

19 I make important decisions.   _____

My overall rating of my placement(s) at this point is:
____Excellent   ____Good   ____ Fair   ____Poor   ____Terrible

Reproduced courtesy of the Ontario Co-operative Education Association (OCEA).

-                    - - - - - - - - -

Prepare a written and a verbal report about your placement. Submit the written report to your teacher and present the verbal report to your class. Gather information from your supervisor and from written information at your placement. In your reports, include the following:

A C T I V I T Y
Reporting on Your Placement

- A brief history and description of the company or organization.
- The duties and responsibilities of your job.
- A summary of the social atmosphere at the company or organization.
- The knowledge and skills you have gained.
- The ways in which your attitudes have changed based on your experience.
- The conclusions you have drawn about the working world from your experience.
- How your work experience has helped you in your career decisions.

- -

Journal Entry

Moving Forward

As a final entry in your journal, write about the effects your work experience has had on you as a person. Think about how your attitudes have changed, in what ways you interact differently with others, and what new knowledge you have about yourself.

ACTIVITY
Looking Back

1 Find a quiet spot to read your journal. Consider your observations and your accomplishments. Highlight items that you would like to share with classmates. If you have trouble choosing what to share, consider these possibilities:

- An entry that you enjoyed writing.
- An entry that shows how much you have changed.
- An entry that is funny.
- An entry that reveals something about you.
- An entry that is worth publishing.

2 In small groups, share these entries. Remember that journals are personal reflections—respond to other people's journal entries with sensitivity.

Make the Connection

▼▼▼▼▼▼▼▼▼▼▼▼▼▼▼▼▼▼▼▼▼▼▼▼▼▼▼▼▼▼▼▼▼▼▼

SAYING GOODBYE

1 Write a letter to your placement supervisor. In your letter, outline what you have gained from your work experience and thank the supervisor (as well as the head of the company) for the opportunity.

2 You may want to ask a co-worker, your supervisor, or your teacher for a letter of recommendation.

3 Revise your résumé based on your new work experience. You may want to try a different résumé format than you used before.

WHAT HAVE YOU LEARNED?

▼ ▼ ▼

1 Explain why self-evaluation is important.

2 How are employees assessed in the workplace?

3 How can an employee contribute to an evaluation?

4 What is the difference between formal and informal employee evaluation?

5 How does your recent work experience affect your career goals and plans?

Glossary

Aggressive	A type of behaviour in which a person attempts to achieve his or her own goals at the expense of others or to impose opinions on others.
Airborne Contaminants	Pollutants in the air.
Anger	The feeling of frustration resulting from a situation that is seen to be wrong or unfair.
Apology	An acknowledgement to another person of a mistake or failure one is responsible for.
Application Form	A request for employment form that some organizations require job applicants to fill out instead of, or in addition to, a résumé.
Apprenticeship	A training program that is required for particular occupations, which involves education (usually at a community college) plus on-the-job training. Apprenticeship programs are regulated by provincial governments and conclude with written examinations that lead to licensing. Many skilled trades require that people complete an apprenticeship program to become, for example, a carpenter, a printer, or an electrician.
Arbitration	A process whereby a union–management dispute is settled by a third party, or arbitrator. Unlike conciliation, the arbitrator's decision is binding on both parties. Labour legislation requires that an arbitration clause be included in all collective agreements.
Assertive	A type of behaviour in which a person expresses feelings, preferences, needs, or opinions while still respecting others.
Attitude	The beliefs and feelings that cause a person to behave in a certain way.
Canada Labour Code	Federal labour legislation that applies to employees of industries under federal authority, such as those involved in air transport, radio and television broadcasting, banking, and telecommunications.
Canadian Charter of Rights and Freedoms	A section of the Canadian constitution that states the human rights of every Canadian citizen. Some of these rights include the right to freedom of conscience and religion; freedom of thought, belief, opinion, and expression; freedom of peaceful assembly; and others.
Canadian Human Rights Act	Federal legislation that applies to the human rights of workers in industries under federal jurisdiction, such as air transport, radio and television broadcasting, banking, and telecommunications.

Career	A person's entire experience in the work world, or a person's work life.
Career Goals	The goals that a person forms prior to and during his or her career; for example, the goal of attaining a management position or starting a business.
Career Planning	The process of identifying your career choices and then forming career goals suited to both your individual needs and the realities of the work world.
Certification	Formal recognition of a union. The process of certification is regulated by labour legislation.
Chief Steward	An employee who serves as an unpaid union representative for a workplace and who is above all the shop stewards.
Chronological Résumé	A résumé style that outlines a person's employment history and other information in chronological order from most recent to least recent.
Collective Action	Action that is taken by a group of people working together; for instance, a union taking action to improve working conditions.
Collective Agreement	The labour contract between a union and an employer. The agreement outlines agreed-upon work conditions, pay rates, employee benefits, and other union–management concerns.
Collective Bargaining	The negotiating with an employer that is carried on by a union on behalf of its members with the purpose of creating a collective agreement.
Combination Résumé	A résumé style that combines features of the chronological and functional résumé styles.
Communication	The process of exchanging information with other people. Communication involves a sender and a receiver of a message in a medium such as writing, speaking, or nonverbal communication.
Communication Barrier	In communication, something that blocks the true intent of a message in the exchange between the sender and the receiver. Some common communication barriers include distractions, lack of concentration on the part of the receiver, or the use of jargon by the sender.
Conciliation	A process whereby a government-appointed officer intervenes to help settle a union–management dispute. Only after conciliation has failed can a union legally call a strike.
Confidentiality	Privacy of information; for example, the confidentiality of a doctor's patient files or a company's employee records.
Conflict	A clash of opposing ideas, interests, or activities.
Court Injunction	A court order sought by a party to prevent another party from taking some sort of action. For instance, employers often seek court injunctions to limit the number of picketers allowed at a company entrance at one time during a strike.

Covering Letter	A letter that accompanies a résumé that is sent to an employer. The purpose of the covering letter is to introduce the applicant and the résumé in order to be granted an interview with the employer.
Craft Union	A union of tradespeople; for example, carpenters, printers, or electricians.
Criticism	Judgements about another person's behaviour or actions, which may involve positive or negative comments.
Customer Service	Conduct that is helpful to and considerate of customers.
Decision Making	The process of identifying a decision in an attempt to solve a problem or meet a challenge.
Demography	The statistical science that deals with the distribution, density, and vital statistics of human populations in order to determine trends.
Discrimination	The act of making distinctions among people on the basis of, for instance, race, place of origin, religion, age, gender, marital or family status, or disability. Usually discrimination involves placing people at a disadvantage because of one or more of these factors.
Employee	A person who works for an organization or another person for pay.
Employer	An organization or a person that hires one or more employees.
Employment Agency	An organization that, for a fee, matches people who are seeking jobs with employers who are seeking employees.
Employment Equity	Equal employment opportunity, or employment practices that are free of any form of discrimination.
Employment Equity Act	Federal legislation that exists to ensure employment equity for all workers under its jurisdiction.
Employment and Immigration Canada	The federal government ministry that addresses employment and immigration issues and operates regional Canada Employment Centres.
Entrepreneurship	The process of pursuing opportunities or fulfilling needs and wants through innovation or the establishment of a business. Entrepreneurs think of new ways of doing things or new products or services to fulfill market needs.
Environment	The outside influences—family, friends, culture, school, media, and so on—that surround a person and have an impact on his or her personality, goals, values, and interests.
Environmental Awareness	Realization of the need to improve, maintain, and protect the conditions and influences that affect the development of living things.
Ergonomics	The study of the physical and mental relationship between a person and his or her work tools, furniture, equipment, and workspace.

Ethics	The rules of right or wrong that form a person's, company's, or society's system of behaviour.
Exchange	The second stage of the job interview process, during which the job, the organization, and the applicant's experience and skills are discussed.
Fatigue	Physical or mental exhaustion.
Feedback	In communication, the receiver's response to a message. This response can take the form of speaking, writing, or nonverbal feedback.
First Aid	Emergency medical care or treatment.
Follow-up	The last stage of the job interview process, when the applicant sends a thank-you letter to the employer and may call to discover the outcome of the interview.
Functional Résumé	A résumé style that emphasizes a person's transferable skills.
Futurist	A person who predicts the future.
Greeting	The first stage of the job interview process, which involves the initial contact between an interviewee and an interviewer.
Grievance Procedure	A process outlined in any collective agreement for settling disputes over a violation of the agreement.
Harassment	Any behaviour that includes unwelcome physical, verbal, or visual conduct. Derogatory comments, threats, actions, or jokes against a person and offensive posters are some forms of harassment.
Hazard	A harmful condition or piece of equipment that could potentially cause injury to someone.
Heredity	The unique genetic information with which a person is born, which can affect physical appearance, gender, ability to learn, emotional tendencies, and other characteristics.
Hidden Job Market	Jobs that are not advertised or available through employment agencies.
Hierarchy of Needs	A model created by psychologist Abraham Maslow that outlines the priority of the five levels of human needs he identified and studied: survival needs, safety needs, love and belonging needs, esteem needs, and self-fulfillment needs.
Honesty	The quality of being honourable and fair in character and actions—refusing to steal, cheat, lie, or misrepresent.
Human Resources Department	In large companies, the department that assists with employee-related matters such as hiring, benefits, and labour negotiations.
Human Rights	The rights that are a part of and that relate to basic human dignity, such as the right to live and work in an environment that is free from discrimination.

Humidity	The moisture content of air.
Illumination	The quality and quantity of light in an area.
Industrial Union	A union whose members include everyone who works for a particular employer regardless of individual skills or occupations; for example, everyone who holds a nonmanagement position at an automobile manufacturing plant.
Information Age	The explosion in the past two decades in industries that create, process, and distribute data.
Injury	A physical hurt suffered by a person.
Integrity	The human quality of having high ethical standards and refusing to compromise those standards.
Interests	The activities, pastimes, and subjects that a person enjoys.
Interpersonal Relations	The pattern of associations and communications among people.
Interview	A meeting between two or more people.
Job	The particular kind of work a person does within an occupation. For example, a person's job may be an employment counsellor in a government employment centre, while the person's occupation is counselling.
Job Benefits	Certain advantages that are offered to an employee in addition to salary or wages. These may include discounts on company merchandise, a company car, health and life insurance, retirement savings programs, and other extras.
Job Interview	An interview whose purpose is to match a job seeker to a particular job.
Job Lead	Information about a possible job opening that may come from a job advertisement, an employment agency, a Canada Employment Centre, or a person's personal and professional contacts. Pursuing job leads can help a person find unadvertised jobs.
Job Rotation	A system in which employees change their work activities periodically to reduce monotony and fatigue.
Job Search	The process of looking for employment.
Journal	A collection of a person's writings that reflects his or her feelings and attitudes.
Labour Union	A formal group of workers who practise a similar craft or are employed in a similar industry whose purpose is to improve economic and social conditions through collective bargaining with an employer and through negotiations with governments.

Letter of Recommendation	A letter written by a former employer, co-worker, or other reference that outlines in positive terms the performance of a worker to help him or her gain future employment.
Lifestyle	How a person lives in terms of work, habits, pastimes, attitudes, accommodation, and material possessions.
Listening	Actively participating in a communication process by attentively receiving and retaining messages. Listening is not the same as hearing, which is passively sensing sounds.
Lockout	A refusal by management to let employees into the workplace in order to pressure a union into accepting management's demands.
Log Sheet	A form you may be required to complete daily or weekly on which you record the tasks you do and the hours you spend at your placement.
Medium	The form a communicated message takes, such as speech, a piece of writing, or a visual display.
Mentor	An experienced adviser who supports, promotes, and nurtures a younger worker by serving as the worker's role model, teacher, and strategist.
Message	The information that a person wishes to communicate.
Monitoring	Observing a person to evaluate her or his performance. Your teacher will monitor your progress at your placement.
Monotony	Wearisome sameness in, for instance, work tasks.
Needs	Necessities that motivate people; for example, the necessities of food, love, or self-fulfillment.
Negotiate	To bargain. In the work world, employees often negotiate with an employer for salary or wages, benefits, and vacation time.
Network	A person's personal and professional contacts that may be able to provide job leads and other information. Networking is the process of contacting these people and building on this base to develop a larger network.
Noise	Unwanted or valueless sound.
Nonverbal Communication	Sometimes called body language, this is a way of expressing a message without using words. Nonverbal communication includes facial expressions, body gestures and movements, posture, attire, grooming, and tone of voice.
Occupation	The field in which a person works; for example, teaching or marine biology.

Occupational Research Interview	An interview with a person who is in a particular occupation. The purpose of an occupational research interview is to find out more about the occupation and one's suitability for it in order to plan a career.
Paradigm	A person's pattern of acting or thinking, or belief system.
Paradigm Shift	A change in a person's paradigms. For example, a person who decides to give up a fast-paced career for a quieter lifestyle exhibits a paradigm shift.
Parting	The third stage of the job interview process, when the interview comes to a close and the interviewee and interviewer part.
Passive	A type of behaviour that allows people to be victimized due to their not expressing themselves and protecting their rights.
Pay Equity	Legislation that requires equal pay for work of equal value.
Performance Review	An exchange between a supervisor and an employee to discuss the employee's work.
Personal Contacts	People you know, such as relatives or friends. In a job search, these contacts may be able to provide leads on unadvertised jobs.
Personality	The individual non-physical characteristics that make a person unique. Personality is a result of heredity, environment, and other factors.
Picket	A job action by striking workers that involves displaying signs during a strike to discourage replacement workers from entering a workplace and to inform the public about the situation. Striking workers often picket in front of a company's premises.
Placement	The workplace at which you complete the out-of-school component of your co-operative education, or work experience, program.
Portfolio	A collection of a person's work that is shown to a prospective employer in order to obtain employment. Artists and writers, for example, often show a portfolio of their work to employers. Students may collect samples from school and work experiences.
Prediction	A forecast of what will happen in the future in order to make decisions about the present and to direct the future.
Probationary Period	A trial period for a new employee, which is usually the first three months of her or his employment. After this period, the employee's performance is assessed in a performance review to determine whether she or he will become a permanent employee.
Problem Solving	The process of identifying problems and developing, selecting, and evaluating solutions for them.
Productivity	A worker's capacity to create or produce during a given period of time.

Professional Contacts	People you know within an occupation. In a job search, these contacts may be able to provide leads on unadvertised jobs.
Radiation	Emissions of light, heat, or other energy that travels in waves.
Raise	A pay increase.
Ratify	To approve an agreement or a contract. In union–management relations, a collective agreement must be ratified by a certain percentage of the union's members in order to be administered by the union and management.
Reading	The mental process of receiving and comprehending a written message.
Receiver	In communication, the person who receives a message—the listener, reader, or viewer.
Reference	A person who recommends you to a potential employer. Employers often ask for references from job candidates in order to check on the candidates' reliability.
Referral	A job lead to a specific company or person. Referrals can help expand a person's network.
Repetition	The act of doing something over and over.
Repression	A defence mechanism people use to put unacceptable or painful emotions or memories out of their minds by not facing them.
Résumé	A summary of a person's education, employment history, and accomplishments that is sent to prospective employers in order to be considered for employment. A résumé may be in chronological, functional, or combination format.
Salary	A fixed rate of pay usually paid to employees bi-weekly or monthly.
Salary Review	An evaluation of an employee's salary, which is usually completed at regular intervals, such as yearly.
Screen	To assess job candidates for an employer. In large companies, a member of the human resources department may screen applicants in a first round of interviews and then invite the most appropriate applicants to return for a second interview with the job supervisor.
Self-Assessment	A process of determining who you are and how you change over time.
Self-Concept	How you feel about yourself. How you believe others feel about you is also part of your self-concept.
Self-Evaluation	Judging your behaviour, performance, skills, knowledge, productivity, and progress.
Self-Management Skills	Skills that are part of a person's personality and that are continually learned; for example, the ability to work with others or to adapt to new situations.

Sender	In communication, the person who originates a message—the speaker, writer, or person who creates a visual display to send a message.
Sexual Harassment	Any conduct that includes unwelcome and repeated sexual advances, requests for sexual favours, and other sexually-related verbal or physical conduct or visual display that interferes with an individual's work or creates an intimidating or unpleasant work environment.
Shop Steward	An employee who is an unpaid union representative in a shop, or section, of a workplace.
Sitdown Strike	A job action by union members in which workers remain at their work stations but refuse to work in order to pressure management to accept their demands.
Skill	A practised or natural ability to do something well; for example, organizing or speaking.
Slowdown	A job action by a union in which employees remain at their work stations but deliberately work slowly in order to pressure management to accept their demands.
Social Insurance Number (SIN)	A nine-digit number used by the federal government to identify people for purposes such as income taxation. Everyone in Canada must have a SIN in order to be employed.
Speaking	Expressing a message verbally.
Stress	Physical, mental, or emotional pressure on a person.
Strike	A temporary refusal of union members to work for the purpose of pressuring management to accept their demands.
Strike Insurance	An insurance policy that employers often buy in order to have a source of compensation in the event of a strike by their workers.
Technical Skills	Specific areas of technical knowledge and ability that a person needs in order to do a particular job; for example, knowledge of computer programming.
Thank-You Letter	A letter sent by a job applicant to an interviewer after a job interview to express appreciation and to show interest in the job.
Time Management	Organizing and planning tasks and events for greater efficiency, productivity, and reduction of stress.
Training Plan	An individualized plan that is developed by you, your teacher, and your placement supervisor before you begin your placement. The plan outlines your placement tasks and learning objectives.
Transferable Skills	Skills that are developed through everyday experiences, such as school, employment, or other activities; for example, the ability to communicate effectively or to make decisions. These skills are common to many situations and can be easily applied to new jobs or industries.

Trend	A general direction in which a society is developing.
Values	The moral principles that a person uses to make decisions.
Ventilation	Air movement.
Vibration	A rapid back and forth motion in, say, a working power tool.
Volunteer Work	Work that is performed without pay. Many community and nonprofit organizations require volunteers in order to continue to operate. In return, volunteers gain valuable work experience and skills as well as the satisfaction of helping others.
Wages	An hourly, daily, or weekly rate of pay paid to employees.
Walkout	A job action in which union members leave their work stations in order to pressure management to accept their demands.
Wildcat Strike	A job action in which employees go on strike without the official consent of their union.
Workers' Compensation	The legislation and the system by which workers are compensated for work-related injuries and illnesses. All employers pay premiums to support this program, which pays for an injured worker's medical costs, hospitalization, rehabilitation, and disability pension, and compensates her or him for lost income.
Working Knowledge	The knowledge and skills required to be a competent worker.
Workplace Hazardous Materials Information System (WHMIS)	A Canada-wide system that provides workers and employers with information about hazardous materials in the workplace and how to handle and store them.
Work-to-Rule	A job action by a union in which employees follow the regulations in their collective agreement to the letter, thus causing work to slow down, in order to pressure management to accept their demands.
Writing	The act of putting a message into words on paper for a reader to receive.